Seven Short

By

Lady Gregory

G. P. Putnam's Sons
New York and London
The Knickerbocker Press
1915

COPYRIGHT, 1903, BY LADY AUGUSTA GREGORY
COPYRIGHT, 1904, BY LADY GREGORY
COPYRIGHT, 1905, BY LADY GREGORY
COPYRIGHT, 1906, BY LADY GREGORY
COPYRIGHT, 1909, BY LADY GREGORY

The Knickerbocker Press, New York

DEDICATION

To you, W. B. YEATS, good praiser, wholesome dispraiser, heavy-handed judge, open-handed helper of us all, I offer a play of my plays for every night of the week, because you like them, and because you have taught me my trade.

AUGUSTA GREGORY

Abbey Theatre,
  May 1 1909.

CONTENTS

	PAGE
SPREADING THE NEWS	1
HYACINTH HALVEY	29
THE RISING OF THE MOON	75
THE JACKDAW	93
THE WORKHOUSE WARD	137
THE TRAVELLING MAN	155
THE GAOL GATE	173
MUSIC FOR THE SONGS IN THE PLAYS	189
NOTES, &C.	196

SPREADING THE NEWS

PERSONS
   Bartley Fallon. — melancholy man
   Mrs. Fallon.
   Jack Smith. — with pitchfork : 'carroty in petticoat'
   Shawn Early.
   Tim Casey.
   James Ryan.
   Mrs. Tarpey. — apple seller — 'cleaning home for village gossip.' never heard accurately.
   Mrs. Tully.
   A Policeman (Jo MULDOON).
   A Removable Magistrate.

SPREADING THE NEWS

Scene: The outskirts of a Fair. An Apple Stall. Mrs. Tarpey sitting at it. Magistrate and Policeman enter.

Magistrate: So that is the Fair Green. Cattle and sheep and mud. No system. What a repulsive sight!
Policeman: That is so, indeed.
Magistrate: I suppose there is a good deal of disorder in this place?
Policeman: There is.
Magistrate: Common assault?
Policeman: It's common enough.
Magistrate: Agrarian crime, no doubt?
Policeman: That is so.
Magistrate: Boycotting? Maiming of cattle? Firing into houses?
Policeman: There was one time, and there might be again.
Magistrate: That is bad. Does it go any farther than that?
Policeman: Far enough, indeed.

Magistrate: Homicide, then! This district has been shamefully neglected! I will change all that. When I was in the Andaman Islands, my system never failed. Yes, yes, I will change all that. What has that woman on her stall?

Policeman: Apples mostly—and sweets.

Magistrate: Just see if there are any unlicensed goods underneath—spirits or the like. We had evasions of the salt tax in the Andaman Islands.

Policeman: (*Sniffing cautiously and upsetting a heap of apples.*) I see no spirits here—or salt.

Magistrate: (*To Mrs. Tarpey.*) Do you know this town well, my good woman?

Mrs. Tarpey: (*Holding out some apples.*) A penny the half-dozen, your honour.

Policeman: (*Shouting.*) The gentleman is asking do you know the town! He's the new magistrate!

Mrs. Tarpey: (*Rising and ducking.*) Do I know the town? I do, to be sure.

Magistrate: (*Shouting.*) What is its chief business?

Mrs. Tarpey: Business, is it? What business would the people here have but to be minding one another's business?

Magistrate: I mean what trade have they?

Mrs. Tarpey: Not a trade. No trade at all but to be talking.

Magistrate: I shall learn nothing here.
>   (*James Ryan comes in, pipe in mouth. Seeing Magistrate he retreats quickly, taking pipe from mouth.*)

Magistrate: The smoke from that man's pipe had a greenish look; he may be growing unlicensed tobacco at home. I wish I had brought my telescope to this district. Come to the post-office, I will telegraph for it. I found it very useful in the Andaman Islands.
>   (*Magistrate and Policeman go out left.*)

Mrs. Tarpey: Bad luck to Jo Muldoon, knocking my apples this way and that way. (*Begins arranging them.*) Showing off he was to the new magistrate.
>   (*Enter Bartley Fallon and Mrs. Fallon.*)

Bartley: Indeed it's a poor country and a scarce country to be living in. But I'm thinking if I went to America it's long ago the day I'd be dead!

Mrs. Fallon: So you might, indeed.
>   (*She puts her basket on a barrel and begins putting parcels in it, taking them from under her cloak.*)

Bartley: And it's a great expense for a poor man to be buried in America.

Mrs. Fallon: Never fear, Bartley Fallon, but I'll give you a good burying the day you'll die.

Bartley: Maybe it's yourself will be buried in

the graveyard of Cloonmara before me, Mary Fallon, and I myself that will be dying unbeknownst some night, and no one a-near me. And the cat itself may be gone straying through the country, and the mice squealing over the quilt.

Mrs. Fallon: Leave off talking of dying. It might be twenty years you'll be living yet.

Bartley: (*With a deep sigh.*) I'm thinking if I'll be living at the end of twenty years, it's a very old man I'll be then!

Mrs. Tarpey: (*Turns and sees them.*) Good morrow, Bartley Fallon; good morrow, Mrs. Fallon. Well, Bartley, you'll find no cause for complaining to-day; they are all saying it was a good fair.

Bartley: (*Raising his voice.*) It was not a good fair, Mrs. Tarpey. It was a scattered sort of a fair. If we didn't expect more, we got less. That's the way with me always; whatever I have to sell goes down and whatever I have to buy goes up. If there's ever any misfortune coming to this world, it's on myself it pitches, like a flock of crows on seed potatoes.

Mrs. Fallon: Leave off talking of misfortunes, and listen to Jack Smith that is coming the way, and he singing.

(*Voice of Jack Smith heard singing:*)
I thought, my first love,
There'd be but one house between you and me,
And I thought I would find

Yourself coaxing my child on your knee.
Over the tide
 I would leap with the leap of a swan,
Till I came to the side
 Of the wife of the Red-haired man!

> (*Jack Smith comes in; he is a red-haired man, and is carrying a hayfork.*)

Mrs. Tarpey: That should be a good song if I had my hearing.

Mrs. Fallon: (*Shouting.*) It's "The Red-haired Man's Wife."

Mrs. Tarpey: I know it well. That's the song that has a skin on it!

> (*She turns her back to them and goes on arranging her apples.*)

Mrs. Fallon: Where's herself, Jack Smith?

Jack Smith: She was delayed with her washing; bleaching the clothes on the hedge she is, and she daren't leave them, with all the tinkers that do be passing to the fair. It isn't to the fair I came myself, but up to the Five Acre Meadow I'm going, where I have a contract for the hay. We'll get a share of it into tramps to-day. (*He lays down hayfork and lights his pipe.*)

Bartley: You will not get it into tramps to-day. The rain will be down on it by evening, and on myself too. It's seldom I ever started on a journey but the rain would come down on me before I'd find any place of shelter.

Jack Smith: If it didn't itself, Bartley, it is my belief you would carry a leaky pail on your head in place of a hat, the way you'd not be without some cause of complaining.

(*A voice heard, "Go on, now, go on out o' that. Go on I say."*)

Jack Smith: Look at that young mare of Pat Ryan's that is backing into Shaughnessy's bullocks with the dint of the crowd! Don't be daunted, Pat, I'll give you a hand with her.

(*He goes out, leaving his hayfork.*)

Mrs. Fallon: It's time for ourselves to be going home. I have all I bought put in the basket. Look at there, Jack Smith's hayfork he left after him! He'll be wanting it. (*Calls.*) Jack Smith! Jack Smith!—He's gone through the crowd—hurry after him, Bartley, he'll be wanting it.

Bartley: I'll do that. This is no safe place to be leaving it. (*He takes up fork awkwardly and upsets the basket.*) Look at that now! If there is any basket in the fair upset, it must be our own basket! (*He goes out to right.*)

Mrs. Fallon: Get out of that! It is your own fault, it is. Talk of misfortunes and misfortunes will come. Glory be! Look at my new egg-cups rolling in every part—and my two pound of sugar with the paper broke——

Mrs. Tarpey: (*Turning from stall.*) God help us, Mrs. Fallon, what happened your basket?

Spreading the News

Mrs. Fallon: It's himself that knocked it down, bad manners to him. (*Putting things up.*) My grand sugar that's destroyed, and he'll not drink his tea without it. I had best go back to the shop for more, much good may it do him!

(*Enter Tim Casey.*)

Tim Casey: Where is Bartley Fallon, Mrs. Fallon? I want a word with him before he'll leave the fair. I was afraid he might have gone home by this, for he's a temperate man.

Mrs. Fallon: I wish he did go home! It'd be best for me if he went home straight from the fair green, or if he never came with me at all! Where is he, is it? He's gone up the road (*jerks elbow*) following Jack Smith with a hayfork.

(*She goes out to left.*)

Tim Casey: Following Jack Smith with a hayfork! Did ever any one hear the like of that. (*Shouts.*) Did you hear that news, Mrs. Tarpey?

Mrs. Tarpey: I heard no news at all.

Tim Casey: Some dispute I suppose it was that rose between Jack Smith and Bartley Fallon, and it seems Jack made off, and Bartley is following him with a hayfork!

Mrs. Tarpey: Is he now? Well, that was quick work! It's not ten minutes since the two of them were here, Bartley going home and Jack going to the Five Acre Meadow; and I had my apples to settle up, that Jo Muldoon of the police had scattered, and when I looked round again Jack Smith was gone, and Bartley Fallon was gone, and Mrs. Fallon's basket upset, and all in it strewed upon the ground—the tea here—the two pound of sugar there—the egg-cups there—Look, now, what a great hardship the deafness puts upon me, that I didn't hear the commencement of the fight! Wait till I tell James Ryan that I see below; he is a neighbour of Bartley's, it would be a pity if he wouldn't hear the news!

(*She goes out. Enter Shawn Early and Mrs. Tully.*)

Tim Casey: Listen, Shawn Early! Listen, Mrs. Tully, to the news! Jack Smith and Bartley Fallon had a falling out, and Jack knocked Mrs. Fallon's basket into the road, and Bartley made an attack on him with a hayfork, and away with Jack, and Bartley after him. Look at the sugar here yet on the road!

Shawn Early: Do you tell me so? Well, that's a queer thing, and Bartley Fallon so quiet a man!

Mrs. Tully: I wouldn't wonder at all. I would never think well of a man that would have that sort of a mouldering look. It's likely he has overtaken Jack by this.

(*Enter James Ryan and Mrs. Tarpey.*)

James Ryan: That is great news Mrs. Tarpey was telling me! I suppose that's what brought the police and the magistrate up this way. I was wondering to see them in it a while ago.

Shawn Early: The police after them? Bartley Fallon must have injured Jack so. They wouldn't meddle in a fight that was only for show!

Mrs. Tully: Why wouldn't he injure him? There was many a man killed with no more of a weapon than a hayfork.

James Ryan: Wait till I run north as far as Kelly's bar to spread the news! (*He goes out.*)

Tim Casey: I'll go tell Jack Smith's first cousin that is standing there south of the church after selling his lambs. (*Goes out.*)

Mrs. Tully: I'll go telling a few of the neighbours I see beyond to the west. (*Goes out.*)

Shawn Early: I'll give word of it beyond at the east of the green.

(*Is going out when Mrs. Tarpey seizes hold of him.*)

Mrs. Tarpey: Stop a minute, Shawn Early, and tell me did you see red Jack Smith's wife, Kitty Keary, in any place?

Shawn Early: I did. At her own house she was, drying clothes on the hedge as I passed.

Mrs. Tarpey: What did you say she was doing?

Shawn Early: (*Breaking away.*) Laying out a sheet on the hedge. (*He goes.*)

Mrs. Tarpey: Laying out a sheet for the dead!

The Lord have mercy on us! Jack Smith dead, and his wife laying out a sheet for his burying! (*Calls out.*) Why didn't you tell me that before, Shawn Early? Isn't the deafness the great hardship? Half the world might be dead without me knowing of it or getting word of it at all! (*She sits down and rocks herself.*) O my poor Jack Smith! To be going to his work so nice and so hearty, and to be left stretched on the ground in the full light of the day!

(*Enter Tim Casey.*)

Tim Casey: What is it, Mrs. Tarpey? What happened since?

Mrs. Tarpey: O my poor Jack Smith!

Tim Casey Did Bartley overtake him?

Mrs. Tarpey: O the poor man!

Tim Casey: Is it killed he is?

Mrs. Tarpey: Stretched in the Five Acre Meadow!

Tim Casey: The Lord have mercy on us! Is that a fact?

Mrs. Tarpey: Without the rites of the Church or a ha'porth!

Tim Casey: Who was telling you?

Mrs. Tarpey: And the wife laying out a sheet for his corpse. (*Sits up and wipes her eyes.*) I suppose they'll wake him the same as another?

(*Enter Mrs. Tully, Shawn Early, and James Ryan.*)

Mrs. Tully: There is great talk about this work in every quarter of the fair.

Mrs. Tarpey: Ochone! cold and dead. And myself maybe the last he was speaking to!

James Ryan: The Lord save us! Is it dead he is?

Tim Casey: Dead surely, and the wife getting provision for the wake.

Shawn Early: Well, now, hadn't Bartley Fallon great venom in him?

Mrs. Tully: You may be sure he had some cause. Why would he have made an end of him if he had not? (*To Mrs. Tarpey, raising her voice.*) What was it rose the dispute at all, Mrs. Tarpey?

Mrs. Tarpey: Not a one of me knows. The last I saw of them, Jack Smith was standing there, and Bartley Fallon was standing there, quiet and easy, and he listening to "The Red-haired Man's Wife."

Mrs. Tully: Do you hear that, Tim Casey? Do you hear that, Shawn Early and James Ryan? Bartley Fallon was here this morning listening to red Jack Smith's wife, Kitty Keary that was! Listening to her and whispering with her! It was she started the fight so!

Shawn Early: She must have followed him from her own house. It is likely some person roused him.

Tim Casey: I never knew, before, Bartley Fallon was great with Jack Smith's wife.

Mrs. Tully: How would you know it? Sure it's not in the streets they would be calling it. If Mrs. Fallon didn't know of it, and if I that have the next house to them didn't know of it, and if Jack Smith himself didn't know of it, it is not likely you would know of it, Tim Casey.

Shawn Early: Let Bartley Fallon take charge of her from this out so, and let him provide for her. It is little pity she will get from any person in this parish.

Tim Casey: How can he take charge of her? Sure he has a wife of his own. Sure you don't think he'd turn souper and marry her in a Protestant church?

James Ryan: It would be easy for him to marry her if he brought her to America.

Shawn Early: With or without Kitty Keary, believe me it is for America he's making at this minute. I saw the new magistrate and Jo Muldoon of the police going into the post-office as I came up—there was hurry on them—you may be sure it was to telegraph they went, the way he'll be stopped in the docks at Queenstown!

Mrs. Tully: It's likely Kitty Keary is gone with him, and not minding a sheet or a wake at all. The poor man, to be deserted by his own wife, and the breath hardly gone out yet from his body that is lying bloody in the field!

(*Enter Mrs. Fallon.*)

Spreading the News

Mrs. Fallon: What is it the whole of the town is talking about? And what is it you yourselves are talking about? Is it about my man Bartley Fallon you are talking? Is it lies about him you are telling, saying that he went killing Jack Smith? My grief that ever he came into this place at all!

James Ryan: Be easy now, Mrs. Fallon. Sure there is no one at all in the whole fair but is sorry for you!

Mrs. Fallon: Sorry for me, is it? Why would any one be sorry for me? Let you be sorry for yourselves, and that there may be shame on you for ever and at the day of judgment, for the words you are saying and the lies you are telling to take away the character of my poor man, and to take the good name off of him, and to drive him to destruction! That is what you are doing!

Shawn Early: Take comfort now, Mrs. Fallon. The police are not so smart as they think. Sure he might give them the slip yet, the same as Lynchehaun.

Mrs. Tully: If they do get him, and if they do put a rope around his neck, there is no one can say he does not deserve it!

Mrs. Fallon: Is that what you are saying, Bridget Tully, and is that what you think? I tell you it's too much talk you have, making yourself out to be such a great one, and to be running down every respectable person! A rope, is it?

It isn't much of a rope was needed to tie up your own furniture the day you came into Martin Tully's house, and you never bringing as much as a blanket, or a penny, or a suit of clothes with you and I myself bringing seventy pounds and two feather beds. And now you are stiffer than a woman would have a hundred pounds! It is too much talk the whole of you have. A rope is it? I tell you the whole of this town is full of liars and schemers that would hang you up for half a glass of whiskey. (*Turning to go.*) People they are you wouldn't believe as much as daylight from without you'd get up to have a look at it yourself. Killing Jack Smith indeed! Where are you at all, Bartley, till I bring you out of this? My nice quiet little man! My decent comrade! He that is as kind and as harmless as an innocent beast of the field! He'll be doing no harm at all if he'll shed the blood of some of you after this day's work! That much would be no harm at all. (*Calls out.*) Bartley! Bartley Fallon! Where are you? (*Going out.*) Did any one see Bartley Fallon?

(*All turn to look after her.*)

James Ryan: It is hard for her to believe any such a thing, God help her!

(*Enter Bartley Fallon from right, carrying hayfork.*)

Bartley: It is what I often said to myself, if

there is ever any misfortune coming to this world it is on myself it is sure to come!

(*All turn round and face him.*)

Bartley: To be going about with this fork and to find no one to take it, and no place to leave it down, and I wanting to be gone out of this —Is that you, Shawn Early? (*Holds out fork.*) It's well I met you. You have no call to be leaving the fair for a while the way I have, and how can I go till I'm rid of this fork? Will you take it and keep it until such time as Jack Smith——

Shawn Early: (*Backing.*) I will not take it, Bartley Fallon, I'm very thankful to you!

Bartley: (*Turning to apple stall.*) Look at it now, Mrs. Tarpey, it was here I got it; let me thrust it in under the stall. It will lie there safe enough, and no one will take notice of it until such time as Jack Smith——

Mrs. Tarpey: Take your fork out of that! Is it to put trouble on me and to destroy me you want? putting it there for the police to be rooting it out maybe. (*Thrusts him back.*)

Bartley: That is a very unneighbourly thing for you to do, Mrs. Tarpey. Hadn't I enough care on me with that fork before this, running up and down with it like the swinging of a clock, and afeard to lay it down in any place! I wish I never touched it or meddled with it at all!

James Ryan: It is a pity, indeed, you ever did.

Bartley: Will you yourself take it, James Ryan? You were always a neighbourly man.

James Ryan: (*Backing.*) There is many a thing I would do for you, Bartley Fallon, but I won't do that!

Shawn Early: I tell you there is no man will give you any help or any encouragement for this day's work. If it was something agrarian now——

Bartley: If no one at all will take it, maybe it's best to give it up to the police.

Tim Casey: There'd be a welcome for it with them surely! (*Laughter.*)

Mrs. Tully: And it is to the police Kitty Keary herself will be brought.

Mrs. Tarpey: (*Rocking to and fro.*) I wonder now who will take the expense of the wake for poor Jack Smith?

Bartley: The wake for Jack Smith!

Tim Casey: Why wouldn't he get a wake as well as another? Would you begrudge him that much?

Bartley: Red Jack Smith dead! Who was telling you?

Shawn Early: The whole town knows of it by this.

Bartley: Do they say what way did he die?

James Ryan: You don't know that yourself, I suppose, Bartley Fallon? You don't know he was followed and that he was laid dead with the stab of a hayfork?

Bartley: The stab of a hayfork!

Shawn Early: You don't know, I suppose, that the body was found in the Five Acre Meadow?

Bartley: The Five Acre Meadow!

Tim Casey: It is likely you don't know that the police are after the man that did it?

Bartley: The man that did it!

Mrs. Tully: You don't know, maybe, that he was made away with for the sake of Kitty Keary, his wife?

Bartley: Kitty Keary, his wife!
   (*Sits down bewildered.*)

Mrs. Tully: And what have you to say now, Bartley Fallon?

Bartley: (*Crossing himself.*) I to bring that fork here, and to find that news before me! It is much if I can ever stir from this place at all, or reach as far as the road!

Tim Casey: Look, boys, at the new magistrate, and Jo Muldoon along with him! It's best for us to quit this.

Shawn Early: That is so. It is best not to be mixed in this business at all.

James Ryan: Bad as he is, I wouldn't like to be an informer against any man.
   (*All hurry away except Mrs. Tarpey, who remains behind her stall. Enter magistrate and policeman.*)

Magistrate: I knew the district was in a bad

state, but I did not expect to be confronted with a murder at the first fair I came to.

Policeman: I am sure you did not, indeed.

Magistrate: It was well I had not gone home. I caught a few words here and there that roused my suspicions.

Policeman: So they would, too.

Magistrate: You heard the same story from everyone you asked?

Policeman: The same story—or if it was not altogether the same, anyway it was no less than the first story.

Magistrate: What is that man doing? He is sitting alone with a hayfork. He has a guilty look. The murder was done with a hayfork!

Policeman: (*In a whisper.*) That's the very man they say did the act; Bartley Fallon himself!

Magistrate: He must have found escape difficult—he is trying to brazen it out. A convict in the Andaman Islands tried the same game, but he could not escape my system! Stand aside—Don't go far—have the handcuffs ready. (*He walks up to Bartley, folds his arms, and stands before him.*) Here, my man, do you know anything of John Smith?

Bartley: Of John Smith! Who is he, now?

Policeman: Jack Smith, sir—Red Jack Smith!

Magistrate: (*Coming a step nearer and tapping him on the shoulder.*) Where is Jack Smith?

Spreading the News

Bartley: (*With a deep sigh, and shaking his head slowly.*) Where is he, indeed?

Magistrate: What have you to tell?

Bartley: It is where he was this morning, standing in this spot, singing his share of songs— no, but lighting his pipe—scraping a match on the sole of his shoe——

Magistrate: I ask you, for the third time, where is he?

Bartley: I wouldn't like to say that. It is a great mystery, and it is hard to say of any man, did he earn hatred or love.

Magistrate: Tell me all you know.

Bartley: All that I know— Well, there are the three estates; there is Limbo, and there is Purgatory, and there is——

Magistrate: Nonsense! This is trifling! Get to the point.

Bartley: Maybe you don't hold with the clergy so? That is the teaching of the clergy. Maybe you hold with the old people. It is what they do be saying, that the shadow goes wandering, and the soul is tired, and the body is taking a rest— The shadow! (*Starts up.*) I was nearly sure I saw Jack Smith not ten minutes ago at the corner of the forge, and I lost him again— Was it his ghost I saw, do you think?

Magistrate: (*To policeman.*) Conscience-struck! He will confess all now!

Bartley: His ghost to come before me! It is likely it was on account of the fork! I to have it and he to have no way to defend himself the time he met with his death!

Magistrate: (*To policeman.*) I must note down his words. (*Takes out notebook.*) (*To Bartley:*) I warn you that your words are being noted.

Bartley: If I had ha' run faster in the beginning, this terror would not be on me at the latter end! Maybe he will cast it up against me at the day of judgment— I wouldn't wonder at all at that.

Magistrate: (*Writing.*) At the day of judgment——

Bartley: It was soon for his ghost to appear to me—is it coming after me always by day it will be, and stripping the clothes off in the night time?— I wouldn't wonder at all at that, being as I am an unfortunate man!

Magistrate: (*Sternly.*) Tell me this truly. What was the motive of this crime?

Bartley: The motive, is it?

Magistrate: Yes; the motive; the cause.

Bartley: I'd sooner not say that.

Magistrate: You had better tell me truly. Was it money?

Bartley: Not at all! What did poor Jack Smith ever have in his pockets unless it might be his hands that would be in them?

Magistrate: Any dispute about land?

Bartley: (*Indignantly.*) Not at all! He never was a grabber or grabbed from any one!

Magistrate: You will find it better for you if you tell me at once.

Bartley: I tell you I wouldn't for the whole world wish to say what it was—it is a thing I would not like to be talking about.

Magistrate: There is no use in hiding it. It will be discovered in the end.

Bartley: Well, I suppose it will, seeing that mostly everybody knows it before. Whisper here now. I will tell no lie; where would be the use? (*Puts his hand to his mouth, and Magistrate stoops.*) Don't be putting the blame on the parish, for such a thing was never done in the parish before—it was done for the sake of Kitty Keary, Jack Smith's wife.

Magistrate: (*To policeman.*) Put on the handcuffs. We have been saved some trouble. I knew he would confess if taken in the right way.

(*Policeman puts on handcuffs.*

Bartley: Handcuffs now! Glory be! I always said, if there was ever any misfortune coming to this place it was on myself it would fall. I to be in handcuffs! There's no wonder at all in that.

(*Enter Mrs. Fallon, followed by the rest. She is looking back at them as she speaks.*)

Mrs. Fallon: Telling lies the whole of the people of this town are; telling lies, telling lies as fast as a dog will trot! Speaking against my poor respectable man! Saying he made an end of Jack Smith! My decent comrade! There is no better man and no kinder man in the whole of the five parishes! It's little annoyance he ever gave to any one! (*Turns and sees him.*) What in the earthly world do I see before me? Bartley Fallon in charge of the police! Handcuffs on him! O Bartley, what did you do at all at all?

Bartley: O Mary, there has a great misfortune come upon me! It is what I always said, that if there is ever any misfortune——

Mrs. Fallon: What did he do at all, or is it bewitched I am?

Magistrate: This man has been arrested on a charge of murder.

Mrs. Fallon: Whose charge is that? Don't believe them! They are all liars in this place! Give me back my man!

Magistrate. It is natural you should take his part, but you have no cause of complaint against your neighbours. He has been arrested for the murder of John Smith, on his own confession.

Mrs. Fallon: The saints of heaven protect us! And what did he want killing Jack Smith?

Magistrate: It is best you should know all. He did it on account of a love affair with the murdered man's wife.

Mrs. Fallon: (*Sitting down.*) With Jack Smith's wife! With Kitty Keary!—Ochone, the traitor!

The Crowd: A great shame, indeed. He is a traitor, indeed.

Mrs. Tully: To America he was bringing her, Mrs. Fallon.

Bartley: What are you saying, Mary? I tell you——

Mrs. Fallon: Don't say a word! I won't listen to any word you'll say! (*Stops her ears.*) O, isn't he the treacherous villain? Ohone go deo!

Bartley: Be quiet till I speak! Listen to what I say!

Mrs. Fallon: Sitting beside me on the ass car coming to the town, so quiet and so respectable, and treachery like that in his heart!

Bartley: Is it your wits you have lost or is it I myself that have lost my wits?

Mrs. Fallon: And it's hard I earned you, slaving, slaving—and you grumbling, and sighing, and coughing, and discontented, and the priest wore out anointing you, with all the times you threatened to die!

Bartley: Let you be quiet till I tell you!

Mrs. Fallon: You to bring such a disgrace into the parish. A thing that was never heard of before!

Bartley: Will you shut your mouth and hear me speaking?

Mrs. Fallon: And if it was for any sort of a fine handsome woman, but for a little fistful of a woman like Kitty Keary, that's not four feet high hardly, and not three teeth in her head unless she got new ones! May God reward you, Bartley Fallon, for the black treachery in your heart and the wickedness in your mind, and the red blood of poor Jack Smith that is wet upon your hand!

(*Voice of Jack Smith heard singing.*)

    The sea shall be dry,
        The earth under mourning and ban!
    Then loud shall he cry
        For the wife of the red-haired man!

Bartley: It's Jack Smith's voice—I never knew a ghost to sing before—. It is after myself and the fork he is coming! (*Goes back. Enter Jack Smith.*) Let one of you give him the fork and I will be clear of him now and for eternity!

Mrs. Tarpey: The Lord have mercy on us! Red Jack Smith! The man that was going to be waked!

James Ryan: Is it back from the grave you are come?

Shawn Early: Is it alive you are, or is it dead you are?

Tim Casey: Is it yourself at all that's in it?

Mrs. Tully. Is it letting on you were to be dead?

Mrs. Fallon: Dead or alive, let you stop Kitty

Keary, your wife, from bringing my man away with her to America!

Jack Smith: It is what I think, the wits are gone astray on the whole of you. What would my wife want bringing Bartley Fallon to America?

Mrs. Fallon: To leave yourself, and to get quit of you she wants, Jack Smith, and to bring him away from myself. That's what the two of them had settled together.

Jack Smith: I'll break the head of any man that says that! Who is it says it? (*To Tim Casey:*) Was it you said it? (*To Shawn Early:*) Was it you?

All together: (*Backing and shaking their heads.*) It wasn't I said it!

Jack Smith: Tell me the name of any man that said it!

All together: (*Pointing to Bartley.*) It was *him* that said it!

Jack Smith: Let me at him till I break his head!

(*Bartley backs in terror. Neighbours hold Jack Smith back.*)

Jack Smith: (*Trying to free himself.*) Let me at him! Isn't he the pleasant sort of a scarecrow for any woman to be crossing the ocean with! It's back from the docks of New York he'd be turned (*trying to rush at him again*), with a lie in his mouth and treachery in his heart, and another

Spreading the News

man's wife by his side, and he passing her off as his own! Let me at him can't you.

(*Makes another rush, but is held back.*)

Magistrate: (*Pointing to Jack Smith.*) Policeman, put the handcuffs on this man. I see it all now. A case of false impersonation, a conspiracy to defeat the ends of justice. There was a case in the Andaman Islands, a murderer of the Mopsa tribe, a religious enthusiast——

Policeman: So he might be, too.

Magistrate: We must take both these men to the scene of the murder. We must confront them with the body of the real Jack Smith.

Jack Smith: I'll break the head of any man that will find my dead body!

Magistrate: I'll call more help from the barracks. (*Blows Policeman's whistle.*)

Bartley: It is what I am thinking, if myself and Jack Smith are put together in the one cell for the night, the handcuffs will be taken off him, and his hands will be free, and murder will be done that time surely!

Magistrate: Come on! (*They turn to the right.*)

HYACINTH HALVEY

PERSONS
Hyacinth Halvey.
James Quirke, a butcher.
Fardy Farrell, a telegraph boy.
Sergeant Carden.
Mrs. Delane, Postmistress at Cloon.
Miss Joyce, the Priest's House-keeper.

HYACINTH HALVEY

Scene: Outside the Post Office at the little town of Cloon. Mrs. Delane at Post Office door. Mr. Quirke sitting on a chair at butcher's door. A dead sheep hanging beside it, and a thrush in a cage above. Fardy Farrell playing on a mouth organ. Train whistle heard.

Mrs. Delane: There is the four o'clock train, Mr. Quirke.

Mr. Quirke: Is it now, Mrs. Delane, and I not long after rising? It makes a man drowsy to be doing the half of his work in the night time. Going about the country, looking for little stags of sheep, striving to knock a few shillings together. That contract for the soldiers gives me a great deal to attend to.

Mrs. Delane: I suppose so. It's hard enough on myself to be down ready for the mail car in the morning, sorting letters in the half dark. It's often I haven't time to look who are the letters from—or the cards.

Mr. Quirke: It would be a pity you not to know any little news might be knocking about. If you did not have information of what is going on who should have it? Was it you, ma'am, was telling me that the new Sub-Sanitary Inspector would be arriving to-day?

Mrs. Delane: To-day it is he is coming, and it's likely he was in that train. There was a card about him to Sergeant Carden this morning.

Mr. Quirke: A young chap from Carrow they were saying he was.

Mrs. Delane: So he is, one Hyacinth Halvey; and indeed if all that is said of him is true, or if a quarter of it is true, he will be a credit to this town.

Mr. Quirke: Is that so?

Mrs. Delane: Testimonials he has by the score. To Father Gregan they were sent. Registered they were coming and going. Would you believe me telling you that they weighed up to three pounds?

Mr. Quirke: There must be great bulk in them indeed.

Mrs. Delane: It is no wonder he to get the job. He must have a great character so many persons to write for him as what there did.

Fardy: It would be a great thing to have a character like that.

Mrs. Delane: Indeed I am thinking it will be long before you will get the like of it, Fardy Farrell.

Fardy: If I had the like of that of a character it is not here carrying messages I would be. It's in Noonan's Hotel I would be, driving cars.

Mr. Quirke: Here is the priest's housekeeper coming.

Mrs. Delane: So she is; and there is the Sergeant a little while after her.

(*Enter Miss Joyce.*)

Mrs. Delane: Good-evening to you, Miss Joyce. What way is his Reverence to-day? Did he get any ease from the cough?

Miss Joyce: He did not indeed, Mrs. Delane. He has it sticking to him yet. Smothering he is in the night time. The most thing he comes short in is the voice.

Mrs. Delane: I am sorry, now, to hear that. He should mind himself well.

Miss Joyce: It's easy to say let him mind himself. What do you say to him going to the meeting to-night? (*Sergeant comes in.*) It's for his Reverence's *Freeman* I am come, Mrs. Delane.

Mrs. Delane: Here it is ready. I was just throwing an eye on it to see was there any news. Good-evening, Sergeant.

Sergeant: (*Holding up a placard.*) I brought this notice, Mrs. Delane, the announcement of the meeting to be held to-night in the Courthouse. You might put it up here convenient to the window. I hope you are coming to it yourself?

Mrs. Delane: I will come, and welcome. I would do more than that for you, Sergeant.

Sergeant: And you, Mr. Quirke.

Mr. Quirke: I'll come, to be sure. I forget what's this the meeting is about.

Sergeant: The Department of Agriculture is sending round a lecturer in furtherance of the moral development of the rural classes. (*Reads.*) "A lecture will be given this evening in Cloon Courthouse, illustrated by magic lantern slides—" Those will not be in it; I am informed they were all broken in the first journey, the railway company taking them to be eggs. The subject of the lecture is "The Building of Character."

Mrs. Delane: Very nice, indeed. I knew a girl lost her character, and she washed her feet in a blessed well after, and it dried up on the minute.

Sergeant: The arrangements have all been left to me, the Archdeacon being away. He knows I have a good intellect for things of the sort. But the loss of those slides puts a man out. The thing people will not see it is not likely it is the thing they will believe. I saw what they call tableaux—standing pictures, you know—one time in Dundrum——

Mrs. Delane: Miss Joyce was saying Father Gregan is supporting you.

Sergeant: I am accepting his assistance. No bigotry about me when there is a question of the welfare of any fellow-creatures. Orange and green will stand together to-night. I myself and the station-master on the one side; your parish priest in the chair.

Miss Joyce: If his Reverence would mind me he would not quit the house to-night. He is no more fit to go speak at a meeting than (*pointing to the one hanging outside Quirke's door*) that sheep.

Sergeant: I am willing to take the responsibility. He will have no speaking to do at all, unless it might be to bid them give the lecturer a hearing. The loss of those slides now is a great annoyance to me—and no time for anything. The lecturer will be coming by the next train.

Miss Joyce: Who is this coming up the street, Mrs. Delane?

Mrs. Delane: I wouldn't doubt it to be the new Sub-Sanitary Inspector. Was I telling you of the weight of the testimonials he got, Miss Joyce?

Miss Joyce: Sure I heard the curate reading them to his Reverence. He must be a wonder for principles.

Mrs. Delane: Indeed it is what I was saying to myself, he must be a very saintly young man.

>(*Enter Hyacinth Halvey. He carries a small bag and a large brown paper parcel. He stops and nods bashfully.*)

Hyacinth: Good-evening to you. I was bid to come to the post office——

Sergeant: I suppose you are Hyacinth Halvey?

I had a letter about you from the Resident Magistrate.

Hyacinth: I heard he was writing. It was my mother got a friend he deals with to ask him.

Sergeant: He gives you a very high character.

Hyacinth: It is very kind of him indeed, and he not knowing me at all. But indeed all the neighbours were very friendly. Anything any one could do to help me they did it.

Mrs. Delane: I'll engage it is the testimonals you have in your parcel? I know the wrapping paper, but they grew in bulk since I handled them.

Hyacinth: Indeed I was getting them to the last. There was not one refused me. It is what my mother was saying, a good character is no burden.

Fardy: I would believe that indeed.

Sergeant: Let us have a look at the testimonials. (*Hyacinth Halvey opens parcel, and a large number of envelopes fall out.*)

Sergeant: (*Opening and reading one by one*). "He possesses the fire of the Gael, the strength of the Norman, the vigour of the Dane, the stolidity of the Saxon"——

Hyacinth: It was the Chairman of the Poor Law Guardians wrote that.

Sergeant: "A magnificent example to old and young"——

Hyacinth: That was the Secretary of the De Wet Hurling Club——

Sergeant: "A shining example of the value conferred by an eminently careful and high class education"——

Hyacinth: That was the National Schoolmaster.

Sergeant: "Devoted to the highest ideals of his Mother-land to such an extent as is compatible with a hitherto non-parliamentary career"——

Hyacinth: That was the Member for Carrow.

Sergeant: "A splendid exponent of the purity of the race"——

Hyacinth: The Editor of the *Carrow Champion*.

Sergeant: "Admirably adapted for the efficient discharge of all possible duties that may in future be laid upon him"——

Hyacinth: The new Station-master.

Sergeant: "A champion of every cause that can legitimately benefit his fellow-creatures"—— Why, look here, my man, you are the very one to come to our assistance to-night.

Hyacinth: I would be glad to do that. What way can I do it?

Sergeant: You are a newcomer—your example would carry weight—you must stand up as a living proof of the beneficial effect of a high character, moral fibre, temperance—there is something about it here I am sure—(*Looks.*) I am sure I saw "unparalleled temperance" in some place——

Hyacinth: It was my mother's cousin wrote that—I am no drinker, but I haven't the pledge taken——

Sergeant: You might take it for the purpose.

Mr. Quirke: (*Eagerly.*) Here is an anti-treating button. I was made a present of it by one of my customers—I'll give it to you (*sticks it in Hyacinth's coat*) and welcome.

Sergeant: That is it. You can wear the button on the platform—or a bit of blue ribbon—hundreds will follow your example—I know the boys from the Workhouse will——

Hyacinth: I am in no way wishful to be an example——

Sergeant: I will read extracts from the testimonials. "There he is," I will say, "an example of one in early life who by his own unaided efforts and his high character has obtained a profitable situation"—(*Slaps his side.*) I know what I'll do. I'll engage a few corner-boys from Noonan's bar, just as they are, greasy and sodden, to stand in a group—there will be the contrast—The sight will deter others from a similar fate—That's the way to do a tableau—I knew I could turn out a success.

Hyacinth: I wouldn't like to be a contrast——

Sergeant: (*Puts testimonials in his pocket.*) I

will go now and engage those lads—sixpence each, and well worth it—Nothing like an example for the rural classes.

(*Goes off, Hyacinth feebly trying to detain him.*)

Mrs. Delane: A very nice man indeed. A little high up in himself, may be. I'm not one that blames the police. Sure they have their own bread to earn like every other one. And indeed it is often they will let a thing pass.

Mr. Quirke: (*Gloomily.*) Sometimes they will, and more times they will not.

Miss Joyce: And where will you be finding a lodging, Mr. Halvey?

Hyacinth: I was going to ask that myself, ma'am. I don't know the town.

Miss Joyce: I know of a good lodging, but it is only a very good man would be taken into it.

Mrs. Delane: Sure there could be no objection there to Mr. Halvey. There is no appearance on him but what is good, and the Sergeant after taking him up the way he is doing.

Miss Joyce: You will be near to the Sergeant in the lodging I speak of. The house is convenient to the barracks.

Hyacinth: (*Doubtfully.*) To the barracks?

Miss Joyce: Alongside of it and the barrack yard behind. And that's not all. It is opposite to the priest's house.

Hyacinth: Opposite, is it?

Miss Joyce: A very respectable place, indeed, and a very clean room you will get. I know it well. The curate can see into it from his window.

Hyacinth: Can he now?

Fardy: There was a good many, I am thinking, went into that lodging and left it after.

Miss Joyce: (*Sharply*) It is a lodging you will never be let into or let stop in, Fardy. If they did go they were a good riddance.

Fardy: John Hart, the plumber, left it——

Miss Joyce: If he did it was because he dared not pass the police coming in, as he used, with a rabbit he was after snaring in his hand.

Fardy: The schoolmaster himself left it.

Miss Joyce: He needn't have left it if he hadn't taken to card-playing. What way could you say your prayers, and shadows shuffling and dealing before you on the blind?

Hyacinth: I think maybe I'd best look around a bit before I'll settle in a lodging——

Miss Joyce: Not at all. *You* won't be wanting to pull down the blind.

Mrs. Delane: It is not likely *you* will be snaring rabbits.

Miss Joyce: Or bringing in a bottle and taking an odd glass the way James Kelly did.

Mrs. Delane: Or writing threatening notices, and the police taking a view of you from the rear.

Miss Joyce: Or going to roadside dances, or running after good-for-nothing young girls——

Hyacinth: I give you my word I'm not so harmless as you think.

Mrs. Delane: Would you be putting a lie on these, Mr. Halvey? (*Touching testimonials.*) I know well the way *you* will be spending the evenings, writing letters to your relations——

Miss Joyce: Learning O'Growney's exercises——

Mrs. Delane: Sticking post cards in an album for the convent bazaar.

Miss Joyce: Reading the *Catholic Young Man*——

Mrs. Delane: Playing the melodies on a melodeon——

Miss Joyce: Looking at the pictures in the *Lives of the Saints*. I'll hurry on and engage the room for you.

Hyacinth: Wait. Wait a minute——

Miss Joyce: No trouble at all. I told you it was just opposite. (*Goes.*)

Mr. Quirke: I suppose I must go upstairs and ready myself for the meeting. If it wasn't for the contract I have for the soldiers' barracks and the Sergeant's good word, I wouldn't go anear it. (*Goes into shop.*)

Mrs. Delane: I should be making myself ready too. I must be in good time to see you being made an example of, Mr. Halvey. It is I myself was the first to say it; you will be a credit to the town. (*Goes.*)

Hyacinth: (*In a tone of agony.*) I wish I had never seen Cloon.

Fardy: What is on you?

Hyacinth: I wish I had never left Carrow. I wish I had been drowned the first day I thought of it, and I'd be better off.

Fardy: What is it ails you?

Hyacinth: I wouldn't for the best pound ever I had be in this place to-day.

Fardy: I don't know what you are talking about.

Hyacinth: To have left Carrow, if it was a poor place, where I had my comrades, and an odd spree, and a game of cards—and a coursing match coming on, and I promised a new greyhound from the city of Cork. I'll die in this place, the way I am. I'll be too much closed in.

Fardy: Sure it mightn't be as bad as what you think.

Hyacinth: Will you tell me, I ask you, what way can I undo it?

Fardy: What is it you are wanting to undo?

Hyacinth: Will you tell me what way can I get rid of my character?

Fardy: To get rid of it, is it?

Hyacinth: That is what I said. Aren't you after hearing the great character they are after putting on me?

Fardy: That is a good thing to have.

Hyacinth: It is not. It's the worst in the world. If I hadn't it, I wouldn't be like a prize mangold at a show with every person praising me.

Fardy: If I had it, I wouldn't be like a head in a barrel, with every person making hits at me.

Hyacinth: If I hadn't it, I wouldn't be shoved into a room with all the clergy watching me and the police in the back yard.

Fardy: If I had it, I wouldn't be but a message-carrier now, and a clapper scaring birds in the summer time.

Hyacinth: If I hadn't it, I wouldn't be wearing this button and brought up for an example at the meeting.

Fardy: (*Whistles.*) Maybe you're not, so, what those papers make you out to be?

Hyacinth: How would I be what they make me out to be? Was there ever any person of that sort since the world was a world, unless it might be Saint Antony of Padua looking down from the chapel wall? If it is like that I was, isn't it in Mount Melleray I would be, or with the Friars at Esker? Why would I be living in the world at all, or doing the world's work?

Fardy: (*Taking up parcel.*) Who would think, now, there would be so much lies in a small place like Carrow?

Hyacinth: It was my mother's cousin did it. He said I was not reared for labouring—he gave me a new suit and bid me never to come back again. I daren't go back to face him—the neighbours knew my mother had a long family—bad luck to them the day they gave me these. (*Tears letters and scatters them.*) I'm done with testimonials. They won't be here to bear witness against me.

Fardy: The Sergeant thought them to be great. Sure he has the samples of them in his pocket. There's not one in the town but will know before morning that you are the next thing to an earthly saint.

Hyacinth: (*Stamping.*) I'll stop their mouths. I'll show them I can be a terror for badness. I'll do some injury. I'll commit some crime. The first thing I'll do I'll go and get drunk. If I never did it before I'll do it now. I'll get drunk—then I'll make an assault—I tell you I'd think as little of taking a life as of blowing out a candle.

Fardy: If you get drunk you are done for. Sure that will be held up after as an excuse for any breaking of the law.

Hyacinth: I will break the law. Drunk or sober I'll break it. I'll do something that will have no excuse. What would you say is the worst crime that any man can do?

Fardy: I don't know. I heard the Sergeant

saying one time it was to obstruct the police in the discharge of their duty——

Hyacinth: That won't do. It's a patriot I would be then, worse than before, with my picture in the weeklies. It's a red crime I must commit that will make all respectable people quit minding me. What can I do? Search your mind now.

Fardy: It's what I heard the old people saying there could be no worse crime than to steal a sheep——

Hyacinth: I'll steal a sheep—or a cow—or a horse—if that will leave me the way I was before.

Fardy: It's maybe in gaol it will leave you.

Hyacinth: I don't care—I'll confess—I'll tell why I did it—I give you my word I would as soon be picking oakum or breaking stones as to be perched in the daylight the same as that bird, and all the town chirruping to me or bidding me chirrup——

Fardy: There is reason in that, now.

Hyacinth: Help me, will you?

Fardy: Well, if it is to steal a sheep you want, you haven't far to go.

Hyacinth: (*Looking round wildly.*) Where is it? I see no sheep.

Fardy: Look around you.

Hyacinth: I see no living thing but that thrush——

Fardy: Did I say it was living? What is that hanging on Quirke's rack?

Hyacinth: It's (*fingers it*) a sheep, sure enough——

Fardy: Well, what ails you that you can't bring it away?

Hyacinth: It's a dead one——

Fardy: What matter if it is?

Hyacinth: If it was living I could drive it before me——

Fardy: You could. Is it to your own lodging you would drive it? Sure everyone would take it to be a pet you brought from Carrow.

Hyacinth: I suppose they might.

Fardy: Miss Joyce sending in for news of it and it bleating behind the bed.

Hyacinth: (*Distracted*). Stop! stop!

Mrs. Delane: (*From upper window.*) Fardy! Are you there, Fardy Farrell?

Fardy: I am, ma'am.

Mrs. Delane: (*From window.*) Look and tell me is that the telegraph I hear ticking?

Fardy: (*Looking in at door.*) It is, ma'am.

Mrs. Delane: Then botheration to it, and I not dressed or undressed. Wouldn't you say, now, it's to annoy me it is calling me down. I'm coming! I'm coming! (*Disappears.*)

Fardy: Hurry on, now! hurry! She'll be coming out on you. If you are going to do it, do it, and if you are not, let it alone.

Hyacinth: I'll do it! I'll do it!

Hyacinth Halvey

Fardy: (Lifting the sheep on his back.) I'll give you a hand with it.

Hyacinth: (Goes a step or two and turns round.) You told me no place where I could hide it.

Fardy: You needn't go far. There is the church beyond at the side of the Square. Go round to the ditch behind the wall—there's nettles in it.

Hyacinth: That'll do.

Fardy: She's coming out—run! run!

Hyacinth: (Runs a step or two.) It's slipping!

Fardy: Hoist it up! I'll give it a hoist! *(Halvey runs out.)*

Mrs. Delane: (Calling out.) What are you doing Fardy Farrell? Is it idling you are?

Fardy: Waiting I am, ma'am, for the message——

Mrs. Delane: Never mind the message yet. Who said it was ready? *(Going to door.)* Go ask for the loan of—no, but ask news of—Here, now go bring that bag of Mr. Halvey's to the lodging Miss Joyce has taken——

Fardy: I will, ma'am. *(Takes bag and goes out.)*

Mrs. Delane: (Coming out with a telegram in her hand.) Nobody here? *(Looks round and calls cautiously.)* Mr. Quirke! Mr. Quirke! James Quirke!

Mr. Quirke: (Looking out of his upper window with soap-suddy face). What is it, Mrs. Delane?

Mrs. Delane: (*Beckoning.*) Come down here till I tell you.

Mr. Quirke: I cannot do that. I'm not fully shaved.

Mrs. Delane: You'd come if you knew the news I have:

Mr. Quirke: Tell it to me now. I'm not so supple as I was.

Mrs. Delane: Whisper now, have you an enemy in any place?

Mr. Quirke: It's likely I may have. A man in business——

Mrs. Delane: I was thinking you had one.

Mr. Quirke: Why would you think that at this time more than any other time?

Mrs. Delane: If you could know what is in this envelope you would know that, James Quirke.

Mr. Quirke: Is that so? And what, now, is there in it?

Mrs. Delane: Who do you think now is it addressed to?

Mr. Quirke: How would I know that, and I not seeing it?

Mrs. Delane: That is true. Well, it is a message from Dublin Castle to the Sergeant of Police!

Mr. Quirke: To Sergeant Carden, is it?

Mrs. Delane: It is. And it concerns yourself.

Mr. Quirke: Myself, is it? What accusation can they be bringing against me? I'm a peaceable man.

Mrs. Delane: Wait till you hear.

Mr. Quirke: Maybe they think I was in that moonlighting case——

Mrs. Delane: That is not it——

Mr. Quirke: I was not in it—I was but in the neighbouring field—cutting up a dead cow, that those never had a hand in——

Mrs. Delane: You're out of it——

Mr. Quirke: They had their faces blackened. There is no man can say I recognized them.

Mrs. Delane: That's not what they're saying——

Mr. Quirke: I'll swear I did not hear their voices or know them if I did hear them.

Mrs. Delane: I tell you it has nothing to do with that. It might be better for you if it had.

Mr. Quirke: What is it, so?

Mrs. Delane: It is an order to the Sergeant bidding him immediately to seize all suspicious meat in your house. There is an officer coming down. There are complaints from the Shannon Fort Barracks.

Mr. Quirke: I'll engage it was that pork.

Mrs. Delane: What ailed it for them to find fault?

Mr. Quirke: People are so hard to please nowadays, and I recommended them to salt it.

Mrs. Delane: They had a right to have minded your advice.

Mr. Quirke: There was nothing on that pig at all but that it went mad on poor O'Grady that owned it.

Mrs. Delane: So I heard, and went killing all before it.

Mr. Quirke: Sure it's only in the brain madness can be. I heard the doctor saying that.

Mrs. Delane: He should know.

Mr. Quirke: I give you my word I cut the head off it. I went to the loss of it, throwing it to the eels in the river. If they had salted the meat, as I advised them, what harm would it have done to any person on earth?

Mrs. Delane: I hope no harm will come on poor Mrs. Quirke and the family.

Mr. Quirke: Maybe it wasn't that but some other thing——

Mrs. Delane: Here is Fardy. I must send the message to the Sergeant. Well, Mr. Quirke, I'm glad I had the time to give you a warning.

Mr. Quirke: I'm obliged to you, indeed. You were always very neighbourly, Mrs. Delane. Don't be too quick now sending the message. There is just one article I would like to put away out of the house before the Sergeant will come. (*Enter Fardy.*)

Mrs. Delane: Here now, Fardy—that's not the way you're going to the barracks. Anyone would think you were scaring birds yet. Put on your uniform. (*Fardy goes into office.*) You have this message to bring to the Sergeant of Police. Get your cap now, it's under the counter.

(*Fardy reappears, and she gives him telegram.*)

Fardy: I'll bring it to the station. It's there he was going.

Mrs. Delane: You will not, but to the barracks. It can wait for him there.

(*Fardy goes off. Mr. Quirke has appeared at door.*)

Mr. Quirke: It was indeed a very neighbourly act, Mrs. Delane, and I'm obliged to you. There is just *one* article to put out of the way. The Sergeant may look about him then and welcome. It's well I cleared the premises on yesterday. A consignment to Birmingham I sent. The Lord be praised isn't England a terrible country with all it consumes?

Mrs. Delane: Indeed you always treat the neighbours very decent, Mr. Quirke, not asking them to buy from you.

Mr. Quirke: Just one article. (*Turns to rack.*) That sheep I brought in last night. It was for a charity indeed I bought it from the widow woman at Kiltartan Cross. Where would the poor make a profit out of their dead meat without me? Where now is it? Well, now, I could have swore that that sheep was hanging there on the rack when I went in——

Mrs. Delane: You must have put it in some other place.

Mr. Quirke: (*Going in and searching and coming out.*) I did not; there is no other place for me to put it. Is it gone blind I am, or is it not in it, it is?

Mrs. Delane: It's not there now anyway.

Mr. Quirke: Didn't you take notice of it there yourself this morning?

Mrs. Delane: I have it in my mind that I did; but it's not there now.

Mr. Quirke: There was no one here could bring it away?

Mrs. Delane: Is it me myself you suspect of taking it, James Quirke?

Mr. Quirke: Where is it at all? It is certain it was not of itself it walked away. It was dead, and very dead, the time I bought it.

Mrs. Delane: I have a pleasant neighbour indeed that accuses me that I took his sheep. I wonder, indeed, you to say a thing like that! I to steal your sheep or your rack or anything that belongs to you or to your trade! Thank you, James Quirke. I am much obliged to you indeed.

Mr. Quirke: Ah, be quiet, woman; be quiet——

Mrs. Delane: And let me tell you, James Quirke, that I would sooner starve and see everyone belonging to me starve than to eat the size of a thimble of any joint that ever was on your rack or that ever will be on it, whatever the soldiers may eat that have no other thing to get, or the English that devour all sorts, or the poor ravenous people that's down by the sea! (*She turns to go into shop.*)

Mr. Quirke: (*Stopping her.*) Don't be talking foolishness, woman. Who said you took my meat? Give heed to me now. There must some other message have come. The Sergeant must have got some other message.

Mrs. Delane: (*Sulkily.*) If there is any way for a message to come that is quicker than to come by the wires, tell me what it is and I'll be obliged to you.

Mr. Quirke: The Sergeant was up here making an excuse he was sticking up that notice. What was he doing here, I ask you?

Mrs. Delane: How would I know what brought him?

Mr. Quirke: It is what he did; he made as if to go away—he turned back again and I shaving —he brought away the sheep—he will have it for evidence against me——

Mrs. Delane: (*Interested.*) That might be so.

Mr. Quirke: I would sooner it to have been any other beast nearly ever I had upon the rack.

Mrs. Delane: Is that so?

Mr. Quirke: I bade the Widow Early to kill

it a fortnight ago—but she would not, she was that covetous!

Mrs. Delane: What was on it?

Mr. Quirke: How would I know what was on it? Whatever was on it, it was the will of God put it upon it—wasted it was, and shivering and refusing its share.

Mrs. Delane: The poor thing.

Mr. Quirke: Gone all to nothing—wore away like a flock of thread. It did not weigh as much as a lamb of two months.

Mrs. Delane: It is likely the Inspector will bring it to Dublin?

Mr. Quirke: The ribs of it streaky with the dint of patent medicines——

Mrs. Delane: I wonder is it to the Petty Sessions you'll be brought or is it to the Assizes?

Mr. Quirke: I'll speak up to them. I'll make my defence. What can the Army expect at fippence a pound?

Mrs. Delane: It is likely there will be no bail allowed?

Mr. Quirke: Would they be wanting me to give them good quality meat out of my own pocket? Is it to encourage them to fight the poor Indians and Africans they would have me? It's the Anti-Enlisting Societies should pay the fine for me.

Mrs. Delane: It's not a fine will be put on you.

I'm afraid. It's five years in gaol you will be apt to be getting. Well, I'll try and be a good neighbour to poor Mrs. Quirke.

(*Mr. Quirke, who has been stamping up and down, sits down and weeps. Halvey comes in and stands on one side.*)

Mr. Quirke: Hadn't I heart-scalding enough before, striving to rear five weak children?

Mrs. Delane: I suppose they will be sent to the Industrial Schools?

Mr. Quirke: My poor wife——

Mrs. Delane: I'm afraid the workhouse——

Mr. Quirke: And she out in an ass-car at this minute helping me to follow my trade.

Mrs. De ane: I hope they will not arrest her along with you.

Mr. Quirke: I'll give myself up to justice. I'll plead guilty! I'll be recommended to mercy!

Mrs. Delane: It might be best for you.

Mr. Quirke: Who would think so great a misfortune could come upon a family through the bringing away of one sheep!

Hyacinth: (*Coming forward.*) Let you make yourself easy.

Mr. Quirke: Easy! It's easy to say let you make yourself easy.

Hyacinth: I can tell you where it is.

Mr. Quirke: Where what is?

Hyacinth: The sheep you are fretting after.

Mr. Quirke: What do you know about it?

Hyacinth: I know everything about it.

Mr. Quirke: I suppose the Sergeant told you?

Hyacinth: He told me nothing.

Mr. Quirke: I suppose the whole town knows it, so?

Hyacinth: No one knows it, as yet.

Mr. Quirke: And the Sergeant didn't see it?

Hyacinth: No one saw it or brought it away but myself.

Mr. Quirke: Where did you put it at all?

Hyacinth: In the ditch behind the church wall. In among the nettles it is. Look at the way they have me stung. (*Holds out hands.*)

Mr. Quirke: In the ditch! The best hiding place in the town.

Hyacinth: I never thought it would bring such great trouble upon you. You can't say anyway I did not tell you.

Mr. Quirke: You yourself that brought it away and that hid it! I suppose it was coming in the train you got information about the message to the police.

Hyacinth: What now do you say to me?

Mr. Quirke: Say! I say I am as glad to hear what you said as if it was the Lord telling me I'd be in heaven this minute.

Hyacinth: What are you going to do to me?

Mr. Quirke: Do, is it? (*Grasps his hand.*)

Hyacinth Halvey

Any earthly thing you would wish me to do, I will do it.

Hyacinth: I suppose you will tell——

Mr. Quirke: Tell! It's I that will tell when all is quiet. It is I will give you the good name through the town!

Hyacinth: I don't well understand.

Mr. Quirke: (*Embracing him.*) The man that preserved me!

Hyacinth: That preserved you?

Mr. Quirke: That kept me from ruin!

Hyacinth: From ruin?

Mr. Quirke: That saved me from disgrace!

Hyacinth: (*To Mrs. Delane.*) What is he saying at all?

Mr. Quirke: From the Inspector!

Hyacinth: What is he talking about?

Mr. Quirke: From the magistrates!

Hyacinth: He is making some mistake.

Mr. Quirke: From the Winter Assizes!

Hyacinth: Is he out of his wits?

Mr. Quirke: Five years in gaol!

Hyacinth: Hasn't he the queer talk?

Mr. Quirke: The loss of the contract!

Hyacinth: Are my own wits gone astray?

Mr. Quirke: What way can I repay you?

Hyacinth: (*Shouting.*) I tell you I took the sheep——

Mr. Quirke: You did, God reward you!

Hyacinth: I stole away with it——

Mr. Quirke: The blessing of the poor on you!

Hyacinth: I put it out of sight——

Mr. Quirke: The blessing of my five children——

Hyacinth: I may as well say nothing——

Mrs. Delane: Let you be quiet now, Quirke. Here's the Sergeant coming to search the shop——

  (*Sergeant comes in: Quirke leaves go of Halvey, who arranges his hat, etc.*)

Sergeant: The Department to blazes!

Mrs. Delane: What is it is putting you out?

Sergeant: To go to the train to meet the lecturer, and there to get a message through the guard that he was unavoidably detained in the South, holding an inquest on the remains of a drake.

Mrs. Delane: The lecturer, is it?

Sergeant: To be sure. What else would I be talking of? The lecturer has failed me, and where am I to go looking for a person that I would think fitting to take his place?

Mrs. Delane: And that's all? And you didn't get any message but the one?

Sergeant: Is that all? I am surprised at you, Mrs. Delane. Isn't it enough to upset a man, within three quarters of an hour of the time of the meeting? Where, I would ask you, am I to find a man that has education enough and wit enough and character enough to put up speaking on the platform on the minute?

Mr. Quirke: (*Jumps up.*) It is I myself will tell you that.

Sergeant: You!

Mr. Quirke: (*Slapping Halvey on the back.*) Look at here, Sergeant. There is not one word was said in all those papers about this young man before you but it is true. And there could be no good thing said of him that would be too good for him.

Sergeant: It might not be a bad idea.

Mr. Quirke: Whatever the paper said about him, Sergeant, I can say more again. It has come to my knowledge—by chance—that since he came to this town that young man has saved a whole family from destruction.

Sergeant: That is much to his credit—helping the rural classes——

Mr. Quirke: A family and a long family, big and little, like sods of turf—and they depending on a—on one that might be on his way to dark trouble at this minute if it was not for his assistance. Believe me, he is the most sensible man, and the wittiest, and the kindest, and the best helper of the poor that ever stood before you in this square. Is not that so, Mrs. Delane?

Mrs. Delane: It is true indeed. Where he gets his wisdom and his wit and his information from

I don't know, unless it might be that he is gifted from above.

Sergeant: Well, Mrs. Delane, I think we have settled that question. Mr. Halvey, you will be the speaker at the meeting. The lecturer sent these notes—you can lengthen them into a speech. You can call to the people of Cloon to stand out, to begin the building of their character. I saw a lecturer do it one time at Dundrum. "Come up here," he said, "Dare to be a Daniel," he said——

Hyacinth: I can't—I won't——

Sergeant: (*Looking at papers and thrusting them into his hand.*) You will find it quite easy. I will conduct you to the platform—these papers before you and a glass of water—That's settled. (*Turns to go.*) Follow me on to the Courthouse in half an hour—I must go to the barracks first—I heard there was a telegram— (*Calls back as he goes.*) Don't be late, Mrs. Delane. Mind, Quirke, you promised to come.

Mrs. Delane: Well, it's time for me to make an end of settling myself—and indeed, Mr. Quirke, you'd best do the same.

Mr. Quirke: (*Rubbing his cheek.*) I suppose so. I had best keep on good terms with him for the present. (*Turns.*) Well, now, I had a great escape this day.

(*Both go in as Fardy reappears whistling.*)

Hyacinth: (*Sitting down.*) I don't know in the world what has come upon the world that the half of the people of it should be cracked!

Fardy: Weren't you found out yet?

Hyacinth: Found out, is it? I don't know what you mean by being found out.

Fardy: Didn't he miss the sheep?

Hyacinth: He did, and I told him it was I took it—and what happened I declare to goodness I don't know— Will you look at these? (*Holds out notes.*)

Fardy: Papers! Are they more testimonials?

Hyacinth: They are what is worse. (*Gives a hoarse laugh.*) Will you come and see me on the platform—these in my hand—and I speaking—giving out advice. (*Fardy whistles.*) Why didn't you tell me, the time you advised me to steal a sheep, that in this town it would qualify a man to go preaching, and the priest in the chair looking on.

Fardy: The time I took a few apples that had fallen off a stall, they did not ask me to hold a meeting. They welted me well.

Hyacinth: (*Looking round.*) I would take apples if I could see them. I wish I had broke my neck before I left Carrow and I'd be better off! I wish I had got six months the time I was caught setting snares—I wish I had robbed a church.

Fardy: Would a Protestant church do?

Hyacinth: I suppose it wouldn't be so great a sin.

Fardy: It's likely the Sergeant would think worse of it—Anyway, if you want to rob one, it's the Protestant church is the handiest.

Hyacinth: (*Getting up.*) Show me what way to do it?

Fardy: (*Pointing.*) I was going around it a few minutes ago, to see might there be e'er a dog scenting the sheep, and I noticed the window being out.

Hyacinth: Out, out and out?

Fardy: It was, where they are putting coloured glass in it for the distiller——

Hyacinth: What good does that do me?

Fardy: Every good. You could go in by that window if you had some person to give you a hoist. Whatever riches there is to get in it then, you'll get them.

Hyacinth: I don't want riches. I'll give you all I will find if you will come and hoist me.

Fardy: Here is Miss Joyce coming to bring you to your lodging. Sure I brought your bag to it, the time you were away with the sheep——

Hyacinth: Run! Run!

(*They go off. Enter Miss Joyce.*)

Miss Joyce: Are you here, Mrs. Delane? Where, can you tell me, is Mr. Halvey?

Mrs. Delane: (*Coming out dressed.*) It's likely he

is gone on to the Courthouse. Did you hear he is to be in the chair and to make an address to the meeting?

Miss Joyce: He is getting on fast. His Reverence says he will be a good help in the parish. Who would think, now, there would be such a godly young man in a little place like Carrow!

(*Enter Sergeant in a hurry, with telegram.*)

Sergeant: What time did this telegram arrive, Mrs. Delane?

Mrs. Delane: I couldn't be rightly sure, Sergeant. But sure it's marked on it, unless the clock I have is gone wrong.

Sergeant: It is marked on it. And I have the time I got it marked on my own watch.

Mrs. Delane: Well, now, I wonder none of the police would have followed you with it from the barracks—and they with so little to do——

Sergeant: (*Looking in at Quirke's shop.*) Well, I am sorry to do what I have to do, but duty is duty.

(*He ransacks shop. Mrs. Delane looks on. Mr. Quirke puts his head out of window.*)

Mr. Quirke: What is that going on inside? (*No answer.*) Is there any one inside, I ask? (*No answer.*) It must be that dog of Tannian's—wait till I get at him.

Mrs. Delane: It is Sergeant Carden, Mr.

Quirke. He would seem to be looking for something——

> (*Mr. Quirke appears in shop. Sergeant comes out, makes another dive, taking up sacks, etc.*)

Mr. Quirke: I'm greatly afraid I am just out of meat, Sergeant—and I'm sorry now to disoblige you, and you not being in the habit of dealing with me——

Sergeant: I should think not, indeed.

Mr. Quirke: Looking for a tender little bit of lamb, I suppose you are, for Mrs. Carden and the youngsters?

Sergeant: I am not.

Mr. Quirke: If I had it now, I'd be proud to offer it to you, and make no charge. I'll be killing a good kid to-morrow. Mrs. Carden might fancy a bit of it——

Sergeant: I have had orders to search your establishment for unwholesome meat, and I am come here to do it.

Mr. Quirke: (*Sitting down with a smile.*) Is that so? Well, isn't it a wonder the schemers does be in the world.

Sergeant: It is not the first time there have been complaints.

Mr. Quirke: I suppose not. Well, it is on their own head it will fall at the last!

Sergeant: I have found nothing so far.

Mr. Quirke: I suppose not, indeed. What is there you could find, and it not in it?

Sergeant: Have you no meat at all upon the premises?

Mr. Quirke: I have, indeed, a nice barrel of bacon.

Sergeant: What way did it die?

Mr. Quirke: It would be hard for me to say that. American it is. How would I know what way they do be killing the pigs out there? Machinery, I suppose, they have—steam hammers——

Sergeant: Is there nothing else here at all?

Mr. Quirke: I give you my word, there is no meat living or dead in this place, but yourself and myself and that bird above in the cage.

Sergeant: Well, I must tell the Inspector I could find nothing. But mind yourself for the future.

Mr. Quirke: Thank you, Sergeant. I will do that. (*Enter Fardy. He stops short.*)

Sergeant: It was you delayed that message to me, I suppose? You'd best mend your ways or I'll have something to say to you. (*Seizes and shakes him.*)

Fardy: That's the way everyone does be faulting me. (*Whimpers.*)

> (*The Sergeant gives him another shake. A half-crown falls out of his pocket.*)

Miss Joyce: (*Picking it up.*) A half-a-crown! Where, now, did you get that much, Fardy?

Fardy: Where did I get it, is it!

Miss Joyce: I'll engage it was in no honest way you got it.

Fardy: I picked it up in the street——

Miss Joyce: If you did, why didn't you bring it to the Sergeant or to his Reverence?

Mrs. Delane: And some poor person, may be, being at the loss of it.

Miss Joyce: I'd best bring it to his Reverence. Come with me, Fardy, till he will question you about it.

Fardy: It was not altogether in the street I found it——

Miss Joyce: There, now! I knew you got it in no good way! Tell me, now.

Fardy: It was playing pitch and toss I won it——

Miss Joyce: And who would play for half-crowns with the like of you, Fardy Farrell? Who was it, now?

Fardy: It was—a stranger——

Miss Joyce: Do you hear that? A stranger! Did you see e'er a stranger in this town, Mrs. Delane, or Sergeant Carden, or Mr. Quirke?

Mr. Quirke: Not a one.

Sergeant: There was no stranger here.

Mrs. Delane: There could not be one here without me knowing it.

Fardy: I tell you there was.

Miss Joyce: Come on, then, and tell who was he to his Reverence.

Sergeant: (*Taking other arm.*) Or to the bench.

Fardy: I did get it, I tell you, from a stranger.

Sergeant: Where is he, so?

Fardy: He's in some place—not far away.

Sergeant: Bring me to him.

Fardy: He'll be coming here.

Sergeant: Tell me the truth and it will be better for you.

Fardy: (*Weeping.*) Let me go and I will.

Sergeant: (*Letting go.*) Now—who did you get it from?

Fardy: From that young chap came to-day, Mr. Halvey.

All: Mr. Halvey!

Mr. Quirke: (*Indignantly.*) What are you saying, you young ruffian you? Hyacinth Halvey to be playing pitch and toss with the like of you!

Fardy: I didn't say that.

Miss Joyce: You did say it. You said it now.

Mr. Quirke: Hyacinth Halvey! The best man that ever came into this town!

Miss Joyce: Well, what lies he has!

Mr. Quirke: It's my belief the half-crown is a bad one. May be it's to pass it off it was given to him. There were tinkers in the town at the time of the fair. Give it here to me. (*Bites it.*)

No, indeed, it's sound enough. Here, Sergeant, it's best for you take it.

(*Gives it to Sergeant, who examines it.*)

Sergeant: Can it be? Can it be what I think it to be?

Mr. Quirke: What is it? What do you take it to be?

Sergeant: It is, it is. I know it. I know this half-crown——

Mr. Quirke: That is a queer thing, now.

Sergeant: I know it well. I have been handling it in the church for the last twelvemonth——

Mr. Quirke: Is that so?

Sergeant: It is the nest-egg half-crown we hand round in the collection plate every Sunday morning. I know it by the dint on the Queen's temples and the crooked scratch under her nose.

Mr. Quirke: (*Examining it.*) So there is, too.

Sergeant: This is a bad business. It has been stolen from the church.

All: O! O! O!

Sergeant: (*Seizing Fardy.*) You have robbed the church!

Fardy: (*Terrified.*) I tell you I never did!

Sergeant: I have the proof of it.

Fardy: Say what you like! I never put a foot in it!

Sergeant: How did you get this, so?

Miss Joyce: I suppose from the *stranger?*

Mrs. Delane: I suppose it was Hyacinth Halvey gave it to you, now?

Fardy: It was so.

Sergeant: I suppose it was he robbed the church?

Fardy: (Sobs.) You will not believe me if I say it.

Mr. Quirke: O! the young vagabond! Let me get at him!

Mrs. Delane: Here he is himself now!

>   (*Hyacinth comes in. Fardy releases himself and creeps behind him.*)

Mrs. Delane: It is time you to come, Mr. Halvey, and shut the mouth of this young schemer.

Miss Joyce: I would like you to hear what he says of you, Mr. Halvey. Pitch and toss, he says.

Mr. Quirke: Robbery, he says.

Mrs. Delane: Robbery of a church.

Sergeant: He has had a bad name long enough. Let him go to a reformatory now.

Fardy: (*Clinging to Hyacinth.*) Save me, save me! I'm a poor boy trying to knock out a way of living; I'll be destroyed if I go to a reformatory. (*Kneels and clings to Hyacinth's knees.*)

Hyacinth: I'll save you easy enough.

Fardy: Don't let me be gaoled!

Hyacinth: I am going to tell them.

Fardy: I'm a poor orphan——

Hyacinth: Will you let me speak?
Fardy: I'll get no more chance in the world——
Hyacinth: Sure I'm trying to free you——
Fardy: It will be tasked to me always.
Hyacinth: Be quiet, can't you.
Fardy: Don't you desert me!
Hyacinth: Will you be silent?
Fardy: Take it on yourself.
Hyacinth: I will if you'll let me.
Fardy: Tell them you did it.
Hyacinth: I am going to do that.
Fardy: Tell them it was you got in at the window.
Hyacinth: I will! I will!
Fardy: Say it was you robbed the box.
Hyacinth: I'll say it! I'll say it!
Fardy: It being open!
Hyacinth: Let me tell, let me tell.
Fardy: Of all that was in it.
Hyacinth: I'll tell them that.
Fardy: And gave it to me.
Hyacinth: (*Putting hand on his mouth and dragging him up.*) Will you stop and let me speak?
Sergeant: We can't be wasting time. Give him here to me.
Hyacinth: I can't do that. He must be let alone.
Sergeant: (*Seizing him.*) He'll be let alone in the lock-up.

Hyacinth: He must not be brought there.
Sergeant: I'll let no man get him off.
Hyacinth: I will get him off.
Sergeant: You will not!
Hyacinth: I will.
Sergeant: Do you think to buy him off?
Hyacinth: I will buy him off with my own confession.
Sergeant: And what will that be?
Hyacinth: It was I robbed the church.
Sergeant: That is likely indeed!
Hyacinth: Let him go, and take me. I tell you I did it.
Sergeant: It would take witnesses to prove that.
Hyacinth: (*Pointing to Fardy.*) He will be witness.
Fardy: O! Mr. Halvey, I would not wish to do that. Get me off and I will say nothing.
Hyacinth: Sure you must. You will be put on oath in the court.
Fardy: I will not! I will not! All the world knows I don't understand the nature of an oath!
Mr. Quirke: (*Coming forward.*) Is it blind ye all are?
Mrs. Delane: What are you talking about?
Mr. Quirke: Is it fools ye all are?
Miss Joyce: Speak for yourself.
Mr. Quirke: Is it idiots ye all are?

Sergeant: Mind who you're talking to.

Mr. Quirke: (*Seizing Hyacinth's hands.*) Can't you see? Can't you hear? Where are your wits? Was ever such a thing seen in this town?

Mrs. Delane: Say out what you have to say.

Mr. Quirke: A walking saint he is!

Mrs. Delane: Maybe so.

Mr. Quirke: The preserver of the poor! Talk of the holy martyrs! They are nothing at all to what he is! Will you look at him! To save that poor boy he is going! To take the blame on himself he is going! To say he himself did the robbery he is going! Before the magistrate he is going! To gaol he is going! Taking the blame on his own head! Putting the sin on his own shoulders! Letting on to have done a robbery! Telling a lie—that it may be forgiven him—to his own injury! Doing all that I tell you to save the character of a miserable slack lad, that rose in poverty.

(*Murmur of admiration from all.*)

Mr. Quirke: Now, what do you say?

Sergeant: (*Pressing his hand.*) Mr. Halvey, you have given us all a lesson. To please you, I will make no information against the boy. (*Shakes him and helps him up.*) I will put back the half-crown in the poor-box next Sunday. (*To Fardy.*) What have you to say to your benefactor?

Fardy: I'm obliged to you, Mr. Halvey. You

behaved very decent to me, very decent indeed. I'll never let a word be said against you if I live to be a hundred years.

Sergeant: (*Wiping eyes with a blue handkerchief.*) I will tell it at the meeting. It will be a great encouragement to them to build up their character. I'll tell it to the priest and he taking the chair——

Hyacinth: O stop, will you——

Mr. Quirke: The chair. It's in the chair he himself should be. It's in a chair we will put him now. It's to chair him through the streets we will. Sure he'll be an example and a blessing to the whole of the town. (*Seizes Halvey and seats him in chair.*) Now, Sergeant, give a hand. Here, Fardy.

> (*They all lift the chair with Halvey in it, wildly protesting.*)

Mr. Quirke: Come along now to the Courthouse. Three cheers for Hyacinth Halvey! Hip! hip! hoora!

> (*Cheers heard in the distance as the curtain drops.*)

THE RISING OF THE MOON

(1909)

PERSONS
  Sergeant.
  Policeman X.
  Policeman B.
  A Ragged Man.

Galway shore in (vaguely) Fenian days

THE RISING OF THE MOON

Scene: Side of a quay in a seaport town. Some posts and chains. A large barrel. Enter three policemen. Moonlight.

>(*Sergeant, who is older than the others, crosses the stage to right and looks down steps. The others put down a pastepot and unroll a bundle of placards.*)

Policeman B: I think this would be a good place to put up a notice. (*He points to barrel.*)

Policeman X: Better ask him. (*Calls to Sergt.*) Will this be a good place for a placard?

(*No answer.*)

Policeman B: Will we put up a notice here on the barrel? (*No answer.*)

Sergeant: There's a flight of steps here that leads to the water. This is a place that should be minded well. If he got down here, his friends might have a boat to meet him; they might send it in here from outside.

Policeman B: Would the barrel be a good place to put a notice up?

Sergeant: It might; you can put it there.

>(*They paste the notice up.*)

Sergeant: (*Reading it.*) Dark hair—dark eyes, smooth face, height five feet five—there's not much to take hold of in that—It's a pity I had no chance of seeing him before he broke out of gaol. They say he's a wonder, that it's he makes all the plans for the whole organization. There isn't another man in Ireland would have broken gaol the way he did. He must have some friends among the gaolers.

Policeman B: A hundred pounds is little enough for the Government to offer for him. You may be sure any man in the force that takes him will get promotion.

Sergeant: I'll mind this place myself. I wouldn't wonder at all if he came this way. He might come slipping along there (*points to side of quay*), and his friends might be waiting for him there (*points down steps*), and once he got away it's little chance we'd have of finding him; it's maybe under a load of kelp he'd be in a fishing boat, and not one to help a married man that wants it to the reward.

Policeman X: And if we get him itself, nothing but abuse on our heads for it from the people, and maybe from our own relations.

Sergeant: Well, we have to do our duty in the force. Haven't we the whole country depending on us to keep law and order? It's those that are down would be up and those that are up would be down, if it wasn't for us. Well, hurry on, you have plenty of other places to placard yet, and come back here then to me. You can take the lantern. Don't be too long now. It's very lonesome here with nothing but the moon.

Policeman B: It's a pity we can't stop with you. The Government should have brought more police into the town, with *him* in gaol, and at assize time too. Well, good luck to your watch.

(*They go out.*)

Sergeant: (*Walks up and down once or twice and looks at placard.*) A hundred pounds and promotion sure. There must be a great deal of spending in a hundred pounds. It's a pity some honest man not to be the better of that.

(*A ragged man appears at left and tries to slip past. Sergeant suddenly turns.*)

Sergeant: Where are you going?

Man: I'm a poor ballad-singer, your honour. I thought to sell some of these (*holds out bundle of ballads*) to the sailors. (*He goes on.*)

Sergeant: Stop! Didn't I tell you to stop? You can't go on there.

Man: Oh, very well. It's a hard thing to be poor. All the world's against the poor!

Sergeant: Who are you?

Man: You'd be as wise as myself if I told you, but I don't mind. I'm one Jimmy Walsh, a ballad-singer.

Sergeant: Jimmy Walsh? I don't know that name.

Man: Ah, sure, they know it well enough in Ennis. Were you ever in Ennis, sergeant?

Sergeant: What brought you here?

Man: Sure, it's to the assizes I came, thinking I might make a few shillings here or there. It's in the one train with the judges I came.

Sergeant: Well, if you came so far, you may as well go farther, for you'll walk out of this.

Man: I will, I will; I'll just go on where I was going. (*Goes towards steps.*)

Sergeant: Come back from those steps; no one has leave to pass down them to-night.

Man: I'll just sit on the top of the steps till I see will some sailor buy a ballad off me that would give me my supper. They do be late going back to the ship. It's often I saw them in Cork carried down the quay in a hand-cart.

Sergeant: Move on, I tell you. I won't have any one lingering about the quay to-night.

Man: Well, I'll go. It's the poor have the hard life! Maybe yourself might like one, sergeant. Here's a good sheet now. (*Turns one over.*) "Content and a pipe"—that's not much. "The Peeler and the goat"—you wouldn't like that. "Johnny Hart"—that's a lovely song.

Sergeant: Move on.

Man: Ah, wait till you hear it. (*Sings:*)

There was a rich farmer's daughter lived near
 the town of Ross;
She courted a Highland soldier, his name was
 Johnny Hart;
Says the mother to her daughter, "I'll go dis-
 tracted mad
If you marry that Highland soldier dressed
 up in Highland plaid."

Sergeant: Stop that noise.

(*Man wraps up his ballads and shuffles towards the steps.*)

Sergeant: Where are you going?

Man: Sure you told me to be going, and I am going.

Sergeant: Don't be a fool. I didn't tell you to go that way; I told you to go back to the town.

Man: Back to the town, is it?

Sergeant: (*Taking him by the shoulder and shoving him before him.*) Here, I'll show you the way. Be off with you. What are you stopping for?

Man: (*Who has been keeping his eye on the notice, points to it.*) I think I know what you're waiting for, sergeant.

Sergeant: What's that to you?

Man: And I know well the man you're waiting for—I know him well—I'll be going.

(*He shuffles on.*)

Sergeant: You know him? Come back here. What sort is he?

Man: Come back is it, sergeant? Do you want to have me killed?

Sergeant: Why do you say that?

Man: Never mind. I'm going. I wouldn't be in your shoes if the reward was ten times as much. (*Goes on off stage to left*). Not if it was ten times as much.

Sergeant: (*Rushing after him.*) Come back here, come back. (*Drags him back.*) What sort is he? Where did you see him?

Man: I saw him in my own place, in the County Clare. I tell you you wouldn't like to be looking at him. You'd be afraid to be in the one place with him. There isn't a weapon he doesn't know the use of, and as to strength, his muscles are as hard as that board (*slaps barrel*).

Sergeant: Is he as bad as that?

Man: He is then.

Sergeant: Do you tell me so?

Man: There was a poor man in our place, a sergeant from Ballyvaughan.—It was with a lump of stone he did it.

Sergeant: I never heard of that.

Man: And you wouldn't, sergeant. It's not everything that happens gets into the papers. And there was a policeman in plain clothes, too . . . It is in Limerick he was. . . . It was after the time of the attack on the police barrack at Kilmallock. . . . Moonlight . . . just like

The Rising of the Moon

this . . . waterside. . . . Nothing was known for certain.

Sergeant: Do you say so? It's a terrible county to belong to.

Man: That's so, indeed! You might be standing there, looking out that way, thinking you saw him coming up this side of the quay (*points*), and he might be coming up this other side (*points*), and he'd be on you before you knew where you were.

Sergeant: It's a whole troop of police they ought to put here to stop a man like that.

Man: But if you'd like me to stop with you, I could be looking down this side. I could be sitting up here on this barrel.

Sergeant: And you know him well, too?

Man: I'd know him a mile off, sergeant.

Sergeant: But you wouldn't want to share the reward?

Man: Is it a poor man like me, that has to be going the roads and singing in fairs, to have the name on him that he took a reward? But you don't want me. I'll be safer in the town.

Sergeant: Well, you can stop.

Man: (*Getting up on barrel.*) All right, sergeant. I wonder, now, you're not tired out, sergeant, walking up and down the way you are.

Sergeant: If I'm tired I'm used to it.

Man: You might have hard work before you to-night yet. Take it easy while you can. There's plenty of room up here on the barrel, and you see farther when you're higher up.

Sergeant: Maybe so. (*Gets up beside him on barrel, facing right. They sit back to back, looking different ways.*) You made me feel a bit queer with the way you talked.

Man: Give me a match, sergeant (*he gives it and man lights pipe*); take a draw yourself? It'll quiet you. Wait now till I give you a light, but you needn't turn round. Don't take your eye off the quay for the life of you.

Sergeant: Never fear, I won't. (*Lights pipe. They both smoke.*) Indeed it's a hard thing to be in the force, out at night and no thanks for it, for all the danger we're in. And it's little we get but abuse from the people, and no choice but to obey our orders, and never asked when a man is sent into danger, if you are a married man with a family.

Man: (*Sings*)—

    As through the hills I walked to view the hills
        and shamrock plain,
    I stood awhile where nature smiles to view the
        rocks and streams,
    On a matron fair I fixed my eyes beneath a
        fertile vale,
    As she sang her song it was on the wrong of
        poor old Granuaile.

Sergeant: Stop that; that's no song to be singing in these times.

The Rising of the Moon

Man: Ah, sergeant, I was only singing to keep my heart up. It sinks when I think of him. To think of us two sitting here, and he creeping up the quay, maybe, to get to us.

Sergeant: Are you keeping a good lookout?

Man: I am; and for no reward too. Amn't I the foolish man? But when I saw a man in trouble, I never could help trying to get him out of it. What's that? Did something hit me?

(*Rubs his heart.*)

Sergeant: (*Patting him on the shoulder.*) You will get your reward in heaven.

Man: I know that, I know that, sergeant, but life is precious.

Sergeant: Well, you can sing if it gives you more courage.

Man: (*Sings*)—

 Her head was bare, her hands and feet with
  iron bands were bound,
 Her pensive strain and plaintive wail mingles
  with the evening gale,
 And the song she sang with mournful air, I am
  old Granuaile.
 Her lips so sweet that monarchs kissed . . .

Sergeant: That's not it. . . . "Her gown she wore was stained with gore." . . . That's it—you missed that.

Man: You're right, sergeant, so it is; I missed

it. (*Repeats line.*) But to think of a man like you knowing a song like that.

Sergeant: There's many a thing a man might know and might not have any wish for.

Man: Now, I daresay, sergeant, in your youth, you used to be sitting up on a wall, the way you are sitting up on this barrel now, and the other lads beside you, and you singing "Granuaile"? . . .

Sergeant: I did then.

Man: And the "Shan Bhean Bhocht"? . . .

Sergeant: I did then.

Man: And the "Green on the Cape?"

Sergeant: That was one of them.

Man: And maybe the man you are watching for to-night used to be sitting on the wall, when he was young, and singing those same songs. . . . It's a queer world. . . .

Sergeant: Whisht! . . . I think I see something coming. . . . It's only a dog.

Man: And isn't it a queer world? . . . Maybe it's one of the boys you used to be singing with that time you will be arresting to-day or to-morrow, and sending into the dock. . . .

Sergeant: That's true indeed.

Man: And maybe one night, after you had been singing, if the other boys had told you some plan they had, some plan to free the country, you might have joined with them . . . and maybe it is you might be in trouble now.

Sergeant: Well, who knows but I might? I had a great spirit in those days.

Man: It's a queer world, sergeant, and it's little any mother knows when she sees her child creeping on the floor what might happen to it before it has gone through its life, or who will be who in the end.

Sergeant: That's a queer thought now, and a true thought. Wait now till I think it out. . . . If it wasn't for the sense I have, and for my wife and family, and for me joining the force the time I did, it might be myself now would be after breaking gaol and hiding in the dark, and it might be him that's hiding in the dark and that got out of gaol would be sitting up where I am on this barrel. . . . And it might be myself would be creeping up trying to make my escape from himself, and it might be himself would be keeping the law, and myself would be breaking it, and myself would be trying maybe to put a bullet in his head, or to take up a lump of a stone the way you said he did . . . no, that myself did. . . . Oh! (*Gasps. After a pause.*) What's that? (*Grasps man's arm.*)

Man: (*Jumps off barrel and listens, looking out over water.*) It's nothing, sergeant.

Sergeant: I thought it might be a boat. I had a notion there might be friends of his coming about the quays with a boat.

Man: Sergeant, I am thinking it was with the

people you were, and not with the law you were, when you were a young man.

Sergeant: Well, if I was foolish then, that time's gone.

Man: Maybe, sergeant, it comes into your head sometimes, in spite of your belt and your tunic, that it might have been as well for you to have followed Granuaile.

Sergeant: It's no business of yours what I think.

Man: Maybe, sergeant, you'll be on the side of the country yet.

Sergeant: (*Gets off barrel.*) Don't talk to me like that. I have my duties and I know them. (*Looks round.*) That was a boat; I hear the oars.

(*Goes to the steps and looks down.*)

Man: (*Sings*)—

    O, then, tell me, Shawn O'Farrell,
      Where the gathering is to be.
    In the old spot by the river
      Right well known to you and me!

Sergeant: Stop that! Stop that, I tell you!

Man: (*Sings louder*)—

    One word more, for signal token,
      Whistle up the marching tune,
    With your pike upon your shoulder,
      At the Rising of the Moon.

Sergeant: If you don't stop that, I'll arrest you.

(*A whistle from below answers, repeating the air.*)

The Rising of the Moon

Sergeant: That's a signal. (*Stands between him and steps.*) You must not pass this way.... Step farther back.... Who are you? You are no ballad-singer.

Man: You needn't ask who I am; that placard will tell you. (*Points to placard.*)

Sergeant: You are the man I am looking for.

Man: (*Takes off hat and wig. Sergeant seizes them.*) I am. There's a hundred pounds on my head. There is a friend of mine below in a boat. He knows a safe place to bring me to.

Sergeant: (*Looking still at hat and wig.*) It's a pity! It's a pity. You deceived me. You deceived me well.

Man: I am a friend of Granuaile. There is a hundred pounds on my head.

Sergeant It's a pity, it's a pity!

Man: Will you let me pass, or must I make you let me?

Sergeant: I am in the force. I will not let you pass.

Man: I thought to do it with my tongue. (*Puts hand in breast.*) What is that?

(*Voice of Policeman X outside:*) Here, this is where we left him.

Sergeant: It's my comrades coming.

Man: You won't betray me . . . the friend of Granuaile. (*Slips behind barrel.*)

(*Voice of Policeman B:*) That was the last of the placards.

Policeman X: (*As they come in.*) If he makes his escape it won't be unknown he'll make it.

(*Sergeant puts hat and wig behind his back.*)

Policeman B: Did any one come this way?

Sergeant: (*After a pause.*) No one.

Policeman B: No one at all?

Sergeant: No one at all.

Policeman B: We had no orders to go back to the station; we can stop along with you.

Sergeant: I don't want you. There is nothing for you to do here.

Policeman B: You bade us to come back here and keep watch with you.

Sergeant: I'd sooner be alone. Would any man come this way and you making all that talk? It is better the place to be quiet.

Policeman B: Well, we'll leave you the lantern anyhow. (*Hands it to him.*)

Sergeant: I don't want it. Bring it with you.

Policeman B: You might want it. There are clouds coming up and you have the darkness of the night before you yet. I'll leave it over here on the barrel. (*Goes to barrel.*)

Sergeant: Bring it with you I tell you. No more talk.

Policeman B: Well, I thought it might be a comfort to you. I often think when I have it in

The Rising of the Moon

my hand and can be flashing it about into every dark corner (*doing so*) that it's the same as being beside the fire at home, and the bits of bogwood blazing up now and again.

(*Flashes it about, now on the barrel, now on Sergeant.*)

Sergeant: (*Furious.*) Be off the two of you, yourselves and your lantern!

(*They go out. Man comes from behind barrel. He and Sergeant stand looking at one another.*)

Sergeant: What are you waiting for?

Man: For my hat, of course, and my wig. You wouldn't wish me to get my death of cold?

(*Sergeant gives them.*)

Man: (*Going towards steps.*) Well, good-night, comrade, and thank you. You did me a good turn to-night, and I'm obliged to you. Maybe I'll be able to do as much for you when the small rise up and the big fall down . . . when we all change places at the Rising (*waves his hand and disappears*) of the Moon.

Sergeant: (*Turning his back to audience and reading placard.*) A hundred pounds reward! A hundred pounds! (*Turns towards audience.*) I wonder, now, am I as great a fool as I think I am?

Curtain.

THE JACKDAW

— benevolent deception,
taken in its
perpetrators.

Obsession with making money for
Jackdaws, because one is purchased at a
ridiculously inflated price to pay a widow
woman's debts.

Logical, madcap, mythologised anarchy.

PERSONS
  JOSEPH NESTOR   *An Army Pensioner.*
  MICHAEL COONEY   *A Farmer.*
  MRS. BRODERICK   *A Small Shopkeeper.*
  TOMMY NALLY   *A Pauper.*
  SIBBY FAHY   *An Orange Seller.*
  TIMOTHY WARD   *A Process Server.*

THE JACKDAW

Scene: Interior of a small general shop at Cloon. Mrs. Broderick sitting down. Tommy Nally sitting eating an orange Sibby has given him. Sibby, with basket on her arm, is looking out of door.

Sibby: The people are gathering to the door of the Court. The Magistrates will be coming there before long. Here is Timothy Ward coming up the street.

Timothy Ward: (*Coming to door.*) Did you get that summons I left here for you ere yesterday, Mrs. Broderick?

Mrs. Broderick: I believe it's there in under the canister. (*Takes it out.*) It had my mind tossed looking at it there before me. I know well what is in it if I made no fist of reading it itself. It's no wonder with all I had to go through if the reading and writing got scattered on me.

Ward: You know it is on this day you have to appear in the Court?

Mrs. Broderick: It isn't easy forget that, though indeed it is hard for me to be keeping anything in my head these times, but maybe remembering to-morrow the thing I was saying to-day.

Ward: Up to one o'clock the magistrates will be able to attend to you, ma'am, before they will go out eating their meal.

Mrs. Broderick: Haven't I the mean, begrudging creditors now that would put me into the Court? Sure it's a terrible thing to go in it and to be bound to speak nothing but the truth. When people would meet with you after, they would remember your face in the Court. What way would they be certain was it in or outside of the dock?

Ward: It is not in the dock you will be put this time. And there will be no bodily harm done to you, but to seize your furniture and your goods. It's best for me to be going there myself and not to be wasting my time. (*Goes out.*)

Mrs. Broderick: Many a one taking my goods on credit and I seeing their face no more. But nothing would satisfy the people of this district. Sure the great God Himself when He came down couldn't please everybody.

Sibby: I am thinking you were talking of some friend, ma'am, might be apt to be coming to your aid.

Mrs. Broderick: Well able he is to do it if the Lord would but put it in his mind. Isn't it a strange thing the goods of this world to shut up the heart of a brother from his own, the same as

Esau and Jacob, and he having a good farm of land in the County Limerick. It is what I heard that in that place the grass does be as thick as grease.

Sibby: I suppose, ma'am, you wrote giving him an account of your case?

Mrs. Broderick: Sure, Mr. Nestor, the dear man, has his fingers wore away writing for me, and I telling him all he had or had not to say. At Christmas I wrote, and at Little Christmas, and at St. Brigit's Day, and on the Feast of St. Patrick, and after that again such time as I had news of the summons being about to be served. And you may ask Mrs. Delane at the Post Office am I telling any lie saying I got no word or answer at all. . . . It's long since I saw him, but it is the way he used to be, his eyes on kippeens and some way suspicious in his heart; a dark weighty tempered man.

Sibby: A person to be crabbed and he young, it is not likely he will grow kind at the latter end.

Tommy Nally: That is no less than true now. There are crabbed people and suspicious people to be met with in every place. It is much that I got a pass from the Workhouse this day, the Master making sure when I asked it that I had in my pocket the means of getting drink.

Mrs. Broderick: It would maybe be best to go join you in the Workhouse, Tommy Nally, when I am out of this, than to go walking the world from end to end.

Tommy Nally: Ah, don't be saying that, ma'am; sure you couldn't be happy within those walls if you had the whole world. Clean outside, but very hard within. No rank but all mixed together, the good, the middling and the bad, the well reared and the rough.

Mrs. Broderick: Sure I'm not asking to go in it. You could never be as stiff in any place as in any sort of little cabin of your own.

Tommy Nally: The tea boiled in a boiler, you should close your eyes drinking it, and ne'er a bit of sugar hardly in it at all. And our curses on them that boil the eggs too hard! What use is an egg that is hard to any person on earth? And as to the dinner, what way would a tasty person eat it not having a knife or a fork?

Mrs. Broderick: That I may live to be in no one's way, but to have some little corner of my own!

Tommy Nally: And to come to your end in it, ma'am! If you were the Lady Mayor herself you'd be brought out to the deadhouse if it was ten o'clock at night, and not a wash unless it was just a Scotch lick, and nobody to wake you at all!

Mrs. Broderick: I will not go in it! I would sooner make any shift and die by the side of the wall. Sure heaven is the best place, heaven and this world we're in now!

Sibby: Don't be giving up now, ma'am. Here

is Mr. Nestor coming, and if any one will give you an advice he is the one will do it. Why wouldn't he, he being, as he is, an educated man, and such a great one to be reading books.

Mrs. Broderick: So he is too, and keeps it in his mind after. It's a wonder to me a man that does be reading to keep any memory at all.

Nally: It's easy for him to carry things light, and his pension paid regular at springtime and harvest.

(*Nestor comes in reading "Tit-Bits."*)

Nestor: There was a servant girl in Austria cut off her finger slicing cabbage. . . .

All: The poor thing!

Nestor: And her master stuck it on again with glue. That now was a very foolish thing to do. What use would a finger be stuck with glue that might melt off at any time, and she to be stirring the pot?

Sibby: That is true indeed.

Nestor: Now, if I myself had been there, it is what I would have advised . . .

Sibby: That's what I was saying, Mr. Nestor. It is you are the grand adviser. What now will you say to poor Mrs. Broderick that has a summons out against her this day for up to ten pounds?

Nestor: It is what I am often saying, it is a very foolish thing to be getting into debt.

Mrs. Broderick: Sure what way could I help

it? It's a very done-up town to be striving to make a living in.

Nestor: It would be a right thing to be showing a good example.

Mrs. Broderick: They would want that indeed. There are more die with debts on them in this place than die free from debt.

Nestor: Many a poor soul has had to suffer from the weight of the debts on him, finding no rest or peace after death.

Sibby: The Magistrates are gone into the Courthouse, Mrs. Broderick. Why now wouldn't you go up to the bank and ask would the manager advance you a loan?

Mrs. Broderick: It is likely he would not do it. But maybe it's as good for me go as to be sitting here waiting for the end.

(*Puts on hat and shawl.*)

Nestor: I now will take charge of the shop for you, Mrs. Broderick.

Mrs. Broderick: It's little call there'll be to it. The time a person is sunk that's the time the custom will go from her. (*She goes out.*)

Nally: I'll be taking a ramble into the Court to see what are the lads doing. (*Goes out.*)

Sibby: (*Following them.*) I might chance some customers there myself.

(*Goes out calling—oranges, good oranges.*)

Nestor: (*Taking a paper from his pocket, sitting*

The Jackdaw

down, and beginning to read.) "Romantic elopement in high life. A young lady at Aberdeen, Missouri, U.S.A., having been left by her father an immense fortune . . ."

> (*Stops to wipe his spectacles, puts them on again and looks for place, which he has lost. Cooney puts his head in at door and draws it out again.*)

Nestor: Come in, come in!

Cooney: (*Coming in cautiously and looking round.*) Whose house now might this be?

Nestor: To the Widow Broderick it belongs. She is out in the town presently.

Cooney: I saw her name up over the door.

Nestor: On business of her own she is gone. It is I am minding the place for her.

Cooney: So I see. I suppose now you have good cause to be minding it?

Nestor: It would be a pity any of her goods to go to loss.

Cooney: I suppose so. Is it to auction them you will or to sell them in bulk?

Nestor: Not at all. I can sell you any article you will require.

Cooney: It would be no profit to herself now, I suppose, if you did?

Nestor: What do you mean saying that? Do you think I would defraud her from her due in anything I would sell for her at all?

Cooney: You are not the bailiff so?

Nestor: Not at all. I wonder any person to take me for a bailiff!

Cooney: You are maybe one of the creditors?

Nestor: I am not. I am not a man to have a debt upon me to any person on earth.

Cooney: I wonder what it is you are at so, if you have no claim on the goods. Is it any harm now to ask what's this your name is?

Nestor: One Joseph Nestor I am, there are few in the district but know me. Indeed they all have a great opinion of me. Travelled I did in the army, and attended school and I young, and slept in the one bed with two boys that were learning Greek.

Cooney: What way now can I be rightly sure that you *are* Joseph Nestor?

Nestor: (*Pulling out envelope.*) There is my pension docket. You will maybe believe that.

Cooney: (*Examining it.*) I suppose you may be him so. I saw your name often before this.

Nestor: Did you now? I suppose it may have travelled a good distance.

Cooney: It travelled as far as myself anyway at the bottom of letters that were written asking relief for the owner of this house.

Nestor: I suppose you are her brother so, Michael Cooney?

Cooney: If I am, there are some questions that

I want to put and to get answers to before my mind will be satisfied. Tell me this now. Is it a fact Mary Broderick to be living at all?

Nestor: What would make you think her not to be living and she sending letters to you through the post?

Cooney: I was saying to myself with myself, there was maybe some other one personating her and asking me to send relief for their own ends.

Nestor: I am in no want of any relief. That is a queer thing to say and a very queer thing. There are many worse off than myself, the Lord be praised!

Cooney: Don't be so quick now starting up to take offence. It is hard to believe the half the things you hear or that will be told to you.

Nestor: That may be so indeed; unless it is things that would be printed on the papers. But I would think you might trust one of your own blood.

Cooney: I might or I might not. I had it in my mind this long time to come hither and to look around for myself. There are seven generations of the Cooneys trusted nobody living or dead.

Nestor: Indeed I was reading in some history of one Ulysses that came back from a journey and sent no word before him but slipped in unknown to all but the house dog to see was his wife minding the place, or was she, as she was, scattering his means.

Cooney: So she would be too. If Mary Broderick is in need of relief I will relieve her, but if she is not, I will bring away what I brought with me to its own place again.

Nestor: Sure here is the summons. You can read that, and if you will look out the door you can see by the stir the Magistrates are sitting in the Court. It is a great welcome she will have before you, and the relief coming at the very nick of time.

Cooney: It is too good a welcome she will give me I am thinking. It is what I am in dread of now, if she thinks I brought her the money so soft and so easy, she will never be leaving me alone, but dragging all I have out of me by little and little.

Nestor: Maybe you might let her have but the lend of it.

Cooney: Where's the use of calling it a lend when I may be sure I never will see it again? It might be as well for me to earn the value of a charity.

Nestor: You might do that and not repent of it.

Cooney: It is likely I'll be annoyed with her to the end of my lifetime if she knows I have as much as that to part with. It might be she would be following me to Limerick.

Nestor: Wait now a minute till I will give you an advice.

Cooney: It is likely my own advice is the best. Look over your own shoulder and do the thing you think right. How can any other person know the reasons I have in my mind?

Nestor: I will know what is in your mind if you will tell it to me.

Cooney: It would suit me best, she to get the money and not to know at the present time where did it come from. The next time she will write wanting help from me, I will task her with it and ask her to give me an account.

Nestor: That now would take a great deal of strategy. . . . Wait now till I think. . . . I have it in my mind I was reading in a penny novel . . . no but on the "Gael" . . . about a boy of Kilbecanty that saved his old sweetheart from being evicted.

Cooney: I never heard my sister had any old sweetheart.

Nestor: It was playing Twenty-five he did it. Played with the husband he did, letting him win up to fifty pounds.

Cooney: Mary Broderick was no cardplayer. And if she was itself she would know me. And it's not fifty pounds I am going to leave with her, or twenty pounds, or a penny more than is needful to free her from the summons to-day.

Nestor: (*Excited.*) I will make up a plan! I am sure I will think of a good one. It is given in to me there is no person so good at making up a plan as myself on this side of the world, not on this side of the world! I will manage all. Leave here what you have for her before she will come in. I will give it to her in some secret way.

Cooney: I don't know. I will not give it to you before I will get a receipt for it . . . and I'll not leave the town till I'll see did she get it straight and fair. Into the Court I'll go to see her paying it.

(*Sits down and writes out receipt.*)

Nestor: I was reading on "Home Chat" about a woman put a note for five pounds into her son's prayer book and he going a voyage. And when he came back and was in the church with her it fell out, he never having turned a leaf of the book at all.

Cooney: Let you sign this and you may put it in the prayer book so long as she will get it safe.

(*Nestor signs. Cooney looks suspiciously at signature and compares it with a letter and then gives notes*)

Nestor: (*Signing.*) Joseph Nestor.

Cooney: Let me see now is it the same handwriting I used to be getting on the letters. It is. I have the notes here.

Nestor: Wait now till I see is there a prayer

book. . . . (*Looks on shelf*). Treacle, castor oil, marmalade. . . . I see no books at all.

Cooney: Hurry on now, she will be coming in and finding me.

Nestor: Here is what will do as well. . . . "Old Moore's Almanac." I will put it here between the leaves. I will ask her the prophecy for the month. You can come back here after she finding it.

Cooney: Amn't I after telling you I wouldn't wish her to have sight of me here at all? What are you at now, I wonder, saying that. I will take my own way to know does she pay the money. It is not my intention to be made a fool of.

(*Goes out.*)

Nestor: You will be satisfied and well satisfied. Let me see now where are the predictions for the month. (*Reads.*) "The angry appearance of Scorpio and the position of the pale Venus and Jupiter presage much danger for England. The heretofore obsequious Orangemen will refuse to respond to the tocsin of landlordism. The scales are beginning to fall from their eyes."

> (*Mrs. Broderick comes in without his noticing her. She gives a groan. He drops book and stuffs notes into his pocket.*)

Mrs. Broderick: Here I am back again and no addition to me since I went.

Nestor: You gave me a start coming in so noiseless.

Mrs. Broderick: It is time for me go to the Court, and I give you my word I'd be better pleased going to my burying at the Seven Churches. A nice slab I have there waiting for me, though the man that put it over me I never saw him at all, and he a far off cousin of my own.

Nestor: Who knows now, Mrs. Broderick, but things might turn out better than you think.

Mrs. Broderick: What way could they turn out better between this and one o'clock?

Nestor: (*Scratching his head.*) I suppose now you wouldn't care to play a game of Twenty-five?

Mrs. Broderick: I am surprised at you, Mr. Nestor, asking me to go cardplaying on such a day and at such an hour as this.

Nestor: I wonder might some person come in and give an order for ten pounds' worth of the stock?

Mrs. Broderick: Much good it would do me. Sure I have the most of it on credit.

Nestor: Well, there is no knowing. Some well-to-do person now passing the street might have seen you and taken a liking to you and be willing to make an advance or a loan.

Mrs. Broderick: Ah, who would be taking a liking to me as they might to a young girl in her bloom.

Nestor. Oh, it's a sort of thing might happen. Sure age didn't catch on to you yet; you are clean and fresh and sound. What's this I was reading in "Answers." (*Looks at it.*) "Romantic elopement . . ."

Mrs. Broderick: I know of no one would be thinking of me for a wife . . . unless it might be yourself, Mr. Nestor. . . .

Nestor: (*Jumping up and speaking fast and running finger up and down paper.*) "Performance of Dick Whittington.". . . There now, there is a story that I read in my reading, it was called Whittington and the Cat. It was the cat led to his fortune. There might some person take a fancy to your cat. . . .

Mrs. Broderick: Ah, let you have done now. I have no cat this good while. I banished it on the head of it threatening the jackdaw.

Nestor: The jackdaw?

Mrs. Broderick: (*Fetches cage from inner room.*) Sure I reared it since the time it fell down the chimney and I going into my bed. It is often you should have seen it, in or out of its cage. Hero his name is. Come out now, Hero.

(*Opens cage.*)

Nestor: (*Slapping his side.*) That is it . . . that's the very thing. Listen to me now, Mrs. Broderick, there are *some* might give a good price for that bird. (*Sitting down to the work.*) It chances now there is a friend of mine in South Africa. A mine owner he is . . . very rich . . . but it is down in the mine he has to live by reason of the Kaffirs . . . it is hard to keep a watch upon them in the half dark, they being black.

Mrs. Broderick: I suppose. . . .

Nestor: He does be lonesome now and again, and he is longing for a bird to put him in mind of old Ireland . . . but he is in dread it would die in the darkness . . . and it came to his mind that it is a custom with jackdaws to be living in chimneys, and that if any birds would bear the confinement it is they that should do it.

Mrs. Broderick: And is it to buy jackdaws he is going?

Nestor: Isn't that what I am coming to. (*He pulls out notes.*) Here now is ten pounds I have to lay out for him. Take them now and good luck go with them, and give me the bird.

Mrs. Broderick: Notes is it? Is it waking or dreaming I am and I standing up on the floor?

Nestor: Good notes and ten of them. Look at them! National Bank they are. . . . Count them now, according to your fingers, and see did I tell any lie.

Mrs. Broderick: (*Counting.*) They are in it sure enough . . . so long as they are good ones and I not made a hare of before the magistrates.

Nestor: Go out now to the Court and show

them to Timothy Ward, and see does he say are they good. Pay them over then, and its likely you will be let off the costs.

Mrs. Broderick: (*Taking shawl.*) I will go, I will go. Well, you are a great man and a kind man, Joseph Nestor, and that you may live a thousand years for this good deed.

Nestor: Look here now, ma'am, I wouldn't wish you to be mentioning my name in this business or saying I had any hand in it at all.

Mrs. Broderick: I will not so long as it's not pleasing to you. Well, it is yourself took a great load off me this day! (*She goes out.*)

Nestor: (*Calling after her.*) I might as well be putting the jackdaw back into the cage to be ready for the journey. (*Comes into shop.*) I hope now he will be well treated by the sailors and he travelling over the sea. . . . Where is he now. . . . (*Chirrups.*) Here now, come here to me, what's this your name is. . . . Nero! Nero! (*Makes pounces behind counter.*) Ah, bad manners to you, is it under the counter you are gone!

(*Lies flat on the floor chirruping and calling, Nero! Nero! Nally comes in and watches him curiously.*)

Nally: Is it catching blackbeetles you are, Mr. Nestor? Where are they and I will give you a hand. . . .

Nestor: (*Getting up annoyed.*) It's that bird I was striving to catch a hold of for to put him back in the cage.

Tommy Nally: (*Making a pounce.*) There he is now. (*Puts bird in cage.*) Wait now till I'll fasten the gate.

Nestor: Just putting everything straight and handy for the widow woman I am before she will come back from the settlement she is making in the Court.

Nally: What way will she be able to do that?

Nestor: I gave her advice. A thought I had, something that came from my reading. (*Taps paper.*) Education and reading and going in the army through the kingdoms of the world; that is what fits a man now to be g:ving out advice.

Tommy: Indeed, it's good for them to have you, all the poor ignorant people of this town.

Cooney: (*Coming in hurriedly and knocking against Nally as he goes out.*) What, now, would you say to be the best nesting place in this town. Nests of jackdaws I should say.

Nestor: There is the old mill should be a good place. To the west of the station it is. Chimneys there are in it. Middling high they are. Wait now till I'll tell you of the great plan I made up. . . .

Cooney: What are you askin͵ for those rakes in the corner? It's no matter, I'll take one on credit, or maybe it is only the lend of it I'll take. . . . I'll be coming back immediately.

(*He goes out with rake.*)

Sibby: (*Coming in excitedly.*) If you went bird-catching, Mr. Nestor, tell me what way would you go doing it?

Nestor: It is not long since I was reading some account of that . . . lads that made a trade of it . . . nets they had and they used to be spreading them in the swamps where the plover do be feeding. . . .

Sibby: Ah, sure where's the use of a plover!

Nestor: And snares they had for putting along the drains where the snipe do be picking up worms. . . . But if I myself saw any person going after things of the sort, it is what I would advise them to stick to the net.

Sibby: What now is the price of that net in the corner?

Nestor: (*Taking it down.*) It is but a little bag that is, suitable for carrying small articles; it would become your oranges well. Twopence I believe, Sibby, is what I should charge you for that.

Sibby: (*Taking money out of handkerchief.*) Give it to me so! Here I'll get the start of you, Timothy Ward, anyway.

(*She takes it and goes out, almost overturning Timothy Ward, who is rushing in.*)

Nestor: Well, Timothy, did you see the Widow Broderick in the Court?

Ward: I did see her. It is in it she is, now, looking as content as in the coffin, and she paying her debt.

Nestor: Did she give you any account of herself?

Ward: She did to be sure, and to the whole Court; but look here now, I have no time to be talking. I have to be back there when the magistrates will have their lunch taken. Now you being so clever a man, Mr. Nestor, what would you say is the surest way to go catching birds?

Nestor: It is a strange thing now, I was asked the same question not three minutes ago. I was just searching my mind. It seems to me I have read in some place it is a very good way to go calling to them with calls; made for the purpose they are. You have but to sit under a tree or whatever place they may perch and to whistle . . . suppose now it might be for a curlew. . . .

    (*Whistles.*)

Timothy Ward: Are there any of those calls in the shop?

Nestor: I would not say there are any made for the purpose, but there might be something might answer you all the same. Let me see now. . . .

    (*Gets down a box of musical toys and turns them over.*)

Ward: Is there anything now has a sound like the croaky screech of a jackdaw?

Nestor: Here now is what we used to be calling a corncrake.... (*Turns it.*) Corncrake, corncrake ... but it seems to me now that to give it but the one creak, this way ... it is much like what you would hear in the chimney at the time of the making of the nests.

Ward: Give it here to me!

(*Puts a penny on counter and runs out.*)

Tommy Nally: (*Coming in shaking with excitement.*) For the love of God, Mr. Nestor, will you give me that live-trap on credit!

Nestor: A trap? Sure there is no temptation for rats to be settling themselves in the Workhouse.

Nally: Or a snare itself ... or any sort of a thing that would make the makings of a crib.

Nestor: What would you want, I wonder, going out fowling with a crib?

Nally: Why wouldn't I want it? Why wouldn't I have leave to catch a bird the same as every other one?

Nestor: And what would the likes of you be wanting with a bird?

Nally: What would I want with it, is it? Why wouldn't I be getting my own ten pounds?

Nestor: Heaven help your poor head this day!

Nally: Why wouldn't I get it the same as Mrs. Broderick got it?

Nestor: Well, listen to me now. You will not get it.

Nally: Sure that man is buying them will have no objection they to come from one more than another.

Nestor: Don't be arguing now. It is a queer thing for you, Tommy Nally, to be arguing with a man like myself.

Nally: Think now all the good it would do me ten pound to be put in my hand! It is not you should be begrudging it to me, Mr. Nestor. Sure it would be a relief upon the rates.

Nestor: I tell you you will not get ten pound or any pound at all. Can't you give attention to what I say?

Nally: If I had but the price of the trap you wouldn't refuse it to me. Well, isn't there great hardship upon a man to be bet up and to have no credit in the town at all.

Nestor: (*Exasperated, and giving him the cage.*) Look here now, I have a right to turn you out into the street. But, as you are silly like and with no great share of wits, I will make you a present of this bird till you try what will you get for it, and till you see will you get as much as will cover its diet for one day only. Go out now looking for customers and maybe you will believe what I say.

Nally: (*Seizing it.*) That you may be doing the

same thing this day fifty years! My fortune's made now! (*Goes out with cage.*)

Nestor: (*Sitting down.*) My joy go with you, but I'm bothered with the whole of you. Everyone expecting me to do their business and to manage their affairs. That is the drawback of being an educated man!

(*Takes up paper to read.*)

Mrs. Broderick: (*Coming in.*) I declare I'm as comforted as Job coming free into the house from the Court!

Nestor: Well, indeed, ma'am, I am well satisfied to be able to do what I did for you, and for my friend from Africa as well, giving him so fine and so handsome a bird.

Mrs. Broderick: Sure Finn himself that chewed his thumb had not your wisdom, or King Solomon that kept order over his kingdom and his own seven hundred wives. There is neither of them could be put beside you for settling the business of any person at a l.

(*Sibby comes in holding up her netted bag.*)

Nestor: What is it you have there, Sibby?

Sibby: Look at them here, look at them here. . . . I wasn't long getting them. Warm they are yet; they will take no injury.

Mrs. Broderick: What are they at all?

Sibby: It is eggs they are . . . look at them. Jackdaws' eggs.

Nestor: (*Suspiciously.*) And what call have you now to be bringing in jackdaws' eggs?

Sibby: Is it ten pound apiece I will get for them do you think, or is it but ten pound I will get for the whole of them?

Nestor: Is it drink, or is it tea, or is it some change that is come upon the world that is fitting the people of this place for the asylum in Ballinasloe?

Sibby: I know of a good clocking hen. I will put the eggs under her. . . . I will rear them when they'll be hatched out.

Nestor: I suppose now, Mrs. Broderick, you went belling the case through the town?

Mrs. Broderick: I did not, but to the Magistrates upon the bench that I told it out of respect to, and I never mentioned your name in it at all.

Sibby: Tell me now, Mrs. Broderick, who have I to apply to?

Mrs. Broderick: What is it you are wanting to apply about?

Sibby: Will you tell me where is the man that is after buying your jackdaw?

Mrs. Broderick: (*Looking at Nestor*) What's that? Where is he, is it?

Nestor: (*Making signs of silence.*) How would you know where he is? It is not in a broken little town of this sort such a man would be stopping, and he having his business finished.

Sibby: Sure he will have to be coming back here for the bird. I will stop till I'll see him drawing near.

Nestor: It is more likely he will get it consigned to the shipping agent. Mind what I say now, it is best not be speaking of him at all.

> (*Timothy Ward comes in triumphantly, croaking his toy. He has a bird in his hand.*)

Ward: I chanced on a starling. It was not with this I tempted him, but a little chap that had him in a crib. Would you say now, Mr. Nestor, would that do as well as a jackdaw? Look now, it's as handsome every bit as the other. And anyway it is likely they will both die before they will reach to their journey's end.

Nestor: (*Lifting up his hands.*) Of all the foolishness that ever came upon the world!

Ward: Hurry on now, Mrs. Broderick, tell me where will I bring it to the buyer you were speaking of. He is fluttering that hard it is much if I can keep him in my hand. Is it at Noonan's Royal Hotel he is or is it at Mack's?

Nestor: (*Shaking his head threateningly.*) How can you tell that and you not knowing it yourself?

Ward: Sure you have a right to know what way did he go, and he after going out of this.

Mrs. Broderick: (*Her eyes apprehensively on Nestor.*) Ah, sure, my mind was tattered on me.

I couldn't know did he go east or west. Standing here in this place I was, like a ghost that got a knock upon its head.

Ward: If he is coming back for the bird it is here he will be coming, and if it is to be sent after him it is likely you will have his address.

Mrs. Broderick: So I should, too, I suppose. Where now did I put it? (*She looks to Nestor for orders, but cannot understand his signs, and turns out pocket.*) That's my specs . . . that's the key of the box . . . that's a bit of root liquorice. . . . Where now at all could I have left down that address?

Ward: There has no train left since he was here. Sure what does it matter so long as he did not go out of this. I'll bring this bird to the railway. Tell me what sort was he till I'll know him.

Mrs. Broderick: (*Still looking at Nestor.*) Well, he was middling tall . . . not very gross . . . about the figure now of Mr. Nestor.

Ward: What aged man was he?

Mrs. Broderick: I suppose up to sixty years. About the one age, you'd say, with Mr. Nestor.

Ward: Give me some better account now; it is hardly I would make him out by that.

Mrs. Broderick: A grey beard he has hanging down . . . and a bald poll, and grey hair like a fringe around it . . . just for all the world like Mr. Nestor!

The Jackdaw

Nestor: (*Jumping up.*) There is nothing so disagreeable in the whole world as a woman that has too much talk.

Mrs. Broderick: Well, let me alone. Where's the use of them all picking at me to say where did I get the money when I am under orders not to tell it?

Ward: Under orders?

Mrs. Broderick: I am, and strong orders.

Ward: Whose orders are those?

Mrs. Broderick: What's that to you, I ask you?

Ward: Isn't it a pity now a woman to be so unneighbourly and she after getting profit for herself?

Mrs. Broderick: Look now, Mr. Nestor, the way they are going on at me, and you saying no word for me at all.

Ward: How would he say any word when he hasn't it to say? The only word could be said by any one is that you are a mean grasping person, gathering what you can for your own profit and keeping yourself so close and so compact. It is back to the Court I am going, and it's no good friend I'll be to you from this out, Mrs. Broderick!

Mrs. Broderick: Amn't I telling you I was bidden not to tell?

Sibby: You were. And is it likely it was you yourself bid yourself and gave you that advice, Mrs. Broderick? It is what I think the bird was never bought at all. It is in some other way she got the money. Maybe in a way she does not like to be talking of. Light weights, light fingers! Let us go away so and leave her, herself and her money and her orders! (*Timothy Ward goes out, but Sibby stops at door.*) And much good may they do her.

Mrs. Broderick: Listen to that, Mr. Nestor! Will you be listening to that, when one word from yourself would clear my character! I leave it now between you and the hearers. Why would I be questioned this way and that way, the same as if I was on the green table before the judges? You have my heart broke between you. It's best for me to heat the kettle and wet a drop of tea.

(*Goes to inner room.*)

Sibby: Tell us the truth now, Mr. Nestor, if you know anything at all about it.

Nestor: I know everything about it. It was to myself the notes were handed in the first place. I am willing to take my oath to you on that. It was a stranger, I said, came in.

Sibby: I wish I could see him and know him if I did see him.

Nestor: It is likely you would know a man of that sort if you did see him, Sibby Fahy. It is likely you never saw a man yet that owns riches would buy up the half of this town.

Sibby: It is not always them that has the most that makes the most show. But it is likely he will have a good dark suit anyway, and shining boots, and a gold chain hanging over his chest.

Nestor: (*Sarcastically.*) He will, and gold rings and pins the same as the King of France or of Spain.

> (*Enter Cooney, hatless, streaked with soot and lime, speechless but triumphant. He holds up a nest with nestlings.*)

Nestor: What has happened you, Mr. Cooney, at all?

Cooney: Look now, what I have got!

Nestor: A nest, is it?

Cooney: Three young ones in it!

Nestor: (*Faintly.*) Is it what you are going to say they are jackdaws!

Cooney: I followed your directions. . . .

Nestor: How do you make that out?

Cooney: You said the mill chimneys were full of them. . . .

Nestor: What has that to do with it?

Cooney: I left my rake after me broken in the loft . . . my hat went away in the millrace . . . I tore my coat on the stones . . . there has mortar got into my eye. . . .

Nestor: The Lord bless and save us!

Cooney: But there is no man can say I did not bring back the birds, sound and living and in good health. Look now, the open mouths of them! (*All gather round.*) Three of them safe and living. . . . I lost one climbing the wall. . . . Where now is the man is going to buy them?

Sibby: (*Pointing at Nestor.*) It is he that can tell you that.

Cooney: Make no delay bringing me to him. I'm in dread they might die on me first.

Nestor: You should know well that no one is buying them.

Sibby: No one! Sure it was you yourself told us that there was!

Nestor: If I did itself there is no such a man.

Sibby: It's not above two minutes he was telling of the rings and the pins he wore.

Nestor: He never was in it at all.

Cooney: What plan is he making up now to defraud me and to rob me?

Sibby: Question him yourself, and you will see what will he say.

Cooney: How can I ask questions of a man that is telling lies?

Nestor: I am telling no lies. I am well able to answer you and to tell you the truth.

Cooney: Tell me where is the man that will give me cash for these birds, the same as he gave it to the woman of this house?

Sibby: That's it, that is it. Let him tell it out now.

Cooney: Will you have me ask it as often as the hairs of my head? If I get vexed I will make you answer me.

Nestor: It seems to me to have set fire to a rick, but I am well able to quench it after. There is no man in South Africa, or that came from South Africa, or that ever owned a mine there at all. Where is the man bought the bird, are you asking? There he is standing among us on this floor. (*Points to Cooney.*) That is himself, the very man!

Cooney: (*Advancing a step.*) What is that you are saying?

Nestor: I say that no one came in here but yourself.

Cooney: Did he say or not say there was a rich man came in?

Sibby: He did, surely.

Nestor: To make up a plan. . . .

Cooney: I know well you have made up a plan.

Nestor: To give it unknownst. . . .

Cooney: It is to keep it unknownst you are wanting!

Nestor: The way she would not suspect. . . .

Cooney: It is I myself suspect and have cause to suspect! Give me back my own ten pounds and I'll be satisfied.

Nestor: What way can I give it back?

Cooney. The same way as you took it, in the palm of your hand.

Nestor: Sure it is paid away and spent. . . .

Cooney: If it is you'll repay it! I know as well as if I was inside you you are striving to make me your prey! But I'll sober you! It is into the Court I will drag you, and as far as the gaol!

Nestor: I tell you I gave it to the widow woman. . . .

(*Mrs. Broderick comes in.*)

Cooney: Let her say now did you.

Mrs. Broderick: What is it at all? What is happening? Joseph Nestor threatened by a tinker or a tramp!

Nestor: I would think better of his behaviour if he was a tinker or a tramp.

Mrs. Broderick: He has drink taken so. Isn't drink the terrible tempter, a man to see flames and punishment upon the one side and drink upon the other, and to turn his face towards the drink!

Cooney: Will you stop your chat, Mary Broderick, till I will drag the truth out of this traitor?

Mrs. Broderick: Who is that calling me by my name? Och! Is it Michael Cooney is in it? Michael Cooney, my brother! O Michael, what will they think of you coming into the town and much like a rag on a stick would be scaring in the wheatfield through the day?

Cooney: (*Pointing at Nestor.*) It was going up in the mill I destroyed myself, following the directions of that ruffian!

Mrs. Broderick: And what call has a man that has drink taken to go climbing up a loft in a mill? A crooked mind you had always, and that's a sort of person drink doesn't suit.

Cooney: I tell you I didn't take a glass over a counter this ten year.

Mrs. Broderick: You would do well to go learn behaviour from Mr. Nestor.

Cooney: The man that has me plundered and robbed! Tell me this now, if you can tell it. Did you find any pound notes in "Old Moore's Almanac"?

Mrs. Broderick: I did not to be sure, or in any other place.

Nestor: She came in at the door and I striving to put them into the book.

Cooney: Look are they in it now, and I will say he is not tricky, but honest.

Nestor: You needn't be looking. . . .

Mrs. Broderick: (*Turning over the leaves.*) Ne'er a thing at all in it but the things that will or will not happen, and the days of the changes of the moon.

Cooney: (*Seizing and shaking it.*) Look at

that now! (*To Nestor.*) Will you believe me now telling you that you are a rogue?

Nestor: Will you listen to me, ma'am. . . .

Cooney: No, but listen to myself. I brought the money to you.

Nestor: If he did he wouldn't trust you with it, ma'am.

Cooney: I intended it for your relief.

Nestor: In dread he was you would go follow him to Limerick.

Mrs. Broderick: It is not likely I would be following the like of him to Limerick, a man that left me to the charity of strangers from Africa!

Cooney: I gave the money to him. . . .

Nestor: And I gave it to yourself paying for the jackdaw. Are you satisfied now, Mary Broderick?

Mrs. Broderick: Satisfied, is it? It would be a queer thing indeed I to be satisfied. My brother to be spending money on birds, and his sister with a summons on her head. Michael Cooney to be passing himself off as a mine-owner, and I myself being the way I am!

Cooney: What would I want doing that? I tell you I ask no birds, black, blue or white!

Mrs. Broderick: I wonder at you now saying that, and you with that clutch on your arm! (*Cooney indignantly flings away nest.*) Searching

The Jackdaw

out jackdaws and his sister without the price of a needle in the house! I tell you, Michael Cooney, it is yourself will be wandering after your burying, naked and perishing, through winds and through frosts, in satisfaction for the way you went wasting your money and your means on such vanities, and she that was reared on the one floor with you going knocking at the Workhouse door! What good will jackdaws be to you that time?

Cooney: It is what I would wish to know, what scheme are the whole of you at? It is long till I will trust any one but my own eyes again in the whole of the living world.

(*She wipes her eyes indignantly. Tommy Nally rushes in the bird and cage still in his hands.*)

Nally: Where is the bird buyer? It is here he is said to be. It is well for me get here the first. It is the whole of the town will be here within half an hour; they have put a great scatter on themselves hunting and searching in every place, but I am the first!

Nestor: What is it you are talking about?

Nally: Not a house in the whole street but is deserted. It is much if the Magistrates themselves didn't quit the bench for the pursuit, the way Tim Ward quitted the place he had a right to be!

Nestor: It is some curse in the air, or some scourge?

Nally: Birds they are getting by the score! Old and young! Where is the bird-buyer? Who is it now will give me my price?

(*He holds up the cage.*)

Cooney: There is surely some root for all this. There must be some buyer after all. It's to keep him to themselves they are wanting. (*Goes to door.*) But I'll get my own profit in spite of them.

(*He goes outside door, looking up and down the street.*)

Mrs. Broderick: Look at what Tommy Nally has. That's my bird.

Nally: It is not, it's my own!

Mrs. Broderick: That is my cage!

Nally: It is not, it is mine!

Mrs. Broderick: Wouldn't I know my own cage and my own bird? Don't be telling lies that way!

Nally: It is no lie I am telling. The bird and the cage were made a present to me.

Mrs. Broderick: Who would make a present to you of the things that belong to myself?

Nally: It was Mr. Nestor gave them to me.

Mrs. Broderick: Do you hear what he says, Joseph Nestor? What call have you to be giving a present of my bird?

The Jackdaw

Nestor: And wasn't I after buying it from you?

Mrs. Broderick: If you were it was not for yourself you bought it, but for the poor man in South Africa you bought it, and you defrauding him now, giving it away to a man has no claim to it at all. Well, now, isn't it hard for any man to find a person he can trust?

Nestor: Didn't you hear me saying I bought it for no person at all?

Mrs. Broderick: Give it up now, Tommy Nally, or I'll have you in gaol on the head of it.

Nally: Oh, you wouldn't do such a thing, ma'am, I am sure!

Mrs. Broderick: Indeed and I will, and have you on the treadmill for a thief.

Nally: Oh, oh, oh, look now, Mr. Nestor, the way you have made me a thief and to be lodged in the gaol!

Nestor: I wish to God you were lodged in it, and we would have less annoyance in this place!

Nally: Oh, that is a terrible thing for you to be saying! Sure the poorhouse itself is better than the gaol! The nuns preparing you for heaven and the Mass every morning of your life. . . .

Nestor: If you go on with your talk and your arguments it's to gaol you will surely go.

Nally: Milk of a Wednesday and a Friday,

the potatoes steamed very good. . . . It's the skins of the potatoes they were telling me you do have to be eating in the gaol. It is what I am thinking, Mr. Nestor, that bird will lie heavy on you at the last!

Nestor: (*Seizing cage and letting the bird out of the door.*) Bad cess and a bad end to it, and that I may never see it or hear of it again!

Mrs. Broderick: Look what he is after doing! Get it back for me! Give it here into my hands I say! Why wouldn't I sell it secondly to the buyer and he to be coming to the door? It is in my own pocket I will keep the price of it that time!

Nally: It would have been as good you to have left it with me as to be sending itself and the worth of it up into the skies!

Mrs. Broderick: (*Taking Nestor's arm.*) Get it back for me I tell you! There it is above in the ash tree, and it flapping its wings on a bough!

Nestor: Give me the cage, if that will content you, and I will strive to entice it to come in.

Cooney: (*Coming in.*) Everyone running this way and that way. It is for birds they are looking sure enough. Why now would they go through such hardship if there was not a demand in some place?

Nestor: (*Pushing him away.*) Let me go now before that bird will quit the branch where it is.

The Jackdaw

Cooney: (*Seizing hold of him.*) Is it striving to catch a bird for yourself you are now?

Nestor: Let me pass if you please. I have nothing to say to you at all.

Cooney: Laying down to me they were worth nothing! I knew well you had made up some plan! The grand adviser is it! It is to yourself you gave good advice that time!

Nestor: Let me out I tell you before that uproar you are making will drive it from its perch on the tree.

Cooney: Is it to rob me of my own money you did and to be keeping me out of the money I earned along with it!

(*Threatens Nestor with "Moore's Almanac," which he has picked up.*)

Sibby: Take care would there be murder done in this place!

(*She seizes Nestor, Mrs. Broderick seizes Cooney. Tommy Nally wrings his hands.*)

Nestor: Tommy Nally, will you kindly go and call for the police.

Cooney: Is it into a den of wild beasts I am come that must go calling out for the police?

Nestor: A very unmannerly person indeed!

Cooney: Everyone thinking to take advantage of me and to make their own trap for my ruin.

Nestor: I don't know what cause has he at all to have taken any umbrage against me.

Cooney: You that had your eye on my notes from the first like a goat in a cabbage garden!

Nestor: Coming with a gift in the one hand and holding a dagger in the other!

Cooney: If you say that again I will break your collar bone!

Nestor: O, but you are the terrible wicked man!

Cooney: I'll squeeze satisfaction out of you if I had to hang for it! I will be well satisfied if I'll kill you!

(*Flings "Moore's Almanac" at him.*)

Nestor: (*Throwing his bundle of newspapers.*) Oh, good jewel!

Ward: (*Coming in hastily.*) Whist the whole of you, I tell you! The Magistrates are coming to the door! (*Comes in and shuts it after him.*)

Mrs. Broderick: The Lord be between us and harm! What made them go quit the Court?

Ward: The whole of the witnesses and of the prosecution made off bird-catching. The Magistrates sent to invite the great mine-owner to go lunch at Noonan's with themselves.

Cooney: Horses of their own to stick him with they have. I wouldn't doubt them at all.

Ward: He could not be found in any place. They are informed he was never seen leaving this house. They are coming to make an investigation.

Nestor: Don't be anyway uneasy. I will explain the whole case.

Ward: The police along with them. . . .

Cooney: Is the whole of this district turned into a trap?

Ward: It is what they are thinking, that the stranger was made away with for his gold!

Cooney: And if he was, as sure as you are living, it was done by that blackguard there!

(*Points at Nestor.*)

Ward: If he is not found they will arrest all they see upon the premises. . . .

Cooney: It is best for me to quit this.

(*Goes to door.*)

Ward: Here they are at the door. Sergeant Carden along with them. Hide yourself, Mr. Nestor, if you've anyway to do it at all.

(*Sounds of feet and talking and knock at the door. Cooney hides under counter. Nestor lies down on top of bench, spreads his newspaper over him. Mrs. Broderick goes behind counter.*)

Nestor: (*Raising paper from his face and looking out.*) Tommy Nally, I will give you five shillings if you will draw "Tit-Bits" over my feet.

Curtain

THE WORKHOUSE WARD

PERSONS
Mike McInerney } PAUPERS
Michael Miskell
Mrs. Donohoe, A COUNTRYWOMAN

THE WORKHOUSE WARD

Scene: A ward in Cloon Workhouse. The two old men in their beds.

Michael Miskell: Isn't it a hard case, Mike McInerney, myself and yourself to be left here in the bed, and it the feast day of Saint Colman, and the rest of the ward attending on the Mass.

Mike McInerney: Is it sitting up by the hearth you are wishful to be, Michael Miskell, with cold in the shoulders and with "speckled shins?" Let you rise up so, and you well able to do it, not like myself that has pains the same as tin-tacks within in my inside.

Michael Miskell: If you have pains within in your inside there is no one can see it or know of it the way they can see my own knees that are swelled up with the rheumatism, and my hands that are twisted in ridges the same as an old cabbage stalk. It is easy to be talking about soreness and about pains, and they maybe not to be in it at all.

Mike McInerney: To open me and to analyse me you would know what sort of a pain and a soreness I have in my heart and in my chest. But I'm not one like yourself to be cursing and praying and tormenting the time the nuns are at hand, thinking to get a bigger share than myself of the nourishment and of the milk.

Michael Miskell: That's the way you do be picking at me and faulting me. I had a share and a good share in my early time, and it's well you know that, and the both of us reared in Skehanagh.

Mike McInerney: You may say that, ind ed, we are both of us reared in Skehanagh. Little wonder you to have good nourishment the time we were both rising, and you bringing away my rabbits out of the snare.

Michael Miskell: And you didn't bring away my own eels, I suppose, I was after spearing in the Turlough? Selling them to the nuns in the convent you did, and letting on they to be your own. For you were always a cheater and a schemer, grabbing every earthly thing for your own profit.

Mike McInerney: And you were no grabber yourself, I suppose, till your land and all you had grabbed wore away from you!

Michael Miskell: If I lost it itself, it was through the crosses I met with and I going through the world. I never was a rambler and a cardplayer like yourself, Mike McInerney, that ran through all and lavished it unknown to your mother!

Mike McInerney: Lavished it, is it? And if I did was it you yourself led me to lavish it or some other one? It is on my own floor I would be to-day and in the face of my family, but for the misfortune I had to be put with a bad next door neighbour that was yourself. What way did my means go from me is it? Spending on fencing, spending on walls, making up gates, putting up doors, that would keep your hens and your ducks from coming in through starvation on my floor, and every four footed beast you had from preying and trespassing on my oats and my mangolds and my little lock of hay!

Michael Miskell: O to listen to you! And I striving to please you and to be kind to you and to close my ears to the abuse you would be calling and letting out of your mouth. To trespass on your crops is it? It's little temptation there was for my poor beasts to ask to cross the mering. My God Almighty! What had you but a little corner of a field!

Mike McInerney: And what do you say to my garden that your two pigs had destroyed on me the year of the big tree being knocked, and they making gaps in the wall.

Michael Miskell: Ah, there does be a great deal of gaps knocked in a twelvemonth. Why wouldn't they be knocked by the thunder, the same as the tree, or some storm that came up from the west?

Mike McInerney: It was the west wind, I suppose, that devoured my green cabbage? And that rooted up my Champion potatoes? And that ate the gooseberries themselves from off the bush?

Michael Miskell: What are you saying? The two quietest pigs ever I had, no way wicked and well ringed. They were not ten minutes in it. It would be hard for them eat strawberries in that time, let alone gooseberries that's full of thorns.

Mike McInerney: They were not quiet, but very ravenous pigs you had that time, as active as a fox they were, killing my young ducks. Once they had blood tasted you couldn't stop them.

Michael Miskell: And what happened myself the fair day of Esserkelly, the time I was passing your door? Two brazened dogs that rushed out and took a piece of me. I never was the better of it or of the start I got, but wasting from then till now!

Mike McInerney: Thinking you were a wild beast they did, that had made his escape out of the travelling show, with the red eyes of you and the ugly face of you, and the two crooked legs of you that wouldn't hardly stop a pig in a gap.

Sure any dog that had any life in it at all would be roused and stirred seeing the like of you going the road!

Michael Miskell: I did well taking out a summons against you that time. It is a great wonder you not to have been bound over through your lifetime, but the laws of England is queer.

Mike McInerney: What ailed me that I did not summons yourself after you stealing away the clutch of eggs I had in the barrel, and I away in Ardrahan searching out a clocking hen.

Michael Miskell: To steal your eggs is it? Is that what you are saying now? (*Holds up his hands.*) The Lord is in heaven, and Peter and the saints, and yourself that was in Ardrahan that day put a hand on them as soon as myself! Isn't it a bad story for me to be wearing out my days beside you the same as a spancelled goat. Chained I am and tethered I am to a man that is ramsacking his mind for lies!

Mike McInerney: If it is a bad story for you, Michael Miskell, it is a worse story again for myself. A Miskell to be next and near me through the whole of the four quarters of the year. I never heard there to be any great name on the Miskells as there was on my own race and name.

Michael Miskell: You didn't, is it? Well, you could hear it if you had but ears to hear it. Go across to Lisheen Crannagh and down to the sea and to Newtown Lynch and the mills of Duras and you'll find a Miskell, and as far as Dublin!

Mike McInerney: What signifies Crannagh and the mills of Duras? Look at all my own generations that are buried at the Seven Churches." And how many generations of the Miskells are buried in it? Answer me that!

Michael Miskell: I tell you but for the wheat that was to be sowed there would be more side cars and more common cars at my father's funeral (God rest his soul!) than at any funeral ever left your own door. And as to my mother, she was a Cuffe from Claregalway, and it's she had the purer blood!

Mike McInerney: And what do you say to the banshee? Isn't she apt to have knowledge of the ancient race? Was ever she heard to screech or to cry for the Miskells? Or for the Cuffes from Claregalway? She was not, but for the six families, the Hyneses, the Foxes, the Faheys, the Dooleys, the McInerneys. It is of the nature of the McInerneys she is I am thinking, crying them the same as a king's children.

Michael Miskell: It is a pity the banshee not to be crying for yourself at this minute, and giving you a warning to quit your lies and your chat and your arguing and your contrary ways; for there is no one under the rising sun could stand you. I tell you you are not behaving as in the presence of the Lord!

Mike McInerney: Is it wishful for my death you are? Let it come and meet me now and welcome so long as it will part me from yourself! And I say, and I would kiss the book on it, I to have one request only to be granted, and I leaving it in my will, it is what I would request, nine furrows of the field, nine ridges of the hills, nine waves of the ocean to be put between your grave and my own grave the time we will be laid in the ground!

Michael Miskell: Amen to that! Nine ridges, is it? No, but let the whole ridge of the world separate us till the Day of Judgment! I would not be laid anear you at the Seven Churches, I to get Ireland without a divide!

Mike McInerney: And after that again! I'd sooner than ten pound in my hand, I to know that my shadow and my ghost will not be knocking about with your shadow and your ghost, and the both of us waiting our time. I'd sooner be delayed in Purgatory! Now, have you anything to say?

Michael Miskell: I have everything to say, if I had but the time to say it!

Mike McInerney: (*Sitting up.*) Let me up out of this till I'll choke you!

Michael Miskell: You scolding pauper you!

Mike McInerney: (*Shaking his fist at him.*) Wait a while!

Michael Miskell: (*Shaking his fist.*) Wait a while yourself!

(*Mrs. Donohoe comes in with a parcel. She is a countrywoman with a frilled cap and a shawl. She stands still a minute. The two old men lie down and compose themselves.*)

Mrs. Donohoe: They bade me come up here by the stair. I never was in this place at all. I don't know am I right. Which now of the two of ye is Mike McInerney?

Mike McInerney: Who is it is calling me by my name?

Mrs. Donohoe: Sure amn't I your sister, Honor McInerney that was, that is now Honor Donohoe.

Mike McInerney: So you are, I believe. I didn't know you till you pushed anear me. It is time indeed for you to come see me, and I in this place five year or more. Thinking me to be no credit to you, I suppose, among that tribe of the Donohoes. I wonder they to give you leave to come ask am I living yet or dead?

Mrs. Donohoe: Ah, sure, I buried the whole string of them. Himself was the last to go. (*Wipes her eyes.*) The Lord be praised he got a fine natural death. Sure we must go through our crosses. And he got a lovely funeral; it would delight you to hear the priest reading the Mass. My poor John Donohoe! A nice clean man, you couldn't but be fond of him. Very severe on the tobacco he was, but he wouldn't touch the drink.

Mike McInerney: And is it in Curranroe you are living yet?

Mrs. Donohoe: It is so. He left all to myself. But it is a lonesome thing the head of a house to have died!

Mike McInerney: I hope that he has left you a nice way of living?

Mrs. Donohoe: Fair enough, fair enough. A wide lovely house I have; a few acres of grass land . . . the grass does be very sweet that grows among the stones. And as to the sea, there is something from it every day of the year, a handful of periwinkles to make kitchen, or cockles maybe. There is many a thing in the sea is not decent, but cockles is fit to put before the Lord!

Mike McInerney: You have all that! And you without ere a man in the house?

Mrs. Donohoe: It is what I am thinking, yourself might come and keep me company. It is no credit to me a brother of my own to be in this place at all.

Mike McInerney: I'll go with you! Let me out of this! It is the name of the McInerneys will be rising on every side!

Mrs. Donohoe: I don't know. I was ignorant of you being kept to the bed.

Mike McInerney: I am not kept to it, but maybe an odd time when there is a colic rises up within me. My stomach always gets better the time there is a change in the moon. I'd like well to draw anear you. My heavy blessing on you, Honor Donohoe, for the hand you have held out to me this day.

Mrs. Donohoe: Sure you could be keeping the fire in, and stirring the pot with the bit of Indian meal for the hens, and milking the goat and taking the tacklings off the donkey at the door; and maybe putting out the cabbage plants in their time. For when the old man died the garden died.

Mike McInerney: I could to be sure, and be cutting the potatoes for seed. What luck could there be in a place and a man not to be in it? Is that now a suit of clothes you have brought with you?

Mrs. Donohoe: It is so, the way you will be tasty coming in among the neighbours at Curranroe.

Mike McInerney: My joy you are! It is well you earned me! Let me up out of this! (*He sits up and spreads out the clothes and tries on coat.*) That now is a good frieze coat . . . and a hat in the fashion . . . (*He puts on hat.*)

Michael Miskell: (*Alarmed.*) And is it going out of this you are, Mike McInerney?

Mike McInerney: Don't you hear I am going? To Curranroe I am going. Going I am to a place where I will get every good thing!

Michael Miskell: And is it to leave me here after you you will?

Mike McInerney: (*In a rising chant.*) Every good thing! The goat and the kid are there, the sheep and the lamb are there, the cow does be running and she coming to be milked! Ploughing and seed sowing, blossom at Christmas time, the cuckoo speaking through the dark days of the year! Ah, what are you talking about? Wheat high in hedges, no talk about the rent! Salmon in the rivers as plenty as turf! Spending and getting and nothing scarce! Sport and pleasure, and music on the strings! Age will go from me and I will be young again. Geese and turkeys for the hundreds and drink for the whole world!

Michael Miskell: Ah, Mike, is it truth you are saying, you to go from me and to leave me with rude people and with townspeople, and with people of every parish in the union, and they having no respect for me or no wish for me at all!

Mike McInerney: Whist now and I'll leave you . . . my pipe (*hands it over*); and I'll engage it is Honor Donohoe won't refuse to be sending you a few ounces of tobacco an odd time, and neighbours coming to the fair in November or in the month of May.

Michael Miskell: Ah, what signifies tobacco? All that I am craving is the talk. There to be no one at all to say out to whatever thought might be rising in my innate mind! To be lying here and no conversible person in it would be the abomination of misery!

Mike McInerney: Look now, Honor. . . . It is what I often heard said, two to be better than one. . . . Sure if you had an old trouser was full of holes . . . or a skirt . . . wouldn't you put another in under it that might be as tattered as itself, and the two of them together would make some sort of a decent show?

Mrs. Donohoe: Ah, what are you saying? There is no holes in that suit I brought you now, but as sound it is as the day I spun it for himself.

Mike McInerney: It is what I am thinking, Honor . . . I do be weak an odd time . . . any load I would carry, it preys upon my side . . . and this man does be weak an odd time with the swelling in his knees . . . but the two of us together it's not likely it is at the one time we would fail. Bring the both of us with you, Honor, and the height of the castle of luck on you, and the both of us together will make one good hardy man!

The Workhouse Ward

Mrs. Donohoe: I'd like my job! Is it queer in the head you are grown asking me to bring in a stranger off the road?

Michael Miskell: I am not, ma'am, but an old neighbour I am. If I had forecasted this asking I would have asked it myself. Michael Miskell I am, that was in the next house to you in Skehanagh!

Mrs. Donohoe: For pity's sake! Michael Miskell is it? That's worse again. Yourself and Mike that never left fighting and scolding and attacking one another! Sparring at one another like two young pups you were, and threatening one another after like two grown dogs!

Mike McInerney: All the quarrelling was ever in the place it was myself did it. Sure his anger rises fast and goes away like the wind. Bring him out with myself now, Honor Donohoe, and God bless you.

Mrs. Donohoe: Well, then, I will not bring him out, and I will not bring yourself out, and you not to learn better sense. Are you making yourself ready to come?

Mike McInerney: I am thinking, maybe . . . it is a mean thing for a man that is shivering into seventy years to go changing from place to place.

Mrs. Donohoe: Well, take your luck or leave it. All I asked was to save you from the hurt and the harm of the year.

Mike McInerney: Bring the both of us with you or I will not stir out of this.

Mrs. Donohoe: Give me back my fine suit so (*begins gathering up the clothes*), till I'll go look for a man of my own!

Mike McInerney: Let you go so, as you are so unnatural and so disobliging, and look for some man of your own, God help him! For I will not go with you at all!

Mrs. Donohoe: It is too much time I lost with you, and dark night waiting to overtake me on the road. Let the two of you stop together, and the back of my hand to you. It is I will leave you there the same as God left the Jews!

(*She goes out. The old men lie down and are silent for a moment.*)

Michael Miskell: Maybe the house is not so wide as what she says.

Mike McInerney: Why wouldn't it be wide?

Michael Miskell: Ah, there does be a good deal of middling poor houses down by the sea.

Mike McInerney: What would you know about wide houses? Whatever sort of a house you had yourself it was too wide for the provision you had into it.

Michael Miskell: Whatever provision I had in my house it was wholesome provision and natural provision. Herself and her periwinkles! Periwinkles is a hungry sort of food.

The Workhouse Ward

Mike McInerney: Stop your impudence and your chat or it will be the worse for you. I'd bear with my own father and mother as long as any man would, but if they'd vex me I would give them the length of a rope as soon as another!

Michael Miskell: I would never ask at all to go eating periwinkles.

Mike McInerney: (*Sitting up.*) Have you anyone to fight me?

Michael Miskell: (*Whimpering.*) I have not, only the Lord!

Mike McInerney: Let you leave putting insults on me so, and death picking at you!

Michael Miskell: Sure I am saying nothing at all to displease you. It is why I wouldn't go eating periwinkles, I'm in dread I might swallow the pin.

Mike McInerney: Who in the world wide is asking you to eat them? You're as tricky as a fish in the full tide!

Michael Miskell: Tricky is it! Oh, my curse and the curse of the four and twenty men upon you!

Mike McInerney: That the worm may chew you from skin to marrow bone! (*Seizes his pillow.*)

Michael Miskell: (*Seizing his own pillow.*) I'll leave my death on you, you scheming vagabone!

Mike McInerney: By cripes! I'll pull out your pin feathers! (*Throwing pillow.*)

Michael Miskell: (*Throwing pillow.*) You tyrant! You big bully you!

Mike McInerney: (*Throwing pillow and seizing mug.*) Take this so, you stobbing ruffian you!

(*They throw all within their reach at one another, mugs, prayer books, pipes, etc.*)

Curtain

THE TRAVELLING MAN

PERSONS
   A Mother.
   A Child.
   A Travelling Man.

THE TRAVELLING MAN

A MIRACLE PLAY

Scene: A cottage kitchen. A woman setting out a bowl and jug and board on the table for breadmaking.

Child: What is it you are going to make, mother?

Mother: I am going to make a grand cake with white flour. Seeds I will put in it. Maybe I'll make a little cake for yourself too. You can be baking it in the little pot while the big one will be baking in the big pot.

Child: It is a pity daddy to be away at the fair on a Samhain night.

Mother: I must make my feast all the same, for Samhain night is more to me than to any other one. It was on this night seven years I first came into this house.

Child: You will be taking down those plates from the dresser so, those plates with flowers on them, and be putting them on the table.

Mother: I will. I will set out the house to-day,

and bring down the best delf, and put whatever thing is best on the table, because of the great thing that happened me seven years ago.

Child: What great thing was that?

Mother: I was after being driven out of the house where I was a serving girl. . . .

Child: Where was that house? Tell me about it.

Mother: (*Sitting down and pointing southward.*) It is over there I was living, in a farmer's house up on Slieve Echtge, near to Slieve na n-Or, the Golden Mountain.

Child: The Golden Mountain! That must be a grand place.

Mother: Not very grand indeed, but bare and cold enough at that time of the year. Anyway, I was driven out a Samhain day like this, because of some things that were said against me.

Child: What did you do then?

Mother: What had I to do but to go walking the bare bog road through the rough hills where there was no shelter to find, and the sharp wind going through me, and the red mud heavy on my shoes. I came to Kilbecanty. . . .

Child: I know Kilbecanty. That is where the woman in the shop gave me sweets out of a bottle.

Mother: So she might now, but that night her door was shut and all the doors were shut; and I saw through the windows the boys and the girls sitting round the hearth and playing their games, and I had no courage to ask for shelter. In dread I was they might think some shameful thing of me, and I going the road alone in the night-time.

Child: Did you come here after that?

Mother: I went on down the hill in the darkness, and with the dint of my trouble and the length of the road my strength failed me, and I had like to fall. So I did fall at the last, meeting with a heap of broken stones by the roadside.

Child: I hurt my knee one time I fell on the stones.

Mother: It was then the great thing happened. I saw a stranger coming towards me, a very tall man, the best I ever saw, bright and shining that you could see him through the darkness; and I knew him to be no common man.

Child: Who was he?

Mother: It is what I thought, that he was the King of the World.

Child: Had he a crown like a King?

Mother: If he had, it was made of the twigs of a bare blackthorn; but in his hand he had a green branch, that never grew on a tree of this world. He took me by the hand, and he led me over the stepping-stones outside to this door, and he bade me to go in and I would find good shelter. I was kneeling down to thank him, but he raised me up and he said, "I will come to see you some other time. And do not shut up your heart in the things I give you," he said, "but have a welcome before me."

Child: Did he go away then?

Mother: I saw him no more after that, but I did as he bade me. (*She stands up and goes to the door.*) I came in like this, and your father was sitting there by the hearth, a lonely man that was after losing his wife. He was alone and I was alone, and we married one another; and I never wanted since for shelter or safety. And a good wife I made him, and a good housekeeper.

Child: Will the King come again to the house?

Mother: I have his word for it he will come, but he did not come yet; it is often your father and myself looked out the door of a Samhain night, thinking to see him.

Child: I hope he won't come in the night time, and I asleep.

Mother: It is of him I do be thinking every year, and I setting out the house, and making a cake for the supper.

Child: What will he do when he comes in?

Mother: He will sit over there in the chair, and maybe he will taste a bit of the cake. I will call in all the neighbours; I will tell them he is here. They will not be keeping it in their mind against me then that I brought nothing, coming to the house. They will know I am before any of them, the time they know who it is has come to visit me. They will all kneel down and ask for his blessing. But the best blessing will be on the house he came to of himself.

Child: And are you going to make the cake now?

Mother: I must make it now indeed, or I will be late with it. I am late as it is; I was expecting one of the neighbours to bring me white flour from the town. I'll wait no longer, I'll go borrow it in some place. There will be a wedding in the stonecutter's house Thursday, it's likely there will be flour in the house.

Child: Let me go along with you

Mother: It is best for you to stop here. Be a good child now, and don't be meddling with the things on the table. Sit down there by the hearth and break up those little sticks I am after bringing in. Make a little heap of them now before me, and we will make a good fire to bake the cake. See now how many will you break. Don't go out the door while I'm away, I would be in dread of you going near the river and it in flood. Behave yourself well now. Be counting the sticks as you break them.

(She goes out.)

Child: (*Sitting down and breaking sticks across his knee.*) One—and two—O I can break this one into a great many, one, two, three, four.—This one is wet—I don't like a wet one—five, six—that is a great heap.—Let me try that great big one.—That is too hard.—I don't think mother could break that one.—Daddy could break it.

  (*Half-door is opened and a travelling man comes in. He wears a ragged white flannel shirt, and mud-stained trousers. He is bareheaded and barefooted, and carries a little branch in his hand.*)

Travelling Man: (*Stooping over the child and taking the stick.*) Give it here to me and hold this.

  (*He puts the branch in the child's hand while he takes the stick and breaks it.*)

Child: That is a good branch, apples on it and flowers. The tree at the mill has apples yet, but all the flowers are gone. Where did you get this branch?

Travelling Man: I got it in a garden a long way off.

Child: Where is the garden? Where do you come from?

Travelling Man: (*Pointing southward.*) I have come from beyond those hills.

Child: Is it from the Golden Mountain you are come? From Slieve na n-Or?

Travelling Man: That is where I come from surely, from the Golden Mountain. I would like to sit down and rest for a while.

Child: Sit down here beside me. We must not go near the table or touch anything, or mother will be angry. Mother is going to make a beautiful cake, a cake that will be fit for a King that might be coming in to our supper.

Travelling Man: I will sit here with you on the floor.

(*Sits down.*)

Child: Tell me now about the Golden Mountain.

Travelling Man: There is a garden in it, and there is a tree in the garden that has fruit and flowers at the one time.

Child: Like this branch?

Travelling Man: Just like that little branch.

Child: What other things are in the garden?

Travelling Man: There are birds of all colours that sing at every hour, the way the people will come to their prayers. And there is a high wall about the garden.

Child: What way can the people get through the wall?

Travelling Man: There are four gates in the wall: a gate of gold, and a gate of silver, and a gate of crystal, and a gate of white brass.

Child: (*Taking up the sticks.*) I will make a garden. I will make a wall with these sticks.

Travelling Man: This big stick will make the first wall.

(*They build a square wall with sticks.*)

Child: (*Taking up branch.*) I will put this in the middle. This is the tree. I will get something to make it stand up. (*Gets up and looks at dresser.*) I can't reach it, get up and give me that shining jug.

    (*Travelling Man gets up and gives him the jug.*)

Travelling Man: Here it is for you.

Child: (*Puts it within the walls and sets the branch in it.*) Tell me something else that is in the garden?

Travelling Man: There are four wells of water in it, that are as clear as glass.

Child: Get me down those cups, those flowery cups, we will put them for wells. (*He hands them down.*) Now I will make the gates, give me those plates for gates, not those ugly ones, those nice ones at the top.

    (*He takes them down and they put them on the four sides for gates. The Child gets up and looks at it.*)

Travelling Man: There now, it is finished.

Child: Is it as good as the other garden? How can we go to the Golden Mountain to see the other garden?

Travelling Man: We can ride to it.

Child: But we have no horse.

Travelling Man: This form will be our horse. (*He draws a form out of the corner, and sits down astride on it, putting the child before him.*) Now, off we go! (*Sings, the child repeating the refrain*)—

> Come ride and ride to the garden,
>   Come ride and ride with a will:
> For the flower comes with the fruit there
>   Beyond a hill and a hill.

Refrain

> Come ride and ride to the garden,
>   Come ride like the March wind;
> There's barley there, and water there,
>   And stabling to your mind.

Travelling Man: How did you like that ride, little horseman?

Child: Go on again! I want another ride!

Travelling Man (sings)—

> The Archangels stand in a row there
>   And all the garden bless,
> The Archangel Axel, Victor the angel
>   Work at the cider press.

Refrain

> Come ride and ride to the garden, &c.

Child: We will soon be at the Golden Mountain now. Ride again. Sing another song.

The Travelling Man

Travelling Man (sings)—

    O scent of the broken apples!
    O shuffling of holy shoes!
    Beyond a hill and a hill there
      In the land that no one knows.

Refrain

Come ride and ride to the garden, &c.

Child: Now another ride.

Travelling Man: This will be the last. It will be a good ride.

    (*The mother comes in. She stares for a second, then throws down her basket and snatches up the child.*)

Mother: Did ever anyone see the like of that! A common beggar, a travelling man off the roads, to be holding the child! To be leaving his ragged arms about him as if he was of his own sort! Get out of that, whoever you are, and quit this house or I'll call to some that will make you quit it.

Child: Do not send him out! He is not a bad man; he is a good man; he was playing horses with me. He has grand songs.

Mother: Let him get away out of this now, himself and his share of songs. Look at the way he has your bib destroyed that I was after washing in the morning!

Child: He was holding me on the horse. We

were riding, I might have fallen. He held me.

Mother: I give you my word you are done now with riding horses. Let him go on his road. I have no time to be cleaning the place after the like of him.

Child: He is tired. Let him stop here till evening.

Travelling Man: Let me rest here for a while, I have been travelling a long way.

Mother: Where did you come from to-day?

Travelling Man: I came over Slieve Echtge from Slieve na n-Or. I had no house to stop in. I walked the long bog road, the wind was going through me, there was no shelter to be got, the red mud of the road was heavy on my feet. I got no welcome in the villages, and so I came on to this place, to the rising of the river at Ballylee.

Mother: It is best for you to go on to the town. It is not far for you to go. We will maybe have company coming in here.

(*She pours out flour into a bowl and begins mixing.*)

Travelling Man: Will you give me a bit of that dough to bring with me? I have gone a long time fasting.

Mother: It is not often in the year I make bread like this. There are a few cold potatoes on the dresser, are they not good enough for you? There is many a one would be glad to get them.

Travelling Man: Whatever you will give me, I will take it.

Mother: (*Going to the dresser for the potatoes and looking at the shelves.*) What in the earthly world has happened all the delf? Where are the jugs gone and the plates? They were all in it when I went out a while ago.

Child: (*Hanging his head.*) We were making a garden with them. We were making that garden there in the corner.

Mother: Is that what you were doing after I bidding you to sit still and to keep yourself quiet? It is to tie you in the chair I will another time! My grand jugs! (*She picks them up and wipes them.*) My plates that I bought the first time I ever went marketing into Gort. The best in the shop they were. (*One slips from her hand and breaks.*) Look at that now, look what you are after doing.

(*She gives a slap at the child.*)

Travelling Man: Do not blame the child. It was I myself took them down from the dresser.

Mother: (*Turning on him.*) It was you took them! What business had you doing that? It's the last time a tramp or a tinker or a rogue of the roads will have a chance of laying his hand on anything in this house. It is jailed you should be! What did you want touching the dresser at all? Is it looking you were for what you could bring away?

Travelling Man: (*Taking the child's hands.*) I would not refuse these hands that were held out for them. If it was for the four winds of the world he had asked, I would have put their bridles into these innocent hands.

Mother: (*Taking up the jug and throwing the branch on the floor.*) Get out of this! Get out of this I tell you! There is no shelter here for the like of you! Look at that mud on the floor! You are not fit to come into the house of any decent respectable person!

(*The room begins to darken.*)

Travelling Man: Indeed, I am more used to the roads than to the shelter of houses. It is often I have spent the night on the bare hills.

Mother: No wonder in that! (*She begins to sweep floor.*) Go out of this now to whatever company you are best used to, whatever they are. The worst of people it is likely they are, thieves and drunkards and shameless women.

Travelling Man: Maybe so. Drunkards and thieves and shameless women, stones that have fallen, that are trodden under foot, bodies that are spoiled with sores, bodies that are worn with fasting, minds that are broken with much sinning, the poor, the mad, the bad. . . .

Mother: Get out with you! Go back to your friends, I say!

Travelling Man: I will go. I will go back to

the high road that is walked by the bare feet of the poor, by the innocent bare feet of children. I will go back to the rocks and the wind, to the cries of the trees in the storm! (*He goes out.*)

Child: He has forgotten his branch!
(*Takes it and follows him.*)

Mother: (*Still sweeping.*) My good plates from the dresser, and dirty red mud on the floor, and the sticks all scattered in every place. (*Stoops to pick them up.*) Where is the child gone? (*Goes to door.*) I don't see him—he couldn't have gone to the river—it is getting dark—the bank is slippy. Come back! Come back! Where are you? (*Child runs in.*)

Mother: O where were you? I was in dread it was to the river you were gone, or into the river.

Child: I went after him. He is gone over the river.

Mother: He couldn't do that. He couldn't go through the flood.

Child: He did go over it. He was as if walking on the water. There was a light before his feet.

Mother: That could not be so. What put that thought in your mind?

Child: I called to him to come back for the branch, and he turned where he was in the river, and he bade me to bring it back, and to show it to yourself.

Mother: (*Taking the branch.*) There are fruit and flowers on it. It is a branch that is not of any earthly tree. (*Falls on her knees.*) He is gone, he is gone, and I never knew him! He was that stranger that gave me all! He is the King of the World!

THE GAOL GATE

PERSONS
- *Mary Cahel* — AN OLD WOMAN
- *Mary Cushin* — HER DAUGHTER-IN-LAW
- *The Gatekeeper*

THE GAOL GATE

Scene: Outside the gate of Galway Gaol. Two countrywomen, one in a long dark cloak, the other with a shawl over her head, have just come in. It is just before dawn.

Mary Cahel: I am thinking we are come to our journey's end, and that this should be the gate of the gaol.

Mary Cushin: It is certain it could be no other place. There was surely never in the world such a terrible great height of a wall.

Mary Cahel: He that was used to the mountain to be closed up inside of that! What call had he to go moonlighting or to bring himself into danger at all?

Mary Cushin: It is no wonder a man to grow faint-hearted and he shut away from the light. I never would wonder at all at anything he might be driven to say.

Mary Cahel: There were good men were gaoled before him never gave in to anyone at all. It is what I am thinking, Mary, he might not have done what they say.

Mary Cushin: Sure you heard what the neighbours were calling the time their own boys were brought away. "It is Denis Cahel," they were saying, "that informed against them in the gaol."

Mary Cahel: There is nothing that is bad or is wicked but a woman will put it out of her mouth, and she seeing them that belong to her brought away from her sight and her home.

Mary Cushin: Terry Fury's mother was saying it, and Pat Ruane's mother and his wife. They came out calling it after me, "It was Denis swore against them in the gaol!" The sergeant was boasting, they were telling me, the day he came searching Daire-caol, it was he himself got his confession with drink he had brought him in the gaol.

Mary Cahel: They might have done that, the ruffians, and the boy have no blame on him at all. Why should it be cast up against him, and his wits being out of him with drink?

Mary Cushin: If he did give their names up itself, there was maybe no wrong in it at all. Sure it's known to all the village it was Terry that fired the shot.

Mary Cahel: Stop your mouth now and don't be talking. You haven't any sense worth while. Let the sergeant do his own business with no help from the neighbours at all.

Mary Cushin: It was Pat Ruane that tempted

them on account of some vengeance of his own. Every creature knows my poor Denis never handled a gun in his life.

Mary Cahel: (*Taking from under her cloak a long blue envelope.*) I wish we could know what is in the letter they are after sending us through the post. Isn't it a great pity for the two of us to be without learning at all?

Mary Cushin: There are some of the neighbours have learning, and you bade me not bring it anear them. It would maybe have told us what way he is or what time he will be quitting the gaol.

Mary Cahel: There is wonder on me, Mary Cushin, that you would not be content with what I say. It might be they put down in the letter that "Denis informed on the rest."

Mary Cushin: I suppose it is all we have to do so, to stop here for the opening of the door. It's a terrible long road from Slieve Echtge we were travelling the whole of the night.

Mary Cahel: There was no other thing for us to do but to come and to give him a warning. What way would he be facing the neighbours, and he to come back to Daire-caol?

Mary Cushin: It is likely they will let him go free, Mary, before many days will be out. What call have they to be keeping him? It is certain they promised him his life.

Mary Cahel: If they promised him his life, Mary Cushin, he must live it in some other place. Let him never see Daire-caol again, or Daroda or Druimdarod.

Mary Cushin: O, Mary, what place will we bring him to, and we driven from the place that we know? What person that is sent among strangers can have one day's comfort on earth?

Mary Cahel: It is only among strangers, I am thinking, he could be hiding his story at all. It is best for him to go to America, where the people are as thick as grass.

Mary Cushin: What way could he go to America and he having no means in his hand? There's himself and myself to make the voyage and the little one-een at home.

Mary Cahel: I would sooner to sell the holding than to ask for the price paid for blood. There'll be money enough for the two of you to settle your debts and to go.

Mary Cushin: And what would yourself be doing and we to go over the sea? It is not among the neighbours you would wish to be ending your days.

Mary Cahel: I am thinking there is no one would know me in the workhouse at Oughterard. I wonder could I go in there, and I not to give them my name?

Mary Cushin: Ah, don't be talking foolishness.

What way could I bring the child? Sure he's hardly out of the cradle; he'd be lost out there in the States.

Mary Cahel: I could bring him into the workhouse, I to give him some other name. You could send for him when you'd be settled or have some place of your own.

Mary Cushin: It is very cold at the dawn. It is time for them open the door. I wish I had brought a potato or a bit of a cake or of bread.

Mary Cahel: I'm in dread of it being opened and not knowing what will we hear. The night that Denis was taken he had a great cold and a cough.

Mary Cushin: I think I hear some person coming. There's a sound like the rattling of keys. God and His Mother protect us! I'm in dread of being found here at all!

(*The gate is opened, and the Gatekeeper is seen with a lantern in his hand.*)

Gatekeeper: What are you doing here, women? It's no place to be spending the night time.

Mary Cahel: It is to speak with my son I am asking, that is gaoled these eight weeks and a day.

Gatekeeper: If you have no order to visit him it's as good for you go away home.

Mary Cahel: I got this letter ere yesterday. It might be it is giving me leave.

Gatekeeper: If that's so he should be under the doctor, or in the hospital ward.

Mary Cahel: It's no wonder if he's down with the hardship, for he had a great cough and a cold.

Gatekeeper: Give me here the letter to read it. Sure it never was opened at all.

Mary Cahel: Myself and this woman have no learning. We were loth to trust any other one.

Gatekeeper: It was posted in Galway the twentieth, and this is the last of the month.

Mary Cahel: We never thought to call at the post office. It was chance brought it to us in the end.

Gatekeeper: (*Having read letter.*) You poor unfortunate women, don't you know Denis Cahel is dead? You'd a right to come this time yesterday if you wished any last word at all.

Mary Cahel: (*Kneeling down.*) God and His Mother protect us and have mercy on Denis's soul!

Mary Cushin: What is the man after saying? Sure it cannot be Denis is dead?

Gatekeeper: Dead since the dawn of yesterday, and another man now in his cell. I'll go see who has charge of his clothing if you're wanting to bring it away.

(*He goes in. The dawn has begun to break.*)

Mary Cahel: There is lasting kindness in Heaven when no kindness is found upon earth.

The Gaol Gate

There will surely be mercy found for him, and not the hard judgment of men! But my boy that was best in the world, that never rose a hair of my head, to have died with his name under blemish, and left a great shame on his child! Better for him have killed the whole world than to give any witness at all! Have you no word to say, Mary Cushin? Am I left here to keen him alone?

Mary Cushin: (*Who has sunk on to the step before the door, rocking herself and keening.*) Oh, Denis, my heart is broken you to have died with the hard word upon you! My grief you to be alone now that spent so many nights in company!

What way will I be going back through Gort and through Kilbecanty? The people will not be coming out keening you, they will say no prayer for the rest of your soul!

What way will I be the Sunday and I going up the hill to the Mass? Every woman with her own comrade, and Mary Cushin to be walking her lone!

What way will I be the Monday and the neighbours turning their heads from the house? The turf Denis cut lying on the bog, and no well-wisher to bring it to the hearth!

What way will I be in the night time, and none but the dog calling after you? Two women to be mixing a cake, and not a man in the house to break it!

What way will I sow the field, and no man to

drive the furrow? The sheaf to be scattered before springtime that was brought together at the harvest!

I would not begrudge you, Denis, and you leaving praises after you. The neighbours keening along with me would be better to me than an estate.

But my grief your name to be blackened in the time of the blackening of the rushes! Your name never to rise up again in the growing time of the year! (*She ceases keening and turns towards the old woman.*) But tell me, Mary, do you think would they give us the body of Denis? I would lay him out with myself only; I would hire some man to dig the grave.

(*The Gatekeeper opens the gate and hands out some clothes.*)

Gatekeeper: There now is all he brought in with him; the flannels and the shirt and the shoes. It is little they are worth altogether; those mountainy boys do be poor.

Mary Cushin: They had a right to give him time to ready himself the day they brought him to the magistrates. He to be wearing his Sunday coat, they would see he was a decent boy. Tell me where will they bury him, the way I can follow after him through the street? There is no other one to show respect to him but Mary Cahel, his mother, and myself.

Gatekeeper: That is not to be done. He is buried since yesterday in the field that is belonging to the gaol.

Mary Cushin: It is a great hardship that to have been done, and not one of his own there to follow after him at all.

Gatekeeper: Those that break the law must be made an example of. Why would they be laid out like a well behaved man? A long rope and a short burying, that is the order for a man that is hanged.

Mary Cushin: A man that was hanged! O Denis, was it they that made an end of you and not the great God at all? His curse and my own curse upon them that did not let you die on the pillow! The curse of God be fulfilled that was on them before they were born! My curse upon them that brought harm on you, and on Terry Fury that fired the shot!

Mary Cahel: (*Standing up.*) And the other boys, did they hang them along with him, Terry Fury and Pat Ruane that were brought from Daire-caol?

Gatekeeper: They did not, but set them free twelve hours ago. It is likely you may have passed them in the night time.

Mary Cushin: Set free is it, and Denis made an end of? What justice is there in the world at all?

Gatekeeper: He was taken near the house. They knew his footmark. There was no witness given against the rest worth while.

Mary Cahel: Then the sergeant was lying and the people were lying when they said Denis Cahel had informed in the gaol?

Gatekeeper: I have no time to be stopping here talking. The judge got no evidence and the law set them free.

(*He goes in and shuts gate after him.*)

Mary Cahel: (*Holding out her hands.*) Are there any people in the streets at all till I call on them to come hither? Did they ever hear in Galway such a thing to be done, a man to die for his neighbour?

Tell it out in the streets for the people to hear, Denis Cahel from Slieve Echtge is dead. It was Denis Cahel from Daire-caol that died in the place of his neighbour!

It is he was young and comely and strong, the best reaper and the best hurler. It was not a little thing for him to die, and he protecting his neighbour!

Gather up, Mary Cushin, the clothes for your child; they'll be wanted by this one and that one. The boys crossing the sea in the springtime will be craving a thread for a memory.

One word to the judge and Denis was free, they offered him all sorts of riches. They brought him drink in the gaol, and gold, to swear away the life of his neighbour!

Pat Ruane was no good friend to him at all, but a foolish, wild companion; it was Terry Fury knocked a gap in the wall and sent in the calves to our meadow.

Denis would not speak, he shut his mouth, he would never be an informer. It is no lie he would have said at all giving witness against Terry Fury.

I will go through Gort and Kilbecanty and Druimdarod and Daroda; I will call to the people and the singers at the fairs to make a great praise for Denis!

The child he left in the house that is shook, it is great will be his boast in his father! All Ireland will have a welcome before him, and all the people in Boston.

I to stoop on a stick through half a hundred years, I will never be tired with praising! Come hither, Mary Cushin, till we'll shout it through the roads, Denis Cahel died for his neighbour!

(*She goes off to the left, Mary Cushin following her.*)

Curtain

MUSIC FOR THE SONGS IN THE PLAYS
NOTES AND CASTS

MUSIC FOR THE SONGS IN THE PLAYS

THE RED-HAIRED MAN'S WIFE

Spreading the News.

I thought, my first love, there'd be but one house be-tween you and me, And I thought I would find your-self coax-ing my child on your knee. O-ver the tide I would leap with the leap of a swan, Till I came to the side of the wife of the red-haired man.

GRANUAILE

The Rising of the Moon.

As through the hills I walked to view the hills and sham-rock plain, I stood a-while where na-ture smiles to view the rocks and streams, On a ma-tron fair I fixed my eyes be-neath a fer-tile vale, As she sang her song — it was on the wrong of poor old Gran-u-aile.

Music for the Songs

Her head was bare, her hands and feet with i-ron bands were bound, Her pen-sive strain and plain-tive wail min-gles with the eve-ning gale, And the song she sang with mourn-ful air, I am old Gran-u-aile, Her lips so sweet that mon-archs kissed—

JOHNNY HART

The Rising of the Moon.

There was a rich far-mer's daugh-ter lived near the town of Ross; She court-ed a High-land sol-dier, His name was John-ny Hart; Says the moth-er to her daugh-ter, "I'll go dis-tract-ed mad If you mar-ry that High-land sol-dier dressed up in his High-land plaid."

THE RISING OF THE MOON

O, then, tell me, Shawn O'Farrell, where the gath'ring is to be. In the old spot by the river, Right well known to you and me. One word more, for signal token whistle up the marching tune, With your pike upon your shoulder at the rising of the moon.

GAOL-GATE

Caione.

Tempo, ad lib.

What way will I be the Sunday
And I going up the hill to the
Mass; Ev'ry woman with her own comrade
And Mary Cushin to be walking her lone.

Spoken. What way—drive the furrow? *Sings.* The
sheaf to be scattered before spring-time that

Music for the Songs

was brought to-geth-er at the har-vest!

Spoken.   *Sings.*

I would not—an estate. But my

grief your name to be black-ened in

the time of the black-'ning of the rush-es

Your   name

nev-er to rise up a-gain In the

grow-ing time of the year.

NOTES

SPREADING THE NEWS

THE idea of this play first came to me as a tragedy. I kept seeing as in a picture people sitting by the roadside, and a girl passing to the market, gay and fearless. And then I saw her passing by the same place at evening, her head hanging, the heads of others turned from her, because of some sudden story that had risen out of a chance word, and had snatched away her good name.

But comedy and not tragedy was wanted at our theatre to put beside the high poetic work, *The King's Threshold, The Shadowy Waters, On Baile's Strand, The Well of the Saints;* and I let laughter have its way with the little play. I was delayed in beginning it for a while, because I could only think of Bartley Fallon as dull-witted or silly or ignorant, and the handcuffs seemed too harsh a punishment. But one day by the sea at Duras a melancholy man who was telling me of the crosses he had gone through at home said—"But I'm thinking if I went to America, its long ago to-day I'd be dead. And its a great expense for a poor man to be buried in America." Bartley was born at that moment, and,

Notes 197

far from harshness, I felt I was providing him with a happy old age in giving him the lasting glory of that great and crowning day of m sfortune.

It has been acted very often by other companies as well as our own, and the Boers have done me the honour of translating and pirating it.

HYACINTH HALVEY

I was pointed out one evening a well-brushed, well-dressed man in the stalls, and was told gossip about him, perhaps not all true, which made me wonder if that appearance and behaviour as of extreme respectability might not now and again be felt a burden.

After a while he translated himself in my mind into Hyacinth; and as one must set one's original a little way off to get a translation rather than a tracing, he found himself in Cloon, where, as in other parts of our country, "charácter" is built up or destroyed by a password or an emotion, rather than by experience and deliberation.

The idea was more of a universal one than I knew at the first, and I have had but uneasy appreciation from some apparently blameless friends.

THE RISING OF THE MOON

When I was a child and came with my elders to Galway for their salmon fishing in the river that rushes past the gaol, I used to look with awe at the window where men were hung, and the dark, closed gate. I used to wonder if ever a prisoner might by some means climb the high, buttressed wall and slip away in the darkness by the canal to the quays and find friends to hide him under a load of kelp in a fishing boat, as happens to my ballad-singing man. The play was considered offensive to some extreme Nationalists before it was acted, because it showed the police in too favourable a light, and a Unionist paper attacked it after it was acted because the policeman was represented "as a coward and a traitor"; but after the Belfast police strike that same paper praised its "insight into Irish character." After all these ups and downs it passes unchallenged on both sides of the Irish Sea.

THE JACKDAW

The first play I wrote was called "Twenty-five." It was played by our company in Dublin and London, and was adapted and translated into Irish and played in America. It was about "A boy of Kilbecanty that saved his old sweetheart from being evicted. It was playing Twenty-five he did it; played with the husband he did, letting him win up to £50."

It was rather sentimental and weak in construction, and for a long time it was an overflowing storehouse of examples of "the faults of my dramatic method." I have at last laid its ghost in "The Jackdaw," and I have not been accused of sentimentality since the appearance of this.

Notes

THE WORKHOUSE WARD

I heard of an old man in the workhouse who had been disabled many years before by, I think, a knife thrown at him by his wife in some passionate quarrel.

One day I heard the wife had been brought in there, poor and sick. I wondered how they would meet, and if the old quarrel was still alive, or if they who knew the worst of each other would be better pleased with one another's company than with that of strangers.

I wrote a scenario of the play, Dr. Douglas Hyde, getting in plot what he gave back in dialogue, for at that time we thought a dramatic movement in Irish would be helpful to our own as well as to the Gaelic League. Later I tried to rearrange it for our own theatre, and for three players only, but in doing this I found it necessary to write entirely new dialogue, the two old men in the original play obviously talking at an audience in the wards, which is no longer there.

I sometimes think the two scolding paupers are a symbol of ourselves in Ireland—Iſ ꞅeaṅṅ imṗeaꞅ na uaiġneaꞅ—"it is better to be quarrelling than to be lonesome." The Rajputs, that great fighting race, when they were told they had been brought under the Pax Britannica and must give up war, gave themselves to opium in its place, but Connacht has not yet planted its poppy gardens.

THE TRAVELLING MAN

An old woman living in a cabin by a bog road on

Slieve Echtge told me the legend on which this play is founded, and which I have already published in "Poets and Dreamers."

"There was a poor girl walking the road one night with no place to stop, and the Saviour met her on the road, and He said—'Go up to the house you see a light in; there's a woman dead there, and they'll let you in.' So she went, and she found the woman laid out, and the husband and other people; but she worked harder than they all, and she stopped in the house after; and after two quarters the man married her. And one day she was sitting outside the door, picking over a bag of wheat, and the Saviour came again, with the appearance of a poor man, and He asked her for a few grains of the wheat. And she said—'Wouldn't potatoes be good enough for you?' And she called to the girl within to bring out a few potatoes. But He took nine grains of the wheat in His hand and went away; and there wasn't a grain of wheat left in the bag, but all gone. So she ran after Him then to ask Him to forgive her; and she overtook Him on the road, and she asked forgiveness. And He said—'Don't you remember the time you had no house to go to, and I met you on the road, and sent you to a house where you'd live in plenty? And now you wouldn't give Me a few grains of wheat.' And she said—'But why didn't you give me a heart that would like to divide it?' That is how she came round on Him. And He said—'From this out, whenever you have plenty in your hands, divide it freely for My sake.'"

And an old woman who sold sweets in a little shop in Galway, and whose son became a great Dominican preacher, used to say—"Refuse not any, for one may be the Christ."

I owe the Rider's Song, and some of the rest, to W. B. Yeats.

THE GAOL GATE

I was told a story some one had heard, of a man who had gone to welcome his brother coming out of gaol, and heard he had died there before the gates had been opened for him.

I was going to Galway, and at the Gort station I met two cloaked and shawled countrywomen from the slopes of Slieve Echtge, who were obliged to go and see some law official in Galway because of some money left them by a kinsman in Australia. They had never been in a train or to any place farther than a few miles from their own village, and they felt astray and terrified "like blind beasts in a bog" they said, and I took care of them through the day.

An agent was fired at on the road from Athenry, and some men were taken up on suspicion. One of them was a young carpenter from my old home, and in a little time a rumour was put about that he had informed against the others in Galway gaol. When the prisoners were taken across the bridge to the courthouse he was hooted by the crowd. But at the trial it was found that he had not informed, that no evidence had been given at all; and bonfires were lighted for him as he went home.

These three incidents coming within a few months wove themselves into this little play, and within three days it had written itself. or been written. I like it better than any in the volume, and I have never changed a word of it.

FIRST PRODUCTIONS OF THE PLAYS

SPREADING THE NEWS was produced for the first time at the opening of the Abbey Theatre, on Tuesday, 27th December, 1904, with the following cast:

Bartley Fallon	W. G. FAY
Mrs. Fallon	SARA ALGOOD
Mrs. Tully	EMMA VERNON
Mrs. Tarpey	MAIRE NI GHARBHAIGH
Shawn Early	J. H. DUNNE
Tim Casey	GEORGE ROBERTS
James Ryan	ARTHUR SINCLAIR
Jack Smith	P. MACSUIBHLAIGH
A Policeman	R. S. NASH
A Removable Magistrate	F. J. FAY

HYACINTH HALVEY was first produced at the Abbey Theatre on 19th February, 1906, with the following cast:

Hyacinth Halvey	F. J. FAY
James Quirke, a butcher	W. G. FAY
Fardy Farrell, a telegraph boy	ARTHUR SINCLAIR
Sergeant Carden	WALTER MAGEE
Mrs. Delane, Postmistress at Cloon	SARA ALLGOOD
Miss Joyce, the Priest's House-keeper	BRIGIT O'DEMPSEY

First Productions

THE GAOL GATE was first produced at the Abbey Theatre, Dublin, on 20th October, 1906, with the following cast:

Mary Cahel	SARA ALLGOOD
Mary Cushin	MAIRE O'NEILL
The Gate Keeper	F. J. FAY

THE JACKDAW was first produced at the Abbey Theatre, Dublin, on 23rd February, 1907, with the following cast:

Joseph Nestor	F. J. FAY
Michael Cooney	W. G. FAY
Mrs. Broderick	SARA ALLGOOD
Tommy Nally	ARTHUR SINCLAIR
Sibby Fahy	BRIGIT O'DEMPSEY
Timothy Ward	J. M. KERRIGAN

THE RISING OF THE MOON was first produced at the Abbey Theatre, Dublin, on 9th March, 1907, with the following cast:

Sergeant	ARTHUR SINCLAIR
Policeman X.	J. A. O'ROURKE
Policeman B.	J. M. KERRIGAN
Ballad Singer	W. G. FAY

WORKHOUSE WARD was first produced at the Abbey Theatre, Dublin, on 20th April, 1908, with the following cast:

Mike M'Inerney	ARTHUR SINCLAIR
Michael Miskell	FRED O'DONOVAN
Mrs. Donohue	MARIE O'NEILL

SEQUENCE DANCING

by

VICTOR SILVESTER

Winner of World's Dancing Championship
Chairman, Imperial Society of Teachers of Dancing Incorporated
Leader of the Victor Silvester Ballroom Orchestra
which records exclusively on Columbia records and
broadcasts regularly for the B.B.C.

Open Hold in Circular Movement

ACKNOWLEDGEMENT

Throughout the period in which I have been writing this book I have enjoyed the co-operation of Miss Netta Brooke, Fellow of the Imperial Society of Teachers of Dancing (Ballroom Branch) and Examiner of the Victorian and Sequence Branch, also a Fellow of the British Association of Teachers of Dancing (Ballroom Branch).

I desire to express my thanks to her for valuable technical advice and for reading the proofs.

V. S.

INTRODUCTORY

DURING the closing weeks of 1949 my book, *Old Time Dancing*, was published. It met with a reception which astonished me. Although in that book I describe no fewer than forty-one dances, I received numerous letters requesting me to furnish details of sequence dances not included in that book.

I have to deal with a very large correspondence arising out of my broadcasts, and it is therefore impossible for me to furnish details of dances to inquirers. It seemed desirable to write a further book and to include in it many popular dances which could not be described in the earlier volume if they were to be given in sufficient detail to make them perfectly clear.

Some of my correspondents have sent me copies of dance descriptions, often the original arrangements of dances, and have asked how one could possibly carry out the instructions given. Sometimes their bewilderment has arisen from the fact that the descriptions they possessed were couched in technical terms of which they did not know the meaning. But this was not always the reason. Many of the descriptions were hopelessly misleading. Indeed, some of the original arrangements which have been largely circulated among Old Time dancers are undanceable—that is, if the dancer does what the arranger tells him to do!

Many of the sequence dances which are popular today were arranged by teachers who could demonstrate their dances clearly enough, but who lacked the ability to describe them simply and clearly *on paper*. It is by no means easy to describe dances in such a way that there can be no doubt as to what is intended, and it is therefore not surprising that many original descriptions are inadequate. Moreover, there has been considerable progress in technique and in teaching methods since many of the dances were introduced.

The Official Board has for some years had a Committee which has been working on the far-from-easy task of standardising Old Time and sequence dances in their best possible form. As more dances are dealt with by this Committee and its findings are published, a considerable advance should be made toward uniformity, so that dancers who have learned a dance from any responsible source will know that wherever they go they can join in that dance without having to learn a local version which may be totally different from the one they already know.

As in my other book, *Old Time Dancing*, I am not concerned in this volume with providing a guide to dances as they were originally presented. My object is to attempt a clear, easily-followed description of the best current ballroom practice, and to include, wherever it has been made known, the technique favoured by the Official Board Committee.

I have tried to use the absolute minimum of technical terms, and instead of devoting much space to the more technical aspects of dancing, have sought to show how the various points of technique are applied *in actual dancing*. This method seems to me particularly appropriate when dealing with Old Time sequence dances, since the majority of Old Time dancers learn as they dance and dance as they learn.

Those who join Old Time clubs or classes see the M.C. or Leader with his partner leading-off the various dances, while there is usually a certain amount of tuition at each session. The object of this book is to supplement what can be learned through membership of such a club or class, and to help the dancer to acquire knowledge of the various figures *by dancing them*, instead of learning first the theory and then trying to apply it.

CONTENTS

	PAGE
INTRODUCTORY	7
ADVICE TO THE BEGINNER IN SEQUENCE DANCING	13
ABBREVIATIONS USED IN DESCRIPTIONS OF DANCES	16
THE DIRECTION OF YOUR STEPS	18
THE FOOT POSITIONS	19
PARTNERS' POSITIONS IN RELATION TO EACH OTHER	23
THE EASIEST WAY TO START	26
THE HARRY LIME FOXTROT	27
THE SAUNTERS: SLOW SEQUENCE FOXTROTS	34
THE YEARNING SAUNTER	36
SAUNTER SERENADE	41
THE OLD TIME WALTZ	51
WALTZ FIGURES IN SEQUENCE DANCES	55
CARINA WALTZ	57
QUAKER GIRL WALTZ	62
HESITATION WALTZ	66
THE EVENING WALTZ	73
CHRYSANTHEMUM WALTZ	78
THE GAVOTTE AS A SEQUENCE DANCE	84
THE BUTTERFLY GAVOTTE	88
THE GAVOTINA	94
THE INTERNATIONAL WALTZ	101
THE MARINE FOUR-STEP	106

	PAGE
Doris Waltz	111
Eva Three-Step	114
Florentine Waltz	120
The Tango as a Sequence Dance	126
Elizabeth Tango	129
The Donella Tango	135
Eugene Tango	141
The Mazurka as a Sequence Dance	145
Oriental Mazurka	147
Marie Mazurka	154
The Dutch Foursome	158
The Western Schottische	164
Blue Danube Waltz	167
The Dream Waltz	170
Tango Fascination	173
The Fylde Waltz	183
Waltz Superbe	187
Other Sequence Dances	191

ADVICE TO THE BEGINNER IN SEQUENCE DANCING

NOWADAYS beginners in sequence dancing may be roughly classified in two groups—those who are absolute beginners in ballroom dancing, and those who have already had some experience of Modern-style dancing.

If you have danced in the Modern style, please be prepared to recognise fully that the Old Time style is something different. Do not attempt to carry your Modern-style dancing into the Old Time ballroom, where the majority of the dances are sequence dances, with all the dancers executing the same steps at the same time.

It would be quite out of place for an Old Time dancer to insist upon dancing an Old Time sequence in a Modern-style ballroom; it is equally wrong for the Modern-style dancer to apply Modern-style methods, including "go-as-you-please" choice of steps, in the Old Time ballroom.

You need not worry—as some do—as to whether your knowledge of Modern style dancing will prejudicially affect your dancing in the Old Time manner. An increasing number of good dancers in the Modern style have added, as a further useful accomplishment, ability to dance the Old Time style, and many whose first introduction to ballroom dancing was in the Old Time ballroom, are nowadays learning the Modern style. Undoubtedly it is well worth knowing both styles, so that one can attend both Old Time and Modern-style dances, both of which are frequently held in most localities.

The revival of the Old Time style has hardly lasted long enough for those who have won notable competition successes in one style to prove equally adept at the other. But for some time one leading demonstration couple—Alex Moore and Pat Kilpatrick—have shown themselves equally at home in both styles of dancing, and in recent years there has been a growing tendency for dancers to participate in dancing competitions in both styles. Thus in 1950 one well-known Provincial dance club, hitherto completely devoted to Modern-style dancing, provided something of a sensation when all its members entered for Butlin's National Veleta Competition, some of them doing very well in it.

Sequence dancing, except in such party or novelty dances as the Lambeth Walk and one or two others, finds little or no place in the Modern-style ballroom. But it is the foundation of the Old Time ballroom. Its popularity has grown enormously, one organisation alone, the International Sequence Dance Circle, which was established during the war, having by the middle of 1950 reached a total affiliated membership of 150,000.

Sequence dancing is very easily learned, and the fact that all the dancers are executing the same steps at the same time makes this kind of dancing ideal for the absolute beginner. Even when teaching Modern-style dancing, whether in newspaper articles or on the radio, I invariably give simple sequences which can be easily learned, remembered, and danced. The reason? Because the beginner, during his earliest visits to the ballroom, has enough to claim his attention without having to try to think quickly which steps to dance. If he knows precisely what to do, he gains a measure of confidence which helps him enormously.

For the beginner, it is a considerable advantage that, in the Old Time ballroom, both he and his partner know exactly which steps must be danced—and these are precisely the same steps as are being danced by all the other people present. Because each dance consists of a set sequence there is little likelihood of treading upon one's partner's toes— as you step forward, she steps back, without having to await your lead. The lady knows which figure follows each other figure, and so is not dependent upon her partner displaying a good knowledge of how to lead, how to carry his weight correctly, and so on.

But if sequence dancing is very easy to learn and to dance, it can also become, when well danced, a national art. The dancing of our best couples, both amateur and professional, proves that. Therefore the beginner should determine not to be content merely to get round the ballroom comfortably, but to dance each sequence in the best possible manner. This comes from practice.

I have seen many reports of quite young children, in various parts of the country, securing medals for dancing in both the Old Time and Modern styles—in fact, one Leicester Dance School has among its pupils three girls, all below the age of 12, each of whom has secured Bronze, Silver, and Gold medals in both Old Time and Modern-style dancing. This should help to disprove the contention —not heard so often now as formerly—that Old Time dancing is of interest only to "old fogies." Yet some of the most successful competitors in Old Time dancing are over 50 years of age.

If you learn sequence dancing thoroughly, then, you have something which will provide you with pleasurable recreation for the rest of your life.

Do not be content to read this book. *Use it.*

Learn the steps of the various dances described. As you do so, you will gradually acquire a useful knowledge of theory, for in the descriptions which follow all the essentials are covered.

ABBREVIATIONS USED IN DESCRIPTIONS OF DANCES

S.—A Slow Step.   Q.—A Quick Step.
R.F.—Right foot.   L.F.—Left foot.

L.O.D.—The Line of Dance, i.e. the direction in which the dancers move round the ballroom—anti-clockwise. (See diagram below.)

P.P.—Promenade Position.   Diag.—diagonally.

The arrows show the ballroom "traffic-line," i.e. the general direction in which the dancers proceed round the room—anti-clockwise.

YOUR POSITION IN THE BALLROOM

POSITIONS OF THE BODY (*indicated by arrows*).

1. Facing L.O.D.   counterpart Back to L.O.D.
2. Back to L.O.D.   „   Facing L.O.D.
3. Facing wall   „   Back to wall.
4. Facing centre   „   Back to centre.
5. Facing diag. to wall   „   Back diag. to wall.
6. Facing diag. to centre „   Back diag. to centre.
7. Facing diag. to wall against L.O.D.   „   Back diag. to wall against L.O.D.
8. Facing diag. to centre against L.O.D. „ Back diag. to centre against L.O.D.

THE DIRECTION OF YOUR STEPS

The diagram below shows you the directions in which steps are taken.

The feet are shown in parallel position in the centre, this being the Starting Position for the Twentieth Century Sequence Dances. For the dances in the traditional style they should be turned out—in 1st Position.

The directions in which steps are taken, as shown below, are exactly the same for both Old Time and Twentieth Century Sequence Dances.

```
                STEP FORWARD   STEP FORWARD
                  WITH L.F.      WITH R.F.
STEP DIAGONALLY FORWARD  |1.|  STEP DIAGONALLY FORWARD
      WITH L.F.                        WITH R.F.
               6.                    5.

STEP TO LEFT SIDE ─────[L.F][R.F]───── STEP TO RIGHT SIDE
      WITH L.F.    4.         3.           WITH R.F.

               8.                    7.
STEP DIAGONALLY BACK    |2.|   STEP DIAGONALLY BACK
      WITH L.F.                        WITH R.F.
                 STEP BACK   STEP BACK
                  WITH L.F.   WITH R.F.
```

THE FOOT POSITIONS

What They Are, and How to Make Use of Them

ALL the sequence dances which are included in present-day dance programmes are based upon one or other of the following styles—

(1) *The Traditional Style*, or genuine Old Time Style, which was danced before the present century began.

(2) *The Twentieth Century Sequence Style*, which is employed for dances inspired by such Twentieth Century dances as the Foxtrot and Tango.

Both these styles are danced in the Old Time ballroom.

Dances in the Traditional Style include the Old Time Waltz and the numerous sequence dances which are based on the Waltz, the Gavottes, Mazurkas, and other Old Time dances.

Dances in the Twentieth Century Sequence Style include the Foxtrots, Saunters (developments of the Foxtrot danced to slow music), and the various sequence varieties of the Tango.

The genuine Old Time dances—i.e. those based on the Traditional Style—were adaptations of ballet technique to ballroom requirements, and these are danced with the feet turned well out.

The Twentieth Century Sequence Dances, on the other hand, are danced with the feet pointing straight forward.

That brings us to the first essential point for you to remember when learning, and executing, sequence dances. It is this—

YOU DANCE THE TRADITIONAL-STYLE DANCES WITH THE FEET TURNED-OUT. YOU DANCE THE TWENTIETH CENTURY SEQUENCE DANCES WITH THE FEET PARALLEL AND POINTING STRAIGHT FORWARD.

If you keep this well in mind, you will find it easy to take your steps in the correct manner for each of the dance-styles mentioned.

WHEN DANCING IN THE TRADITIONAL STYLE your feet should be kept turned-out at an angle of about forty-five degrees from the direction you are facing. In other words, the feet should be turned-out like this—

This foot position is known as 1st Position, and you should keep your feet turned out, as shown above, right throughout the dance.

When you step forward with R.F., *take care to keep that foot turned out* as the step is taken, and to keep it turned out at the completion of the step—as in 1st Position.

The same rule applies to any step taken with L.F. It applies equally to steps taken forward or backward, or to the side.

Now you know how to take steps forward, backward, or to the side, and also the fundamental principle which governs all foot-movements in the Traditional Style. These foot-movements, and also those which are used when the dancer closes one foot to the other, are known as the Five Positions. They are easily learned, and it is desirable that you should learn them at this stage, because they serve the very useful purpose of making dance descriptions very much simpler than they otherwise would be.

THE FOOT POSITIONS

Thus, it saves much space and needless repetition to say: "Close L.F. to 3rd position" instead of having to describe, for each step, exactly what is intended. Please, therefore, note carefully the Five Positions, as follows—

1st Position: Heels together, toes turned-out.

2nd Position: One foot placed away from, and to side of, the other—*exactly* to the side, not forward or rearward of the other foot.

3rd Position: Heel of one foot placed against instep of other foot.

4th Position: One foot placed directly forward—i.e. starting from 1st Position, it is moved straight forward.

5TH POSITION: Heel of one foot is placed close to toe of other foot.

You should not only learn these positions, but should accustom yourself to moving the feet from one position to another. Starting with weight on R.F., move L.F. to 2nd, 3rd, 4th and 5th positions. Then resume 1st position and, keeping the weight on L.F., move R.F. to 2nd, 3rd, 4th, and 5th positions. Next, practise them rearwards.

WHEN DANCING IN THE TWENTIETH CENTURY SEQUENCE STYLE you keep the feet parallel instead of turned-out.

When you step forward, you keep the toes pointing straight ahead. The same applies when you step back or to the side.

PARTNERS' POSITIONS IN RELATION TO EACH OTHER

IN all the round sequence dances (as distinct from the set or square dances, which are sequence dances executed by sets of dancers) the dancers participate in partnerships of two—a lady and a gentleman. As soon as they prepare to dance they adopt a position—a Starting Position. All the time they are dancing they are in some position in relation to each other. It may be the one with which they started, or it may be some other position. It is necessary for them to understand clearly what the various positions are, and to know the terms which denote them.

THE STARTING POSITION is the position taken up prior to beginning a dance.

THE MOST FREQUENTLY USED STARTING POSITION is the Waltz Hold, in which the lady always stands in front of her partner. Therefore if a Starting Position is given as "Waltz Hold, Gentleman facing wall," this is a sufficient explanation of one Starting Position, since if the gentleman faces the wall, clearly the lady, who faces him, must have her back to the wall.

THE WALTZ HOLD is employed not only for many of the sequence dances which are based on the Waltz, but for various others. It is used for most of the Twentieth Century Sequence dances—i.e. for the sequence varieties of the Foxtrot, Saunter, and Tango.

For an explanation of the Waltz Hold, see the Starting Position for the Old Time Waltz on page 51.

THE OPEN POSITION is also frequently used. Here the partners stand side by side, facing the L.O.D., and with the lady on the gentleman's right (i.e. nearer to the wall).

The Gentleman holds his partner's left hand in his own right hand, which he keeps palm upward. His left hand is held lightly on his left hip, thumb to rear, and with fingers forward and grouped.

The Lady places her left hand palm downwards on her partner's right hand. She holds her gown with her right thumb and first finger, the other fingers being neatly grouped. Her right arm should be gracefully curved.

In most sequence dances changes of Hold and Position occur instead of the Starting Position being maintained all through the dance. Where these occur they are indicated in the descriptions of the dances.

Not only do the dancers sometimes "open-out" from Waltz Hold to the Open Position. In some figures they partially "open-out," the gentleman turning slightly to his left, and the lady slightly to her right, as follows—

PROMENADE POSITION: in which the partners open-out fanwise from each other and travel in a V formation. Those who have danced in the Modern style should note that in Old Time dancing the partners usually open-out rather more than in Modern-style dancing. Consequently the steps taken in Promenade Position are not so much to the side (moving sideways along L.O.D.) as forward along L.O.D.

CONTRA PROMENADE POSITION: in which, after the partners have taken a number of steps in P.P., they turn inwards, so as to face the opposite direction to that in which they were formerly proceeding. When in Contra Promenade Position the gentleman should ease his Hold slightly with the right hand. If he does not slightly release that hand he will have to keep his right shoulder forward, thus possibly prejudicing his balance and certainly spoiling his "line." In other words, failure to ease the Hold has the effect of causing the gentleman to incline sideways instead of remaining naturally erect.

THE EASIEST WAY TO START

YOU do not need to know much about dancing before you begin to dance. Indeed, it is desirable that you should dance as you learn, and learn as you dance.

Far too many people have the utterly erroneous impression that dancing is difficult, and some are convinced that they never could learn to dance. It is therefore encouraging and helpful if, right at the start, you prove to yourself how simple sequence dancing is, by learning a dance.

It is for that reason that I invite the reader, before proceeding further, to learn the dance which I describe on the next page. It is built up entirely on movements such as we all employ every day of our lives. By learning to dance it right at the beginning, you will learn more about sequence dancing than you will from reading pages of theory.

Before you attempt to learn the Harry Lime Foxtrot, please note that this is a Twentieth Century Sequence dance. It makes an excellent introduction to that important group of dances, in all of which you keep the feet pointing straight forward all the time—not turned out.

THE HARRY LIME FOXTROT

EVEN if you have never before danced a step in your life, you can learn this dance easily and quickly.

It is danced to familiar music—the Harry Lime Theme. This is a considerable advantage to the beginner. You can hum the tune as you try the steps.

This dance has been selected for use here, as No. 1 in the book, because of its simplicity. But do not regard it merely as an exercise. It is, in fact, a very popular dance, and well worth learning even if you already know a good deal about sequence dancing.

This dance, one of the outstanding successes of the 1949–50 season, was arranged by Henry Clarke. Partnered by Mae Thickens, he demonstrated it before a huge audience at the Fifth Anniversary Pageant of Old Time Dancing held by the International Sequence Dance Circle at the Empress Ballroom, Blackpool. It was later demonstrated at other large I.S.D.C. balls in various parts of Britain. Not only was it danced at these big balls, the dancers quickly picking up the very simple steps, but it was adopted by hundreds of village clubs.

Timing: as for all the Foxtrots and Saunters. A slow step equals two beats of the music, and a quick step one beat.

Time: 4/4. *Tempo:* 32 bars per minute.

Starting position: Waltz hold. Gentleman facing L.O.D. Both partners stand with feet together and broadside on, i.e. toe-to-toe and heel-to-heel, ready to begin.

The Point and Side Step, with which this dance begins, should be practised very slowly at first. Speed up the steps when you can dance them quite easily and without having to think hard.

GENTLEMAN

The Point and Side Step (Left)—	COUNT	BARS
Point L.F. to L. side, keeping weight on R.F.	Q.	
Close L.F. back to R.F.	Q.	
Point L.F. to L. side, keeping weight on R.F.	Q.	
Close L.F. back to R.F.	Q.	
Step to L. side with L.F.	S.	
Close R.F. to L.F., keeping weight on L.F.	S.	2

The Point and Side Step (Right)—		
Point R.F. to R. side, keeping weight on L.F.	Q.	
Close R.F. back to L.F.	Q.	
Point R.F. to R. side, keeping weight on L.F.	Q.	
Close R.F. back to L.F.	Q.	
Step to R. side with R.F.	S.	
Close L.F. to R.F., keeping weight on R.F.	S.	2

The Walk and Chassé (Left)—		
Step forward with L.F.	S.	
Step forward with R.F.	S.	

Chassé—		
Step forward with L.F. (short step)	Q.	
Close R.F. to L.F.	Q.	
Step forward with L.F.	S.	2

	COUNT	BARS

The Walk and Chassé (Right)—
Step forward with R.F. — S.
Step forward with L.F. — S.

Chassé—
Step forward with R.F. (short step) — Q.
Close L.F. to R.F. — Q.
Step forward with R.F. — S. — 2

The Side Steps (Left)—
Rising on to balls of feet,
Step to L. side with L.F. (short step) — Q.
Close R.F. to L.F. — Q.
Step to L. side with L.F. (short step) — Q.
Close R.F. to L.F. — Q.
Lower on to flat foot, then—
Step to L. side with L.F. — S.
Close R.F. to L.F., keeping weight on L.F. — S. — 2

The Side Steps (Right)—
Rising on to balls of feet,
Step to R. side with R.F. (short step) — Q.
Close L.F. to R.F. — Q.
Step to R. side with R.F. (short step) — Q.
Close L.F. to R.F. — Q.
Lower on to flat foot, then—
Step to R. side with R.F. — S.
Close L.F. to R.F., keeping weight on R.F. — S. — 2

SEQUENCE DANCING

	COUNT	BARS
The Walk and Twinkle (Left)—		
Step forward with L.F.	S.	
Step forward with R.F.	S.	
Twinkle—		
Step back with L.F. (short step)	Q.	
Close R.F. to L.F.	Q.	
Step forward with L.F.	S.	2
The Walk and Twinkle (Right)—		
Step forward with R.F.	S.	
Step forward with L.F.	S.	
Twinkle—		
Step back with R.F. (short step)	Q.	
Close L.F. to R.F.	Q.	
Step forward with R.F.	Q.	
Close L.F. to R.F., keeping weight on R.F., ready to repeat the sequence from the beginning.	Q.	2
		16

Note. The 3rd step of the Twinkle is normally slow, but in the last bar is taken quickly so that there is time to close L.F. up to R.F., thus bringing the dancer into original Starting Position, ready to begin the sequence again on the next bar.

LADY

The Point and Side Step (Right)—	COUNT	BARS
Point R.F. to R. side, keeping weight on L.F.	Q.	
Close R.F. back to L.F.	Q.	
Point R.F. to R. side, keeping weight on L.F.	Q.	
Close R.F. back to L.F.	Q.	
Step to R. side with R.F.	S.	
Close L.F. to R.F., keeping weight on R.F.	S.	2

The Point and Side Step (Left)—		
Point L.F. to L. side, keeping weight on R.F.	Q.	
Close L.F. back to R.F.	Q.	
Point L.F. to L. side, keeping weight on R.F.	Q.	
Close L.F. back to R.F.	Q.	
Step to L. side with L.F.	S.	
Close R.F. to L.F., keeping weight on L.F.	S.	2

The Walk and Chassé (Right)—		
Step back with R.F.	S.	
Step back with L.F.	S.	

Chassé—		
Step back with R.F. (short step)	Q.	
Close L.F. to R.F.	Q.	
Step back with R.F.	S.	2

The Walk and Chassé (Left)—		
Step back with L.F.	S.	
Step back with R.F.	S.	

Chassé—

	COUNT	BARS
Step back with L.F. (short step)	Q.	
Close R.F. to L.F.	Q.	
Step back with L.F.	S.	2

The Side Steps (Right)—

Rising on to balls of feet,

	COUNT	BARS
Step to R. side with R.F. (short step)	Q.	
Close L.F. to R.F.	Q.	
Step to R. side with R.F. (short step)	Q.	
Close L.F. to R.F.	Q.	
Lower on to flat foot, then—		
Step to R. side with R.F.	S.	
Close L.F. to R.F., keeping weight on R.F.	S.	2

The Side Steps (Left)—

Rising on to balls of feet,

	COUNT	BARS
Step to L. side with L.F. (short step)	Q.	
Close R.F. to L.F.	Q.	
Step to L. side with L.F. (short step)	Q.	
Close R.F. to L.F.	Q.	
Lower on to flat foot, then—		
Step to L. side with L.F.	S.	
Close R.F. to L.F., keeping weight on L.F.	S.	2

The Walk and Twinkle (Right)—

	COUNT	BARS
Step back with R.F.	S.	
Step back with L.F.	S.	

Promenade Position

Contra Promenade Position

	COUNT	BARS

Twinkle—

Step forward with R.F. (short step)	Q.	
Close L.F. to R.F.	Q.	
Step back with R.F.	S.	2

The Walk and Twinkle (Left)—

| Step back with L.F. | S. | |
| Step back with R.F. | S. | |

Twinkle—

Step forward with L.F. (short step)	Q.	
Close R.F. to L.F.	Q.	
Step back with L.F.	Q.	
Close R.F. to L.F., keeping weight on L.F., ready to repeat the sequence from the beginning.	Q.	2

$$\overline{16}$$

Note. The 3rd step of the Twinkle is normally slow, but in the last bar it is taken quickly so that there is time to close R.F. to L.F., thus bringing the dancer into original Starting Position, ready to begin the sequence again on the next bar.

THE SAUNTERS: SLOW SEQUENCE FOXTROTS

IN the Old Time ballroom various sequence Foxtrots are danced, those in normal Foxtrot tempo (32 bars per minute) being generally called Foxtrots (e.g. On Leave Foxtrot) and those in a slower tempo (28 bars per minute) being called Saunters. There are, of course, Foxtrots (Slow Foxtrot and Quickstep, or Quick Foxtrot) in the Modern-style ballroom. But the Saunter, a slow, leisurely, graceful dance based on precisely the same technique as the Old Time Foxtrot, finds a place only in Old Time programmes.

Between the two great wars a great many Foxtrots were introduced as sequence dances. Most of them were extremely poor imitations of the Modern-style Foxtrot, and they did not last long. But the Saunters have proved very popular indeed. The steps of the various sequence Saunters are easily learned, but because they are danced to slow music they are rather more difficult to dance than those of the Foxtrots. There is more time to be taken over each step, and thus the demands upon balance are somewhat heavier.

THE SAUNTER HOLD is similar to that for the Waltz. The lady is held in front of the Gentleman. Both partners should keep their weight forward—i.e. keep weight towards your partner. Take care, however, not to lean forward. You should remain naturally erect.

THE SAUNTER WALK is a long, gliding step, taken forward or backward, with the leg swinging freely from the hip. The feet should point straight ahead and not be turned out as for the dances of the traditional style. When stepping forward or backward, the foot with which you are stepping should pass close to the other foot, almost touching it in passing.

THE WALK FORWARD is a natural-length step, the heel of the moving foot touching the floor first, then the whole of the foot touching the floor.

THE WALK BACKWARD is a natural-length step, the leg swinging well back from the hip, and the toe of the moving foot touching the floor first, then the whole of the foot touching the floor.

TIMING for the Saunters is the same as for the Foxtrots, namely: *A slow step equals two beats of the music, and a quick step equals one beat of the music.*

It is easier to count in Quicks and Slows rather than in numbers of beats where the Foxtrots and Saunters are concerned, and in the descriptions of Saunter sequence dances I accordingly employ that method.

THE YEARNING SAUNTER

THIS dance is one of the easiest of the Saunters to learn. It was arranged by Harry Boyle in 1919, and it has remained steadily popular throughout the years. For the beginner it makes an ideal introduction to the dances of the Saunter group.

Time: 4/4. *Tempo:* 28 bars per minute.

Starting position: Waltz hold. Gentleman facing L.O.D.

GENTLEMAN

The Forward Walk—	COUNT	BARS
Step forward with L.F.	s.	
Step forward with R.F.	s.	
Step forward with L.F.	s.	
Step forward with R.F.	s.	2
The Rock—		
Without moving feet, balance back on to L.F.	s.	
Balance forward on to R.F.	s.	
Balance back on to L.F.	s.	
Balance forward on to R.F.	s.	2
The Forward Walk—		
Repeat Bars 1, 2		2

The Rock and Swivel—

	COUNT	BARS
Repeat Bars 3, 4, and on last Rock Forward swivel slightly to R. (to face diag. to wall)		2

Scissors Step—

	COUNT	BARS
Step diag. to R., over and across R.F., with L.F.	S.	
Point R.F. to side, toe to floor (towards wall)	S.	
Swivelling to L. on both feet, step diag. to L., over and across L.F. with R.F.	S.	
Point L.F. to side, toe to floor (towards centre)	S.	2
Repeat Scissors Step, i.e. the last two bars.		2

Chassé (Left)—

	COUNT	BARS
Step diag. forward with L.F.	Q.	
Close R.F. to L.F.	Q.	
Step diag. forward with L.F.	S.	1

Chassé (Right)—

	COUNT	BARS
Step diag. forward with R.F.	Q.	
Close L.F. to R.F.	Q.	
Step diag. forward with R.F.	S.	1

Chassé Turn—

	COUNT	BARS
Step to L. side with L.F., turning to R.	Q.	
Close R.F. to L.F., still turning	Q.	
Step back with L.F., turning to R.	S.	
Step to R. side with R.F., still turning	Q.	

	COUNT	BARS
Close L.F. to R.F., still turning	Q.	
Step forward with R.F.	S.	2
		16

This sequence is repeated *ad lib.*

LADY

	COUNT	BARS
The Backward Walk—		
Step back with R.F.	S.	
Step back with L.F.	S.	
Step back with R.F.	S.	
Step back with L.F.	S.	2
The Rock—		
Without moving feet, balance forward on to R.F.	S.	
Balance back on to L.F.	S.	
Balance forward on to R.F.	S.	
Balance back on to L.F.	S.	2
The Backward Walk—		
Repeat Bars 1, 2		2
The Rock and Swivel—		
Repeat Bars 3, 4, and on last Rock back swivel slightly to R. (now backing diag. to wall)		2

Scissors Step—   COUNT   BARS

	Count	Bars
Step diag. to L., and across behind L.F. with R.F.	S.	
Point L.F. to side, toe to floor	S.	
Swivelling to L. on both feet, step diag. to R., and across behind R.F. with L.F.	S.	
Point R.F. to side, toe to floor (towards centre)	S.	2
Repeat Scissors Step, i.e. last 2 bars		2

Chassé (Right)—

Step diag. back with R.F.	Q.	
Close L.F. to R.F.	Q.	
Step diag. back with R.F.	S.	1

Chassé (Left)—

Step diag. back with L.F.	Q.	
Close R.F. to L.F.	Q.	
Step diag. back with L.F.	S.	1

Chassé Turn—

Step to R. side with R.F., turning to R.	Q.	
Close L.F. to R.F., still turning	Q.	
Step forward with R.F., turning to R.	S.	
Step to L. side with L.F., still turning	Q.	
Close R.F. to L.F., still turning	Q.	
Step back with L.F.	S.	2
		—
		16

This sequence is repeated *ad lib.*

How to Improve Your Dance

THE ROCK. The ideal here is a gentle rocking motion, first back, then forward (Lady: forward, then back). There must be nothing hurried or jerky about it. You finish bar 2 with your weight on the right foot (Lady, left foot) and the Rock, in the following bar, involves transferring your weight back on to the left foot (Lady, forward on to right foot). Relax knee on each of the Rock steps.

CHASSÉ TURN. Throughout this figure both partners keep turning to the right, until the last step, which is of course straight forward (Lady, straight back). Take care to turn your body as you take the steps—not, as is sometimes seen, stepping first and then, as an after-thought, starting to turn the body.

Finally, bear in mind that your Yearning Saunter should be a continuous, flowing dance, with no breaks to spoil the flow. I have described it in sections, each of one short figure, for the purpose of simplicity, but when dancing you should pass from one figure to another without any pause between them.

SAUNTER SERENADE

THIS is one of the newer sequence dances of the Saunter group, for it was introduced in 1949. It aroused immediate interest.

Miss Dorothy Bullars, of the British Association of Teachers of Dancing, arranged this dance. It differs from most of the Saunters in that it does not include many Slow walking steps; nevertheless, the figures are based on the underlying Saunter technique, and it is not only its name which makes this one of the Saunter dances.

The only descriptions I have seen of this dance have given the steps one after the other, all through without a break, which makes it look rather forbidding, and much harder than it really is. I have, therefore, broken it up into readily-learned figures. If each of these is learned thoroughly before proceeding to the next figure, this dance will prove no more difficult than most of the others in this book.

Time: 4/4. *Tempo:* 28 bars per minute.

Starting position: Waltz hold. Gentleman facing L.O.D.

GENTLEMAN

Diagonal Chassé (Left)—	COUNT	BARS
Step diag. forward with L.F.	Q.	
Close R.F. to L.F.	Q.	
Step diag. forward with L.F.	S.	1

	COUNT	BARS
Diagonal Chassé (Right)—		
Step diag. forward with R.F.	Q.	
Close L.F. to R.F.	Q.	
Step diag. forward with R.F.	S.	1
		—
		2
The Salutes—		
Turning slightly to R., so as to face diag. to wall,		
Step to L. side with L.F.	S.	
Place R.F. behind L.F., keeping weight on L.F., withdraw right hand and relax both knees	S.	1
Turning slightly to L.,		
Step to R. side with R.F.	S.	
Place L.F. behind R.F., keeping weight on R.F., withdraw left hand and relax both knees	S.	1
		—
		4
Repeat the whole sequence (Bars 1 to 4), so far described, and open-out at the finish into P.P., facing diag. to centre		4
		—
		8
The Point Step (Twice)—		
Step forward with L.F. in P.P.	Q.	
Close R.F. to L.F.	Q.	
Point L.F. forward	S.	1

SAUNTER SERENADE

	COUNT	BARS
Step forward with L.F. in P.P.	Q.	
Close R.F. to L.F.	Q.	
Point L.F. forward	S.	1
		—
		10

The Salute—

Turning slightly to R., so as to face diag. to wall,

Step to L. side with L.F.	S.	
Place R.F. behind L.F., still turning, and keeping weight on L.F. Relax both knees. (Now backing diag. to centre.)	S.	1

The Three-Step—

Step forward with R.F. (diag. to wall against L.O.D.)	Q.	
Step forward with L.F.	Q.	
Step forward with R.F., turning to face diag. to centre, in P.P.	S.	1
		—
		12
Repeat Bars 9–12 (the last four bars), turning to face L.O.D. at end		4
		—
		16

The Promenade Walk—

Still in P.P., facing L.O.D.,

Step forward with L.F. in P.P.	S.	
Step forward with R.F. in P.P.	S.	1

	COUNT	BARS

The Heel–Toe Promenade—

Still in P.P., facing L.O.D.,

Short step forward on heel of L.F.	Q.	
Close R. toe to L. heel	Q.	
Short step forward on heel of L.F.	Q.	
Close R. toe to L. heel	Q.	1
		18

The Solo Turn—

Release hold, and

Step forward with L.F., turning to L.	S.	
Step forward with R.F., still turning	S.	1
Step forward with L.F. (against L.O.D.)	S.	
Point R.F. forward, and resume Holds	S.	1
		20

Repeat Bars 17–20, beginning with R.F., against L.O.D., finishing in P.P., pointing L.F. forward along L.O.D.   4

24

Salute—

Step forward with L.F.	S.	
Close R.F. to L.F.	S.	
Hold position while partner curtseys	S.	
Bow slightly	S.	2
		26

SAUNTER SERENADE

	COUNT	BARS
The Left Wheel—		
Joining L. hands,		
Step forward with L.F., turning to L.	S.	
Step forward with R.F., still turning	S.	
Step forward with L.F., still turning	S.	
Close R.F. to L.F., now facing wall, and slightly behind partner, with right shoulder behind her left shoulder, taking partner's R. hand in own R. hand	S.	2
		28
Side Steps and Points—		
Step to L. side with L.F.	Q.	
Close R.F. to L.F.	Q.	
Point L.F. to L. side (along L.O.D.)	S.	1
Repeat Side Step and Point (Bar 29)		1
		30
Final Salute—		
Release hands,		
Step to L. side with L.F.	S.	
Close R.F. to L.F., keeping weight on L.F.	S.	1
Turning slightly to L.,		
Step to R. side with R.F.	S.	
Place L.F. behind R.F., keeping weight on R.F., withdraw left hand and relax both knees	S.	1
		32

At finish, resume Waltz Hold, and repeat the sequence *ad lib*.

LADY

	COUNT	BARS
Diagonal Chassé (Right)—		
Step diag. back with R.F.	Q.	
Close L.F. to R.F.	Q.	
Step diag. back with L.F.	S.	1
Diagonal Chassé (Left)—		
Step diag. back with L.F.	Q.	
Close R.F. to L.F.	Q.	
Step diag. back with L.F.	S.	1
		—
		2
The Salutes—		
Turning slightly to R., now facing diag. to centre against L.O.D.,		
Step to R. side with R.F.	S.	
Cross L.F. behind and to R. of R.F., keeping weight on R.F., and relax both knees	S.	1
Turning slightly to L.,		
Step to L. side with L.F.	S.	
Cross R.F. behind and to L. of L.F., keeping weight on L.F., and relax both knees	S.	1
		—
		4
Repeat the whole sequence (Bars 1–4) so far described, and open-out at finish into P.P., facing diag. to centre		4
		—
		8

	COUNT	BARS
The Point Step (*Twice*)—		
Step forward with R.F. in P.P.	Q.	
Close L.F. to R.F.	Q.	
Point R.F. forward	S.	1
Step forward with R.F. in P.P.	Q.	
Close L.F. to R.F.	Q.	
Point R.F. forward	S.	1
		10
The Salute—		
Turning slightly to R., so as to back diag. to wall,		
Step to R. side with R.F.	S.	
Place L.F. behind and to R. of R.F., keeping weight on R.F. and relax both knees. (Now facing diag. to centre.)	S.	1
The Three-Step—		
Step back with L.F. (diag. to wall against L.O.D.)	Q.	
Step back with R.F.	Q.	
Step back with L.F., turning to back centre diag.	S.	1
		12
Repeat Bars 9 *to* 12, turning to face L.O.D. at end		4
		16

SEQUENCE DANCING

	COUNT	BARS
The Promenade Walk—		
Still in P.P., facing L.O.D.,		
Step forward with R.F. in P.P.	S.	
Step forward with L.F. in P.P.	S.	1
The Heel-Toe Promenade—		
Still in P.P., facing L.O.D.,		
Short step forward on heel of R.F.	Q.	
Close L. toe to R. heel	Q.	
Short step forward on heel of R.F.	Q.	
Close L. toe to R. heel	Q.	1
		—
		18
The Solo Turn—		
Release hold, and		
Step forward with R.F., turning to R.	S.	—
Step forward with L.F., still turning	S.	1
Step forward with R.F. (against L.O.D.)	S.	
Point L.F. forward (against L.O.D.) and resume Hold	S.	1
		—
		20
Repeat Bars 17–20, beginning with L.F., against L.O.D., finishing in P.P., pointing R.F. along L.O.D.		4
		—
		24
Salute—		
Step forward with R.F.	S.	
Step forward with L.F. turning to L.	S.	1

	COUNT	BARS
Turning to face partner,		
Step to R. side with R.F.	S.	
Step across behind R.F. with L.F., and curtsey	S.	1
		——
		26

The Left Wheel—
Giving left hand in partner's left,

	COUNT	BARS
Step forward with L.F., turning to L.	S.	
Step forward with R.F., still turning	S.	1
Step forward with L.F., still turning	S.	
Close R.F. to L.F., finishing facing wall, slightly in front of partner (his right shoulder behind own left shoulder)	S.	1
		——
		28

Side Step and Points—

	COUNT	BARS
Step to L. side with L.F.	Q.	
Close R.F. to L.F.	Q.	
Point L.F. to L. side (along L.O.D.)	S.	1
		——
		29
Repeat Side Step and Point (Bar 29)		1
		——
		30

Final Salute—
Release hands,

	COUNT	BARS
Step to R. side with R.F.	S.	
Close L.F. to R.F., keeping weight on R.F.	S.	1
Turning to face partner,		

	COUNT	BARS
Step to L. side with L.F.	S.	
Place R.F. behind and to L. of L.F., keeping weight on L.F., withdraw left hand, and relax both knees	S.	1
		$\overline{\overline{32}}$

At finish, resume Waltz Hold, and repeat the sequence *ad lib.*

General Notes on the Saunter Serenade

It will be noted, from the above description, that in the Salutes which occur in Bars 2 and 3 (as well as later in this dance) both partners relax the knees. The result is what might be termed a semi-curtsey—though in actual practice it is hardly as marked a salutation as that. The relaxation of the knees should not be overdone; just the *suggestion* of a curtsey is all that is required, and this by both partners—not the lady only.

In Bar 26, the Salutation takes a different form; there, the gentleman bows slightly, while the lady does a curtsey.

Note that in the Left Wheel (Bars 27 and 28) both partners begin with L.F. and move round to the left. This figure finishes with the partners in Maxina Position—the gentleman's right shoulder behind the lady's left shoulder.

In the Side Steps and Points (Bars 29 and 30) the partners continue to dance exactly the same steps, both beginning with L.F.

THE OLD TIME WALTZ

IN order to enjoy sequence dancing you must be able to dance the Old Time Waltz. Some people dance it moderately well almost from the start; others find it difficult. If you experience any difficulty in mastering this essential basic dance, for such it is, you should consult a good teacher. A few lessons in the Waltz will be well worth while, and the small cost in time and money amply repaid by the subsequent pleasure derived from dancing this most-popular-of-all dances both as a dance in itself, and as part of the many sequence dances in which it figures.

You take a step to each beat of the music. The beats occur regularly and consistently throughout—1-2-3, 1-2-3, and so on, and you can readily distinguish them.

In the two main figures—the Natural Turn and the Reverse Turn, the partners both dance the same steps, although not at the same time. The Lady dances the second half of the Turn while the Gentleman dances the first half and vice versa.

Time: 3/4. *Tempo:* 48 bars per minute.

Starting position: Partners stand facing each other.

Gentleman faces wall, and stands naturally erect. His right hand is placed just above the lady's waist. His left arm is extended, with hand at shoulder-level.

Lady stands with back to wall, naturally erect. Her left hand is on gentleman's right shoulder, and her right hand is placed in his left hand.

THE NATURAL TURN

STEP		COUNT	BARS
1	Glide L.F. diag. forward, turning to R.	1	
2	Place toe of R.F. behind heel of L.F., still turning	2	
3	Pivot to R., with weight on balls of feet, until R.F. is in 5th position in front	3	1
4	Glide R.F. forward between partner's feet (short step) turning to R.	1	
5	Glide L.F. to L. side, still turning	2	
6	Draw L.F. to R.F., in 5th position in front, still turning	3	1
			2

THE LADY dances steps 4, 5, 6 above while the Gentleman dances 1, 2, 3, and vice versa. In other words, she begins at step 4, and dances 4, 5, 6; 1, 2, 3.

Practise the steps slowly at first. Then, when you have mastered the foot-movements, try them to Waltz music, first without, then with, a partner.

THE REVERSE TURN

STEP		COUNT	BARS
1	Glide L.F. forward between partner's feet (short step) turning to L.	1	
2	Glide R.F. to R. side, still turning	2	
3	Draw L.F. to R.F., in 5th position in front, still turning	3	1
4	Glide R.F. back, and slightly to the side, still turning	1	

		COUNT	BARS
5	Place toe of L.F. behind heel of R.F., still turning	2	
6	Pivot to L., with weight on balls of feet until L.F. is in 5th position in front	3	1 — 2 =

THE LADY dances 4, 5, 6 above, while the Gentleman dances 1, 2, 3, and vice versa. In other words, she begins at step 4, and dances 4, 5, 6; 1, 2, 3.

THE PAS DE VALSE

This figure is used as a link between the two Turns.
It may be danced either forward or backward, as follows—

Pas de Valse Forward: Starting with either foot, step forward (1 beat); Step forward with the other foot (1 beat); Close foot first moved to 3rd position rear.

Pas de Valse Backward: Starting with either foot, step back (1 beat); Step back with the other foot (1 beat); Close foot first moved to 3rd position in front.

The Gentleman dances the Pas de Valse Forward while his partner dances the Pas de Valse Backward, and vice versa.

How to Link the Waltz Turns Together

To Change from Natural to Reverse Turn—
Dance steps 1, 2, 3 of Natural Turn;
Pas de Valse Forward (Lady, Backward) curving steps slightly towards L.O.D.
Then dance the Reverse Turn, and if desired, continue to dance that figure.

To Change from Reverse to Natural Turn—

Dance a complete Reverse Turn;

Pas de Valse Forward (along L.O.D.);

Then dance steps 4, 5, 6 of Natural Turn, and if desired, continue to dance that figure.

WALTZ FIGURES IN SEQUENCE DANCES

BY far the largest group of sequence dances consists of those which are based on the Waltz. These dances are Waltz-like in character and are danced in Waltz (3/4) time.

Waltz figures are included in some of the sequence dances which are not Waltz-like in character, and which are not danced in Waltz-time.

WHEN DANCING WALTZ FIGURES TO NON-WALTZ MUSIC (in those dances which are in 4/4 or 6/8 time) the counting is "1 and 2" instead of 1, 2, 3.

This does not prove at all difficult in practice; the music almost tells the dancer how to time the steps. Care must be taken to ensure that the steps are taken smoothly and without jerkiness.

THE PAS DE VALSE sometimes occurs with the partners side-by-side instead of facing each other.

THE SOLO WALTZ is, as its name implies, the Waltz danced independently of one's partner. It may be danced in two ways, as follows—

Solo Waltz Outward, in which the dancer turns away from his or her partner.

Solo Waltz Inward, in which the dancer turns towards his or her partner.

The Gentleman's Solo Waltz Outward is a Gentleman's Reverse Turn.

The Gentleman's Solo Waltz Inward is a Lady's Natural Turn.

The Lady's Solo Waltz Outward is a Lady's Natural Turn.
The Lady's Solo Waltz Inward is a Gentleman's Reverse Turn.

When dancing a Solo Waltz, whether Outward or Inward, the Gentleman keeps his left hand on his left hip. He retains normal Waltz position with his right hand. This enables him, on rejoining his partner, to resume the normal Waltz Hold easily and naturally.

When dancing a Solo Waltz, whether Outward or Inward, the Lady holds her skirt with her right hand. She retains normal Waltz position with her left hand. This enables her, on rejoining her partner, to resume the normal Waltz Hold easily and naturally.

WALTZ FINALES. Many of the sequence dances conclude with a short spell of Waltzing. It is necessary that this should end with the dancers back in their original Starting Position, ready to repeat the dance from the beginning. *Where Open Position has to be regained,* on the final bar the Gentleman dances a Pas de Valse to enable him to finish facing in the desired direction.

Thus, assuming a 4-bar spell of Waltzing—

The Gentleman dances one complete Natural Turn, then half a Natural Turn (3 bars in all) followed by one Pas de Valse (1 bar).

The Lady dances two complete Natural Turns (4 bars).

When the closed Waltz position has to be regained, with Gentleman facing L.O.D., the Lady dances a Pas de Valse in the last bar.

CARINA WALTZ

THIS is one of the simplest sequence dances based on the Waltz, and it is therefore eminently suitable for beginners.

Tom Hayton, a Past President of the British Association of Teachers of Dancing, arranged this dance.

Note that when pointing a foot, either forward or backward (as in the first two bars) the weight of the body should be on the opposite foot; i.e. point R.F., keep weight on L.F., and vice versa.

Time: 3/4. *Tempo:* 46 bars per minute.

Starting position: Open.

GENTLEMAN

	COUNT	BARS
The Points—		
Point L.F. forward, toe to floor, heel raised	1, 2, 3	
Point L.F. back, toe to floor, heel raised	1, 2, 3	2
Chassé Forward—		
Step forward with L.F.	1, 2	
Close R.F. to 3rd position rear	3	
Step forward with L.F.	1, 2, 3	2
		4

SEQUENCE DANCING

	COUNT	BARS
Now turn to opposite direction, i.e. facing against L.O.D.—		
Repeat the first 4 bars beginning with R.F., as follows—		
Point R.F. forward, then back	1, 2, 3 twice	2
Step forward with R.F.	1, 2	
Close L.F. to 3rd position rear	3	
Step forward with R.F.	1, 2, 3	2
		—
		8
Turning L. to face partner, take her right hand in own left, her left in own right, and—		
Step forward with L.F. (towards wall)	1, 2, 3	
Step forward with R.F.	1, 2, 3	
Step to L. side with L.F.	1, 2, 3	
Step over L.F. and to L. side with R.F.	1, 2, 3	4
		—
		12
Waltz Finale—		
Take Waltz Hold and Waltz (Natural Turn) opening-out at finish to original Starting Position ready to repeat the sequence *ad lib*.	1, 2, 3 four times	4
		—
		16

CARINA WALTZ

LADY

	COUNT	BARS
The Points—		
Point R.F. forward, toe to floor, heel raised	1, 2, 3	
Point R.F. back, toe to floor, heel raised	1, 2, 3	2
Chassé Forward—		
Step forward with R.F.	1, 2	
Close L.F. to 3rd position rear	3	
Step forward with R.F.	1, 2, 3	2
		—
		4

Now turn to opposite direction, i.e. facing against L.O.D.—

Repeat the first 4 bars beginning with L.F., as follows—

Point L.F. forward, then back	1, 2, 3 twice	2
Step forward with L.F.	1, 2	
Close R.F. to 3rd position rear	3	
Step forward with L.F.	1, 2, 3	2
		—
		8

Turning to R. to face partner, give right hand in his left, and left hand in his right, and—

Step back with R.F. (towards wall)	1, 2, 3	
Step back with L.F.	1, 2, 3	
Step to R. side with R.F.	1, 2, 3	
Step over R.F. and to R. side with L.F.	1, 2, 3	4
		—
		12

Waltz Finale—	COUNT	BARS
Take Waltz Hold and Waltz (Natural Turn) opening-out at finish to original Starting Position ready to repeat the sequence *ad lib*.	1, 2, 3 four times	4
		16

How to Improve Your Dance

The feet should be kept turned-out throughout the Carina Waltz, i.e. the dancer should maintain correct 1st Position. This applies to the Waltz sequence dances generally, and if the feet are kept correctly turned out, they tend to move easily and naturally into the appropriate positions for each step.

When pointing a foot, as in the first two bars, take care to keep the foot well turned-out and stretch the instep in order to point the toe downward. By keeping the weight of the body well back, i.e. on the supporting foot, you help to produce a good "line." In other words, your whole body provides a pleasing picture, which is really the aim in all our dances.

Thus, although you learn the dances by way of foot-movements, or steps, you are all the time dancing with your whole body, and once you have mastered the steps you should devote more attention to the style with which you dance them.

Try to respond, in your dancing, to the gentle lilt which occurs in Waltz music, and which encourages you to rise slightly throughout each bar. For instance, in the Chassé Forward you should rise on the balls of the feet during the counts of 2 and 3, but gently lower the heel at the end of the bar.

The same applies to the forward steps (lady, backward steps) in bars 9 and 10. Rise on to the balls of the feet during counts 2 and 3, but gently lower the heel at the end of the bar.

Finally, bear in mind that your Carina Waltz should be a continuous, flowing dance, with no breaks to spoil the flow. I have described it in separate figures for the purpose of simplicity, but when dancing you should pass from one figure to another without any pause between them.

QUAKER GIRL WALTZ

ALTHOUGH not, perhaps, so well-known as some of the other dances arranged by F. J. Mainey, this pleasant Waltz sequence has long been included in the programmes at Northern and Midland ballrooms, while of late it has found favour at many of the London resorts of Old Time dancers.

It is very easily learned, and, as will be seen from the following description, makes considerable use of the Pas de Valse figure.

Time: 3/4. *Tempo:* 46 bars per minute.

Starting position: Partners stand facing each other, the Gentleman facing L.O.D., and Lady facing him, with back to L.O.D.

Partners join both hands. The Gentleman holds Lady's right hand in his left hand, and her left hand in his right hand. The arms are extended, the joined hands being at shoulder-height.

GENTLEMAN

Pas de Valse Forward (3 times)—	COUNT	BARS
Step forward with L.F.	1	
Step forward with R.F.	2	
Close L.F. to 3rd position rear	3	1
Repeat Bar 1, but starting with R.F.	1, 2, 3	1
Repeat Bar 1	1, 2, 3	1
		3

QUAKER GIRL WALTZ

	COUNT	BARS
Balancé Forward—		
Step forward with R.F.	1	
Close L.F. to 3rd position rear, keeping weight on R.F.	2, 3	1
		—
		4
Pas de Valse Rearward (3 times)—		
Step back with L.F.	1	
Step back with R.F.	2	
Close L.F. to 3rd position in front	3	1
Repeat Bar 5, but starting with R.F.	1, 2, 3	1
Repeat Bar 5	1, 2, 3	1
		—
		7
Balancé Rearward—		
Step back with R.F.	1	
Close L.F. to R.F., opening-out to Open Position, side-by-side with partner, and taking her left hand in own right hand. (Both facing L.O.D.)	2, 3	1
		—
		8
Pas de Valse Forward (Twice)—		
Step forward with L.F.	1	
Step forward with R.F.	2	
Close L.F. to 3rd position rear	3	1
		—
		9
Repeat Bar 9, but starting with R.F.	1, 2, 3	1
		—
		10
Allemande—		
Repeat Bar 9, raising right arm while partner Waltzes beneath it	1, 2, 3	1

	COUNT	BARS
Repeat Bar 9, but starting with R.F., partner still Waltzing under raised arm, and take Waltz Hold at end	1, 2, 3	1
		12

Waltz Finale—

	COUNT	BARS
Waltz (Natural Turn), opening-out at finish to original Starting Position ready to repeat the whole sequence *ad lib*.	1, 2, 3 four times	4
		16

LADY

Pas de Valse Rearward (3 times)—

	COUNT	BARS
Step back with R.F.	1	
Step back with L.F.	2	
Close R.F. to 3rd position in front	3	1
Repeat Bar 1, but starting with L.F.	1, 2, 3	1
Repeat Bar 1	1, 2, 3	1
		3

Balancé Rearward—

Step back with L.F.	1	
Close R.F. to 3rd position in front	2, 3	1
		4

Pas de Valse Forward (3 times)—

Step forward with R.F. (against L.O.D.)	1	
Step forward with L.F.	2	
Close R.F. to 3rd position rear	3	1
		5

	COUNT	BARS
Repeat Bar 5, but starting with L.F.	1, 2, 3	1
Repeat Bar 5	1, 2, 3	1
		7

Change Position—

Step forward with L.F., turning to R.	1	
Close R.F. to L.F., now facing L.O.D., side-by-side with partner, and joining left hand to his right	2, 3	1
		8

Pas de Valse Forward (Twice)—

Step forward with R.F.	1	
Step forward with L.F.	2	
Close R.F. to 3rd position rear	3	1
		9
Repeat Bar 9, but starting with L.F.	1, 2, 3	1
		10

Allemande—

| Waltz two bars under partner's raised right arm, and finish by taking Waltz Hold | 1, 2, 3 twice | 2 |
| | | 12 |

Waltz Finale—

| Waltz (Natural Turn), opening-out at finish to original Starting Position ready to repeat the whole sequence *ad lib.* | 1, 2, 3 four times | 4 |
| | | 16 |

HESITATION WALTZ

THIS dance includes many steps of what might be called a Waltz Walk—steps which take up three beats of the music instead of the dancer taking one step to each beat as in the normal Waltz. These steps (as in Bars 1-4 and 9-12) should be long, the leg swinging well forward or backward from the hip, and each step occupying the full time allotted to it—3 beats.

Time: 3/4. *Tempo:* 46 bars per minute.
Starting position: Waltz hold. Gentleman facing wall.

GENTLEMAN

	COUNT	BARS
Backward and Forward Glide—		
Step back with L.F. (towards centre)	1, 2, 3	
Step back with R.F., drawing L.F. towards R.F., heel raised from floor	1, 2, 3	
Step forward with L.F. (towards wall)	1, 2, 3	
Step forward with R.F.	1, 2, 3	4
Chassé to Left—		
Still facing wall,		
Step to L. side with L.F.	1	
Close R.F. to L.F. on balls of feet	2	
Lower heels at end of bar	3	1
Step to L. side with L.F., turning slightly to L. and opening-out into P.P.	1, 2, 3	1
		6

	COUNT	BARS
The Promenade—		
In P.P., facing L.O.D.,		
Step forward with R.F.	1, 2, 3	1
Swivel to R. so as to face partner and close L.F. to R.F.	1, 2, 3	1
		8
Backward and Forward Glide—		
Step back with R.F. (towards centre)	1, 2, 3	
Step back with L.F., drawing R.F. towards L.F., heel raised from floor	1, 2, 3	
Step forward with R.F. (towards wall)	1, 2, 3	
Step forward with L.F.	1, 2, 3	4
		12
Chassé to Right—		
Still facing wall,		
Step to R. side with R.F.	1	
Close L.F. to R.F., on balls of feet	2	
Lower heels at end of bar	3	1
Step to R. side with R.F., turning slightly to R. and opening-out into Contra P.P.	1, 2, 3	1
		14
The Contra Promenade—		
In Contra P.P., back to L.O.D.,		
Step forward with L.F. (against L.O.D.)	1, 2, 3	1
Swivel to L. so as to face partner, and close R.F. to L.F.	1, 2, 3	1
		16

	COUNT	BARS

Waltz—

Dance one complete Natural Turn, opening-out at finish into P.P. ... 1, 2, 3 twice ... 2

— 18

The Promenade—

In P.P., facing L.O.D.,
Step forward with L.F. ... 1, 2, 3 ... 1
Step forward with R.F., turning to face partner ... 1, 2, 3 ... 1

— 20

Waltz—

Dance one complete Natural Turn, opening-out at finish into P.P. ... 1, 2, 3 twice ... 2

— 22

The Promenade—

In P.P., facing L.O.D.,
Step forward with L.F. ... 1, 2, 3 ... 1
Step forward with R.F., turning slightly to R. ... 1, 2, 3 ... 1

— 24

Backward and Forward Chassé—

Step back with L.F. (towards centre) ... 1
Close R.F. to L.F., on balls of feet ... 2
Lower heels ... 3 ... 1
Step back with L.F. ... 1, 2, 3 ... 1
Step forward with R.F. (towards wall) ... 1

HESITATION WALTZ

	COUNT	BARS
Close L.F. to R.F., on balls of feet	2	
Lower heels at end of bar	3	1
Step forward with R.F.	1, 2, 3	1
		28

Waltz Finale—

Waltz (Natural Turn) finishing in original Starting Position, ready to repeat the sequence *ad lib.*	1, 2, 3 four times	4
		32

LADY

Forward and Backward Glide—   COUNT   BARS

Step forward with R.F. (towards centre)	1, 2, 3	
Step forward with L.F., drawing R.F. towards L.F., heel raised from floor	1, 2, 3	
Step back with R.F. (towards wall)	1, 2, 3	
Step back with L.F.	1, 2, 3	4

Chassé to Right—

Now with back to wall,

Step to R. side with R.F.	1	
Close L.F. to R.F.	2	
Lower heels at end of bar	3	1
Step to R. side with R.F., turning slightly to R. and opening-out into P.P.	1, 2, 3	1
		6

SEQUENCE DANCING

	COUNT	BARS

The Promenade—
In P.P., facing L.O.D.,
Step forward with L.F. — 1, 2, 3 — 1
Swivel to L. so as to face partner and close R.F. to L.F. — 1, 2, 3 — 1
                                                                    —
                                                                    8

Forward and Backward Glide—
Step forward with L.F. (towards centre) — 1, 2, 3
Step forward with R.F., drawing L.F. towards R.F., heel raised from floor — 1, 2, 3
Step back with L.F. (towards wall) — 1, 2, 3
Step back with R.F. — 1, 2, 3 — 4
                                 —
                                 12

Chassé to Left—
Still with back to wall,
Step to L. side with L.F. — 1
Close R.F. to L.F., on balls of feet — 2
Lower heels at end of bar — 3 — 1
Step to L. side with L.F., turning slightly to L. and opening-out into Contra P.P. — 1, 2, 3 — 1
                                                                                             —
                                                                                             14

The Contra Promenade—
In Contra P.P., back to L.O.D.,
Step forward with R.F. (against L.O.D.) — 1, 2, 3 — 1
Swivel to R. so as to face partner, and close L.F. to R.F. — 1, 2, 3 — 1
                                                                      —
                                                                      16

HESITATION WALTZ

	COUNT	BARS
Waltz—		
Dance one complete Natural Turn, opening-out at finish into P.P.	1, 2, 3 twice	2
		18
The Promenade—		
In P.P., facing L.O.D.,		
Step forward with R.F.	1, 2, 3	1
Step forward with L.F., turning to face partner	1, 2, 3	1
		20
Waltz—		
Dance one complete Natural Turn, opening-out at finish into P.P.	1, 2, 3 twice	2
		22
The Promenade—		
In P.P., facing L.O.D.,		
Step forward with R.F.	1, 2, 3	1
Step forward with L.F., turning slightly to L. so as to face centre	1, 2, 3	1
		24
Forward and Backward Chassé—		
Step forward with R.F. (towards centre)	1	
Close L.F. to R.F., on balls of feet	2	
Lower heels	3	1
Step forward with R.F.	1, 2, 3	1

	COUNT	BARS
Step back with L.F. (towards wall)	1	
Close R.F. to L.F., on balls of feet	2	
Lower heels at end of bar	3	1
Step back with L.F.	1, 2, 3	1
		28

Waltz Finale—

Waltz (Natural Turn) finishing in original Starting Position ready to repeat the sequence *ad lib*.	1, 2, 3 four times	4
		32

THE EVENING WALTZ

IT is widely believed that this attractive dance was introduced during the second Great War, for the music, published by Ross, Grey & Co. (of *Visions of Vienna*, by J. W. Tattersall) is preceded by a description of the steps "copyright, 1944, by F. J. Mainey."

This was, however, really the re-introduction of the dance, for it had been danced long before then. I am unable to state precisely when it was arranged, but I have seen dance programmes which included it as far back as 1937— including one of a Coronation Ball organised by Mr. Mainey.

When Mr. Mainey found that his efforts to revive Old Time dancing during the war were meeting with success he arranged for publication of the Evening Waltz, and thus brought it before a wider public than hitherto.

It is hardly surprising that this dance has become well-established as a favourite sequence dance, not only in the International Sequence Dance Circle, but in Old Time ballrooms generally. It possesses the great virtue of simplicity. It is also invaluable as a means of improving reverse Waltzing. Many dancers are not nearly so comfortable in the Reverse as in the Natural Turn, and some competitions have been held with a view to improving the standard of reverse Waltzing. For this purpose the Evening Waltz is ideal, for it is built up entirely upon reverse figures, even the Waltz Finale being the Reverse Turn.

Time: 3/4. *Tempo:* 46 bars per minute.
Starting position: Waltz hold. Gentleman facing L.O.D.

GENTLEMAN

	COUNT	BARS
The Waltz Walk—		
Step forward with L.F.		
Step forward with R.F.		
Step forward with L.F.		
Step forward with R.F.	1, 2, 3 four times	4
The Waltz Walk Rearward—		
Step back with L.F. (against L.O.D.)		
Step back with R.F.		
Step back with L.F.		
Step back with R.F.	1, 2, 3 four times	4
		8
Reverse Waltz—		
Dance two complete Waltz Reverse Turns along L.O.D.	1, 2, 3 four times	4
Dance two complete Waltz Reverse Turns against L.O.D.	1, 2, 3 four times	4
		16
The Side Movement (Left)—		
Step to L. side with L.F.	1, 2, 3	1
Step with R.F. over and across L.F., and to L. side, turning body slightly to L.	1, 2, 3	1

THE EVENING WALTZ

	COUNT	BARS
Step to L. side with L.F.	1, 2, 3	1
Close R.F. to L.F., turning to face partner	1, 2, 3	1
		20

The Side Movement (Right)—

	COUNT	BARS
Step to R. side with R.F.	1, 2, 3	1
Step with L.F. over and across R.F., and to R. side, turning body slightly to R.	1, 2, 3	1
Step to R. side with R.F.	1, 2, 3	1
Close L.F. to R.F., turning slightly to L. (Now facing L.O.D.)	1, 2, 3	1
		24

Pas de Valse and Balancé—

	BARS
Pas de Valse Forward (along L.O.D.)	1
Balancé Forward (on R.F.)	1
Pas de Valse Rearward (against L.O.D.)	1
Balancé Rearward (on R.F.)	1
	28

Reverse Waltz Finale—

	BARS
Dance 4 bars of Waltz (Reverse Turn) along L.O.D., finishing in original Starting Position ready to repeat the whole sequence *ad lib.*	4
	32

LADY

The Waltz Walk—

	COUNT	BARS
Beginning with R.F., take 4 steps backward	1, 2, 3 four times	4
Beginning with R.F., take 4 steps forward	1, 2, 3 four times	4
		8

Reverse Waltz—

Dance 2 complete Waltz Reverse Turns along L.O.D.	1, 2, 3 four times	4
Dance 2 complete Waltz Reverse Turns against L.O.D.	1, 2, 3 four times	4
		16

The Side Movement (Right)—

Step to R. side with R.F.	1, 2, 3	1
Step with L.F. over and across R.F. and to R. side, turning body slightly to L.	1, 2, 3	1
Step to R. side with R.F.	1, 2, 3	1
Close L.F. to R.F., turning to face partner	1, 2, 3	1
		20

	COUNT	BARS
The Side Movement (Left)—		
Step to L. side with L.F.	1, 2, 3	1
Step with R.F. over and across L.F., and to L. side, turning body slightly to R.	1, 2, 3	1
Step to L. side with L.F.	1, 2, 3	1
Close R.F. to L.F., turning slightly to L. (Now with back to L.O.D.)	1, 2, 3	1
		24
Pas de Valse and Balancé—		
Pas de Valse Rearward (against L.O.D.)	1, 2, 3	1
Balancé Rearward (on L.F.)	1, 2, 3	1
Pas de Valse Forward (along L.O.D.)	1, 2, 3	1
Balancé Rearward (on L.F.)	1, 2, 3	1
		28
Reverse Waltz Finale—		
Dance 4 bars of Waltz (Reverse Turn), finishing in original Starting Position, ready to repeat the whole sequence *ad lib*.		4
		32

CHRYSANTHEMUM WALTZ

THIS dance has suffered much as the result of incorrect descriptions, and I have received many inquiries from dancers as to where they could obtain details of the correct steps. Not only has this dance usually been described in technical terms which have made it appear very difficult to many, but the Starting Position is often given as "Waltz Hold" which, of course, is misleading, as both partners face Line of Dance at the start.

Failure to mention that the partners take Waltz Hold *in P.P.* accounts for much of the confusion which has arisen.

The Chrysanthemum Waltz was arranged by James Telford and A. Bell.

Time: 3/4. *Tempo:* 46 bars per minute.

Starting position: Waltz hold, in P.P., Partners facing L.O.D.

GENTLEMAN

The Rondé, Pivot and Point—	COUNT	BARS
Step forward with L.F. in P.P.	1, 2, 3	1
Step forward with R.F. in P.P.	1, 2, 3	1
Move L.F. out to L. then forward with a semi-circular movement, drawing the foot back at end of step, knee raised, toe pointed down	1, 2, 3	1

CHRYSANTHEMUM WALTZ

	COUNT	BARS
Step forward with L.F., turning on it to R. so as to back L.O.D., and point R.F. against L.O.D.	1, 2 3	1 — 4
Beginning with R.F., repeat Bars 1–4 against L.O.D., finishing by pointing L.F. along L.O.D.		4 — 8

Glissade—

Turning to face partner,	1	
Step to L. side with L.F.		
Close R.F. to L.F.	2, 3	1

Pas Glissé—

Step to L. side with L.F.	1	
Close R.F. to L.F., keeping weight on L.F.	2, 3	1 — 10
Beginning with R.F., dance a Glissade and a Pas Glissé to R., relinquishing Waltz Hold at finish	1, 2, 3 twice	2 — 12

Change Hold—

Take partner's hands, her right in own left, her left in own right, and with arms extended. Still facing partner and wall.

SEQUENCE DANCING

The Salute—	COUNT	BARS
Step to L. side with L.F.	1, 2, 3	1
Cross R.F. behind L.F., relaxing both knees	1, 2, 3	1
Straightening knees, step to R. side with R.F. (against L.O.D.)	1, 2, 3	1
Cross L.F. behind R.F., relaxing both knees, and turning slightly to L., to face L.O.D.	1, 2, 3	1
		16

Pas de Valse and Balancé—		
Placing left hand on left hip,		
Pas de Valse Forward	1, 2, 3	1
Step forward with R.F.	1	
Close L.F. to R.F., keeping weight on R.F.	2, 3	1
		18
Repeat Bars 17 and 18 backwards, against L.O.D., beginning with L.F. back		2
		20

Glide and Solo Waltz—		
Step forward with L.F.	1, 2, 3	1
Step forward with R.F.	1, 2, 3	1
Solo Waltz Outward (Reverse Turn) (Now facing L.O.D.)	1, 2, 3 twice	2
		24

The Points—		
Take partner's left hand in own right (own left on left hip).		
Point L.F. forward, toe to floor, heel slightly raised	1, 2, 3	1

CHRYSANTHEMUM WALTZ

	COUNT	BARS
Point L.F. to L. side	1, 2, 3	1
Point L.F. back, relaxing right knee	1, 2, 3	1
Close L.F. behind R.F., keeping weight on R.F., and turning to R. to face partner	1, 2, 3	1

$$\overline{28}$$

Waltz Finale—

Taking Waltz Hold, Waltz (Natural Turn) opening-out at finish to original Starting Position, ready to repeat the sequence *ad lib.*   4

$$\overline{\overline{32}}$$

LADY

The Rondé, Pivot and Point—	COUNT	BARS
Step forward with R.F. in P.P.	1, 2, 3	1
Step forward with L.F. in P.P.	1, 2, 3	1
Move R.F. out to R. then forward with a semi-circular movement, drawing the foot back at end of step, knee raised, toe pointed down	1, 2, 3	1
Step forward with R.F., turning inwards so as to back L.O.D., and point L.F. against L.O.D.	1, 2 3	1

$$\overline{4}$$

Beginning with L.F., repeat Bars 1–4 against L.O.D., finishing by pointing R.F. along L.O.D.   4

$$\overline{8}$$

Glissade—

	COUNT	BARS
Turning to face partner,		
Step to R. side with R.F.	1	
Close L.F. to R.F.	2, 3	1

Pas Glissé—

Step to R. side with R.F.	1	
Close L.F. to R.F., keeping weight on R.F.	2, 3	1
		—
		10
Beginning with L.F., dance a Glissade and a Pas Glissé to L., relinquishing Waltz Hold at finish	1, 2, 3 twice	2
		—
		12

Change Hold—

Give right hand in partner's left, and left hand in his right, with arms extended. Still facing partner and centre.

The Salute—

Step to R. side with R.F.	1, 2, 3	1
Cross L.F. behind R.F., relaxing both knees	1, 2, 3	1
Straightening knees, step to L. side with L.F. (against L.O.D.)	1, 2, 3	1
Cross R.F. behind L.F., relaxing both knees and turning slightly to face L.O.D.	1, 2, 3	1
		—
		16

CHRYSANTHEMUM WALTZ

	COUNT	BARS
Pas de Valse and Balancé—		
Pas de Valse Forward, beginning with R.F.	1, 2, 3	1
Step forward with L.F.	1	
Close R.F. to L.F., keeping weight on L.F.	2, 3	1
		18
Repeat Bars 17 and 18 backwards, against L.O.D., beginning with R.F. back		2
		20
Glide and Solo Waltz—		
Step forward with R.F.	1, 2, 3	1
Step forward with L.F.	1, 2, 3	1
Solo Waltz Outward. Finish facing L.O.D.	1, 2, 3 twice	2
		24
The Points—		
Give right hand in partner's left, and Point R.F. forward, toe to floor, heel slightly raised	1, 2, 3	1
Point R.F. to R. side	1, 2, 3	1
Point R.F. back, relaxing left knee	1, 2, 3	1
Close R.F. to L.F., keeping weight on L.F., and turning to face partner	1, 2, 3	1
		28
Waltz Finale—		
Taking Waltz Hold, Waltz (Natural Turn) opening-out at finish to original Starting Position, ready to repeat the sequence *ad lib*.	1, 2, 3 four times	4
		32

THE GAVOTTE AS A SEQUENCE DANCE

ONE sometimes hears Old Time enthusiasts urging that our ballroom dances should be executed "just as they were in the old days." But which days? Most of the dances have changed from time to time, and many people would doubtless be shocked if they were to enter a present-day Old Time ballroom and see some of their favourite dances being executed in the manner which has found favour at some time or other in the past.

The Gavotte provides an example of this. The reader may have enjoyed the spectacle of a large company of dancers moving gracefully round a large ballroom in the popular Butterfly Gavotte. But if he had read some of the accounts which have been published of the way in which the Gavotte was danced in the seventeenth and eighteenth centuries, he might have wondered when the kissing was going to begin! For, truth to tell, the dancers used to stand in a row or circle, according to the space available, and one couple would dance into the centre, pause, then salute each other with a kiss.

But that was merely the beginning. The partners, having kissed each other, then proceeded to deal out similar treatment all round. The lady kissed all the gentlemen in turn; the gentleman kissed all the ladies in turn. Those, it seems, were the days!

Do not imagine that this was a freakish departure from the generally accepted procedure. The best professional guidance was available to those who wished to do things properly. Thus in one old book I note: "Arbeau tells the dancer not to lift his lady partner into the air, but only to kiss her while performing sundry small leapings."

In her book, *Dancing*, published in 1895, Mrs. L. Groves, F.R.G.S., includes the Gavotte among the dances of France. She states that it was originally a peasant's dance, deriving its name from Gap, the inhabitants of which are called Gavots. According to this writer, the Gavotte was introduced into Paris in 1600.

Various arrangements of the Gavotte were danced in Britain during the nineteenth century, towards the close of which Louis d'Egville, a well-known teacher, recommended two sequence dances based on the Gavotte—the Kaiserin Gavotte, described as "a capital arrangement, suitable in every way for either the drawing-room or stage performance," and the Gavotte de Vestris.

THE PRESENT-DAY GAVOTTE

In the present-day ballrooms, the Gavotte has become much more popular than formerly, almost invariably as a sequence dance. Such dances as the Gavotina and the Butterfly Gavotte have been featured in radio programmes, and the latter is now regularly danced at many Old Time clubs as well as at the large dance halls.

THE GAVOTTE STEP, or Pas de Gavotte, is easily learned so far as the actual foot-movements are concerned, but it is necessary to dance this figure in a free, light, spontaneous manner, without the slightest suggestion of stiffness, and without undue haste. This is largely a matter of practice and experience.

The Gavotte Step Forward can be begun with either foot. It consists of four steps as follows—

	COUNT
Step forward with one foot . . .	1
Close other foot to 3rd position rear .	2

	COUNT
Step forward with foot first moved .	3
Bring rear foot to 4th position in front, off the floor and with toe pointed down	4

When bringing the rear foot to the forward position aerial, i.e. raised off the floor, take care to pass it close to the other foot as it moves through to the forward position.

The Gavotte Step Backward can be begun with either foot. It consists of four steps as follows—

	COUNT
Step back with one foot . .	1
Close other foot to 3rd position front .	2
Step back with foot first moved . .	3
Bring forward foot close to, and in front of other foot, off the floor and with toe pointed down	4

The Gavotte is usually danced to 4/4 time. Where, however, it is danced in 2/4 time (as in the Gavotina) the steps described above are counted: 1, 2; 1, 2.

THE GAVOTTE SEQUENCE DANCES are all in the traditional style. *The feet must therefore be kept turned-out as in 1st Position throughout these dances.*

In the sequence Gavottes, when the Partners are facing each other, the Gentleman dances the Gavotte Step Forward, while the Lady dances the Gavotte Step Backward, and vice versa.

When the partners are side-by-side (in Open Position) both may dance the figure forward or backward at the same time.

The Pas de Basque, a figure much used in ballet and in theatrical dancing, finds a place in many of the Gavotte

THE GAVOTTE AS A SEQUENCE DANCE

sequence dances. This figure was described by Edward Scott, a leading authority of the nineteenth century, as "one of the most beautiful steps used in dancing, and frequently employed in Gavottes and other ornamental dances." All who aspire to competition success should thoroughly master this figure, which is described in detail in the description of the Butterfly Gavotte, in which dance the Pas de Basque occurs four times. Its use is not restricted to dances of the Gavotte group, and it is one of the most important basic figures of the Old Time style.

THE BUTTERFLY GAVOTTE

THIS dance has become very popular since, in March, 1950, it was included in the "Take Your Partners" radio programme. Little appears to be known of its history, but it is hardly surprising that present-day Old Time dancers have accepted this dance with enthusiasm, for it bears a close resemblance to the very popular Latchford Schottische.

Time: 4/4. *Tempo:* 28 bars per minute.

Starting position: Open.

GENTLEMAN

	COUNT	BARS
Pas de Basque Outward—		
Step to L. side with L.F., moving the foot forward and to L. with a semi-circular movement	1	
Close R.F., with semi-circular movement, in front of L.F., with heel raised.	and	
With weight on R.F., hop on L.F., and at the same time raise right knee, toe pointing to floor	2	
Pas de Basque Inward—		
Step to R. side with R.F., moving the foot forward and to R. with a semi-circular movement	3	

THE BUTTERFLY GAVOTTE

	COUNT	BARS
Close L.F., with semi-circular movement, in front of R.F., with heel raised.	and	
With weight on L.F., hop on R.F., and at the same time raise left knee, toe pointing to floor	4	1

Gavotte Step Forward—

Step forward with L.F.	1	
Close R.F. to L.F. (3rd position rear)	2	
Step forward with L.F.	3	
Bring R.F. from rear to 4th position in front, off the floor, toe pointed down	4	1

Pas de Basque Inward—

Beginning with R.F., dance the second half of Bar 1 again   1 and 2

Pas de Basque Outward—

Beginning with L.F., dance the first half of Bar 1 again   3 and 4   1

Gavotte Step Forward—

Beginning with R.F., repeat steps of Bar 2, i.e. Forward R.F., close L.F. to R.F., Forward R.F., Forward L.F. to 4th position in front   1 and 2
3 and 4   1

Solo Waltz Outward—

Dance one complete Reverse Turn, Solo Waltz, finishing facing partner.   1 and 2
3 and 4   1

The Salute— | COUNT | BARS

	COUNT	BARS
Glide L.F. to L. side.	1	
Close R.F. to L.F., 3rd position in front, and make a slight bow	2	
Glide R.F. slightly forward	3	
Close L.F. to R.F., 3rd position rear, keeping weight on R.F., and taking Waltz Hold	4	1

Waltz Finale—

	COUNT	BARS
Dance 2 bars of Waltz (Natural Turn), opening-out at finish to original Starting Position, ready to repeat the sequence *ad lib.*	1 and 2 3 and 4 twice	2
		—
		8

LADY

Pas de Basque Outward— | COUNT | BARS

	COUNT	BARS
Step to R. side with R.F., moving the foot forward and to R. with a semi-circular movement	1	
Close L.F., with semi-circular movement, in front of R.F., with heel raised	and	
With weight on L.F., hop on R.F., and at the same time raise left knee, toe pointing to floor	2	

Pas de Basque Inward—

Step to L. side with L.F., moving the foot forward and to L. with a semi-circular movement   3

THE BUTTERFLY GAVOTTE

	COUNT	BARS
Close R.F., with semi-circular movement, in front of L.F., with heel raised	and	
With weight on R.F., hop on L.F., and at the same time raise right knee, toe pointing to floor	4	1

Gavotte Step Forward—

Step forward with R.F.	1	
Close L.F. to R.F. (3rd position rear)	2	
Step forward with R.F.	3	
Bring L.F. from rear to 4th position in front, off the floor, toe pointed down	4	1

Pas de Basque Inward—

Beginning with L.F., dance the second half of Bar 1 again	1 and 2	

Pas de Basque Outward—

Beginning with R.F., dance the first half of Bar 1 again	3 and 4	1

Gavotte Step Forward—

Beginning with L.F., repeat steps of Bar 2, i.e. Forward L.F., close R.F. to L.F., Forward L.F., Forward R.F. to 4th position in front	1 and 2 3 and 4	1

Solo Waltz Outward—

Dance one complete Natural Turn, Solo Waltz, finishing facing partner	1 and 2 3 and 4	1

The Salute—   COUNT   BARS

	COUNT	BARS
Step to R. side with R.F.	1	
Step behind and to R. side of R.F. with L.F. and curtsey. (Keep weight on R.F.)	2	
Step diagonally forward with L.F.	3	
Close R.F. to 3rd position in front, keeping weight on L.F., and take Waltz Hold	4	1

Waltz Finale—

	COUNT	BARS
Dance 2 bars of Waltz (Natural Turn), opening-out at finish to original Starting Position, ready to repeat the sequence *ad lib.*	1 and 2 3 and 4 twice	2
		8

How to Improve Your Dance

THE PAS DE BASQUE figure which occurs in Bars 1 and 3 requires perfect timing. Often there is a tendency for dancers to execute the steps in a jerky, hurried manner. The ability to fit the steps perfectly to the music, without the slightest suggestion of haste, comes with practice. When danced lightly, yet with complete control, and in perfect time with the music, this is a particularly satisfying figure to dance and one which provides a pleasing spectacle.

THE SALUTE: The Gentleman's Bow and Lady's Curtsey, in Bar 6, require special care. The detailed description which I give above of the foot-movements should enable the reader, with practice, to achieve correct execution and timing, thus greatly enhancing the appearance of this figure. The Salute is an essential part of the dance, and it is necessary to treat it seriously. Incidentally, this Salute, both for Gentleman and Lady, is similar to that in the Championship dance, the Latchford Schottische, and it should be mastered by all who wish to dance the Old Time style well.

When the Lady curtseys, she should keep the hips well forward and the knees out. Her weight should be on her forward foot while she circles her other foot to the rear (and across to right behind L.F.) on the count of 2; this ensures freedom of movement for the rear foot, so that on the count of 3 it can be moved easily and smoothly as she rises from her curtsey.

The Gentleman makes only a slight bow. He should take care not to prolong it unduly, for if he does, the timing is spoiled and he has to make a hurried movement in order to catch up. He should resume an erect position on the count of 3.

Finally, here is a further reminder that although I describe this dance and others in short combinations of steps, this is for the purpose of simplicity. When dancing, you should pass from one figure to another without any pause between them.

THE GAVOTINA

THIS charming dance has aroused interest since its inclusion in some of Mr. Sydney Thompson's "Take Your Partners" broadcasts, and although it appeals primarily to the keenest Old Time dancers rather than to the masses, it is included here because it has distinct possibilities for use (either in full or in part) in formation dancing.

It is a somewhat novel dance in that it is really two dances combined—the first a sequence dance based on the Gavotte, and the second the Old Time Waltz (Natural Turn). The latter is danced in Waltz time; consequently this dance starts in 2/4 time, but ends in 3/4 time.

This Gavotte-Waltz combination was arranged by Charles d'Albert, and it is danced to *The Gavotina*, by G. Proust.

The dance is preceded by an introduction of 8 bars of music. During this, the Gentleman bows to his partner, and the Lady curtseys.

Time: 2/4 for the first 16 bars.
3/4 for the last 16 bars.

Tempo: 24 bars per minute for the first 16 bars.
48 bars per minute for the last 16 bars.

Starting position: Open.

GENTLEMAN

	COUNT	BARS
Gavotte Step Forward—		
Step forward with L.F.	1	
Close R.F. to L.F. (3rd position rear)	2	

	COUNT	BARS
Step forward with L.F.	1	
Bring R.F. forward, raised from floor, and with toe pointed down. At the same time, pivot to R. on L.F. to face partner	2	2

Gavotte Step Diagonally Forward—

	COUNT	BARS
Step diagonally forward with R.F.	1	
Close L.F. to R.F. (3rd position rear)	2	
Step diagonally forward with R.F.	1	
Bring L.F. forward, raised from floor, toe pointed down. At the same time, pivot to L. on R.F. to face L.O.D. Release partner's left hand, and take her right hand in own right hand	2	2
		4

Gavotte Step Diagonally Backward—

	COUNT	BARS
Step diagonally back with L.F.	1	
Close R.F. to L.F. (3rd position front)	2	
Step diagonally back with L.F.	1	
Bring R.F. close to L.F., raised from floor, toe pointed down. At the same time, pivot slightly to L. on L.F., preparing to walk round partner	2	2
		6

The Walk—

	COUNT	BARS
Walk round partner (R, L, R, L) turning to face her on last step	1, 2 1, 2	2
		8

SEQUENCE DANCING

Balancé Forward—   COUNT   BARS

Step forward with R.F.   1

Close L.F. to R.F. (3rd position rear), keeping weight on R.F.   2   1

Balancé Backward—

Step back with L.F.   1

Close R.F. to L.F. (3rd position front) and pivoting to L. to face L.O.D.   2   1

Release partner's hand

    10

The Glide to Right—

    In this figure, the Gentleman moves to his right and passes behind his partner.

With left hand on left hip,

Glide to R. side with R.F.   1

Step over R.F. and across to R. with L.F.   2

Glide to R. side with R.F.   1

Point L.F. forward   2   2

    12

The Glide to Left—

    In this figure the Gentleman moves to his left, and passes behind his partner.

Glide to L. side with L.F.   1

Step over L.F. and across to L. with R.F.   2

Glide to L. side with L.F.   1

Point R.F. forward, and pivot to face partner   2   2

    14

THE GAVOTINA

The Salute—   COUNT   BARS

Bow to partner   2

     ―

     16

(*Here the music changes to 3/4 time.*)

Waltz Figure—

Taking Waltz Hold, dance 16 bars of Waltz (Natural Turn) opening-out at finish to original starting position, ready to repeat the sequence *ad lib.*   1, 2, 3   16 times   16

     ―

     32

LADY

Gavotte Step Forward—   COUNT   BARS

	COUNT	BARS
Step forward with R.F.	1	
Close L.F. to R.F. (3rd position rear)	2	
Step forward with R.F.	1	
Bring L.F. forward, raised from floor, and with toe pointed down. At the same time, pivot to L. on R.F. to face partner	2	1
		―
		2

Gavotte Step Diagonally Back—

Step diagonally back with L.F.	1	
Close R.F. to L.F. (3rd position front)	2	

	COUNT	BARS

Step diagonally back with L.F. — 1

Bring R.F. forward, raised from floor, and with toe pointed down. At the same time pivot to R. on L.F. to face L.O.D. — 2 — 2

$$\frac{}{4}$$

Release hold with left hand and give right hand to partner.

Gavotte Step Diagonally Forward—

Step diagonally forward with R.F. — 1

Close L.F. to R.F. (3rd position rear) — 2

Step diagonally forward with R.F. — 1

Bring L.F. forward, raised from floor, and with toe pointed down. At the same time, pivot to L. on R.F. preparing to walk round partner — 2 — 2

$$\frac{}{6}$$

The Walk—

Walk round partner (L, R, L, R) turning to face him on last step — 1, 2 / 1, 2 — 2

$$\frac{}{8}$$

Balancé Forward—

Step forward with L.F. — 1

Close R.F. to L.F. (3rd position rear) keeping weight on L.F. — 2 — 1

THE GAVOTINA

Balancé Backward—   COUNT   BARS

Step back with R.F.   1

Close L.F. to R.F. (3rd position front) and pivoting to R. to face L.O.D. Release hand   2   1

                                                                                             10

The Glide to Left—

In this figure, the Lady moves to her left and passes in front of her partner.

Glide to L. side with L.F.   1

Step over L.F. and across to L. side with R.F.   2

Glide to L. side with L.F.   1

Point R.F. forward   2   2

                                                                                           12

The Glide to Right—

In this figure the Lady moves to her right, and passes in front of her partner.

Glide to R. side with R.F.   1

Step over R.F. and across to R. side with L.F.   2

Glide to R. side with R.F.   1

Point L.F. forward, and pivot to face partner   2   2

                                                                                           14

The Salute—

Curtsey to partner   2   2

                                                                                           16

(*Here the music changes to 3/4 time.*)

Waltz Figure—   COUNT   BARS

Taking Waltz Hold, dance 16 bars of Waltz (Natural Turn), opening-out at finish to original Starting Position ready to repeat the sequence *ad lib.*   1, 2, 3
16 times   16

                                                              32

THE INTERNATIONAL WALTZ

WELL-KNOWN as the theme song and dance of the International Sequence Dance Circle, The International Waltz was arranged by F. J. Mainey, the Founder and Director of that largest of all Old Time and Sequence organisations. He fitted steps to the music of J. W. Tattersall. The Mainey-Tattersall co-operation has proved exceedingly happy in its results, for it has given to dancers a number of excellent sequence dances which are ideal interpretations of the lilting music to which they are executed.

Time: 3/4. *Tempo:* 46 bars per minute.

Starting position: Open.

GENTLEMAN

	COUNT	BARS
Pas de Valse (L.F., R.F., L.F.)	1, 2, 3	1
Balancé Forward (on R.F.)	1, 2, 3	1
Pas de Valse Rearward (L.F., R.F., L.F.)	1, 2, 3	1
Balancé Rearward (on R.F.) and turn to face partner at end	1, 2, 3	1
		4

The Swing Steps—

Joining both hands, partner's left in own right, her right in own left, and facing wall, Step to L. side with L.F. (along L.O.D.)	1

	COUNT	BARS
Swing R.F. over L.F. and to L. side, foot raised from floor, toe pointed down	2, 3	1
Step to R. side with R.F. (against L.O.D.)	1	
Swing L.F. over R.F. and to R. side, foot raised from floor, toe pointed down	2, 3	1
		—
		6
Glissade along L.O.D., i.e.,		
Step to L. side with L.F.	1	
Close R.F. to L.F.	2, 3	1
Pas Glissé along L.O.D., i.e., similar to previous bar, but when closing feet keep weight on L.F.	1	
	2, 3	1
		—
		8
Turning to R., now dance the whole sequence above, Bars 1 to 8, against L.O.D., beginning Pas de Valse with R.F.		8
		—
		16
Still with both hands joined,		
Balancé towards partner (on R.F.), own right shoulder to her right shoulder	1, 2, 3	1
Balancé Rearward (on L.F.)	1, 2, 3	1
Turning slightly to R.,		
Balancé Forward (on R.F.), own left shoulder to partner's left shoulder	1, 2, 3	1
Balancé Rearward (on L.F.)	1, 2, 3	1
		—
		20

THE INTERNATIONAL WALTZ

	COUNT	BARS
Step forward with R.F. (Allemande)	1, 2, 3	1
Step forward with L.F.	1, 2, 3	1
Partner Waltzing under own raised right arm.	—	
		22
Without moving feet, sway gently forward	1, 2, 3	1
Without moving feet, sway gently backward	1, 2, 3	1
		24
Waltz (Natural Turn) opening-out at finish to original Starting Position ready to repeat the sequence *ad lib*.		8
		32

LADY

	COUNT	BARS
Pas de Valse (R.F., L.F., R.F.)	1, 2, 3	1
Balancé Forward (on L.F.)	1, 2, 3	1
Pas de Valse Rearward	1, 2, 3	1
Balancé Rearward (on L.F.) and turn to face partner at end	1, 2, 3	1
		4
Joining both hands,		
Step to R. side with R.F.	1	
Swing L.F. over R.F., and to R. side, foot raised from floor, toe pointed down	2, 3	1
Step to L. side with L.F.	1	
Swing R.F. over L.F., and to L. side, foot raised from floor, toe pointed down	2, 3	1
		6

	COUNT	BARS
Step to R. side with R.F.	1	
Close L.F. to R.F.	2, 3	1
Step to R. side with R.F.	1	
Close L.F. to R.F., keeping weight on R.F.	2, 3	1
		8
Turning to L., dance the whole sequence above, Bars 1 to 8, against L.O.D., beginning Pas de Valse with L.F.		8
		16
Balancé towards partner (on R.F.), own right shoulder to his right shoulder	1, 2, 3	1
Balancé Rearward (on L.F.)	1, 2, 3	1
Turning slightly to R.,		
Balancé Forward (on R.F.), own left shoulder to partner's left shoulder	1, 2, 3	1
Balancé Rearward (on L.F.)	1, 2, 3	1
		20
Allemande: Waltz under partner's raised right arm, and finishing in normal Waltz position	1, 2, 3 twice	2
		22
Without moving feet, sway gently backward (along L.O.D.)	1, 2, 3	1
Without moving feet, sway gently forward	1, 2, 3	1
		24

	COUNT	BARS
Waltz (Natural Turn) opening-out at finish to original Starting Position ready to repeat the sequence *ad lib*.		8
		32

THE MARINE FOUR-STEP

THIS lively dance was arranged by James Finnigan, who was particularly adept at devising dances based on the military march, his "classic" being the Military Two-step, one of the Championship dances.

The Marine Four-step is danced to rousing military marches, and the reader who has studied this book so far will be able to learn the dance easily, for it is entirely built up on figures already described.

This dance is often executed in a frolicsome, rather rompish manner which, while it provides good fun, is not in keeping with the real idea behind the dance. As its name suggests, it should be danced with that soldierlike precision which we all associate with the Royal Marines.

Year after year, at the Royal Tournament at Olympia, the King's Squad of the Royal Marines gives a display of simple drill movements which are in no way remarkable in themselves. Yet they always win rounds of applause. Why? Because of the fine precision with which they are performed. And the secret of this precision lies in *perfect timing*, resulting from much practice.

The same applies to the Marine Four-step. Simple though it is to learn and to dance, only plenty of practice produces the perfect balance and timing which enables the dancer to display the characteristics of the dance. Not only should the marching steps and hops, whether forward or backward, be danced with military precision, but the Pas de Basque and all the other figures should convey the impression of military smartness.

It pays to practice simple dances assiduously. They then

become more enjoyable to dance and much more pleasing to the onlooker. It is, indeed, these simple dances, well executed, which raise Old Time dancing at its best to the high level of a national art.

Time: 6/8. *Tempo:* 56 bars per minute.

Starting position: Open.

GENTLEMAN

	COUNT	BARS
March and Hop Forward—		
Step forward with L.F.	1	
Step forward with R.F.	2	
Step forward with L.F.	1	
Hop on L.F., point R.F. forward, off floor, toe pointed down	2	2
March and Hop Backward—		
Step back with R.F. (against L.O.D.)	1	
Step back with L.F.	2	
Step back with R.F.	1	
Hop on R.F., point L.F. forward, off floor, toe pointed down	2	2
		4
Pas de Basque Outward	1 and 2	
Pas de Basque Inward	1 and 2	2
		6
Solo Waltz Outward	1 and 2 twice	2
		8

Side Step to Left—

Join both hands, partner's left in own right, her right in own left. (Now facing wall.)

	COUNT	BARS
Step to L. side with L.F. (along L.O.D.)	1	
Step over L.F., and to L. side, with R.F.	2	
Step to L. side with L.F.	1	
Draw R.F. close to L.F. while swivelling to R. slightly	2	2
		10

Side Step to Right—

	COUNT	BARS
Step to R. side with R.F. (against L.O.D.)	1	
Step over R.F., and to R. side, with L.F.	2	
Step to R. side with R.F.	1	
Draw L.F. close to R.F. while swivelling to L. slightly	2	2
		12

Waltz Finale—

	COUNT	BARS
Taking Waltz Hold, Waltz (Natural Turn), opening-out at finish to original Starting Position, ready to repeat the sequence *ad lib.*	1 and 2 four times	4
		16

LADY

March and Hop Forward—

	COUNT	BARS
Step forward with R.F.	1	
Step forward with L.F.	2	
Step forward with R.F.	1	

	COUNT	BARS
Hop on R.F., point L.F. forward, off floor, toe pointed down	2	2

March and Hop Backward—

	COUNT	BARS
Step back with L.F. (against L.O.D.)	1	
Step back with R.F.	2	
Step back with L.F.	1	
Hop on L.F., point R.F. forward, off floor, toe pointed down	2	2
		4
Pas de Basque Outward	1 and 2	
Pas de Basque Inward	1 and 2	2
		6
Solo Waltz Outward, finishing facing centre	1 and 2 twice	2
		8

Side Step to Right—

Join both hands (left in partner's right; right in partner's left).

	COUNT	BARS
Step to R. side with R.F. (along L.O.D.)	1	
Step over R.F., and to R. side, with L.F.	2	
Step to R. side with R.F.	1	
Draw L.F. close to R.F., while swivelling slightly to L.	2	2
		10

Side Step to Left—

	COUNT	BARS
Step to L. side with L.F. (against L.O.D.)	1	
Step over L.F., and to L. side, with R.F.	2	
Step to L. side with L.F.	1	
Draw R.F. close to L.F., while swivelling slightly to R.	2	2
		12

Waltz Finale—

Taking Waltz Hold, Waltz (Natural Turn), opening-out at finish to original Starting Position, ready to repeat the sequence *ad lib.*   1 and 2 four times   4

16

DORIS WALTZ

WHEN this dance first appeared, in 1908, it was described as "a novelty dance." It has long ceased to be anything of the kind, for it is firmly founded upon the well-recognised principles of the traditional style, and has remained steadily popular in Old Time ballrooms. Like so many dances worthy of such treatment, it has been featured in radio programmes, with the result that it is now danced by far more people than ever in its history.

This dance was arranged by J. H. Bickerstaffe, who dedicated it "to my little daughter, Doris"—hence its name.

Throughout this dance, with the exception of Bar 8, and of course during the brief spell of Waltzing which concludes the sequence, the steps of both partners are precisely the same. I therefore depart from my usual practice of describing Gentleman's and Lady's steps separately, since this would involve unnecessary repetition.

Time: 3/4. *Tempo:* 48 bars per minute.

Starting position: Gentleman stands slightly behind Lady, his right shoulder behind her left shoulder. Hands are joined left-to-left and right-to-right, and are held at shoulder level.

STEPS FOR BOTH PARTNERS

	COUNT	BARS
Step diagonally forward with L.F.		
Close R.F. to 3rd position rear	1, 2, 3	1
Step diagonally back with R.F.		
Close L.F. to 3rd position front	1, 2, 3	1

	COUNT	BARS
Chassé diagonally forward:		
Step diagonally forward with L.F.	1, 2	
Close R.F. to L.F.	3	1
Step forward with L.F., swivelling to face opposite direction	1, 2, 3	1
		—
		4
Now facing diagonally to wall against L.O.D., Step diagonally forward with R.F.		
Close L.F. to R.F. (weight on R.F.)	1, 2, 3	1
Step diagonally back with L.F.		
Close R.F. to L.F. (weight on L.F.)	1, 2, 3	1
Step diagonally forward with R.F.		
Close L.F. to R.F.	1, 2, 3	1
		—
		7

Gentleman:

    Diag. forward with R.F.
    Close L.F. to R.F.

Lady:

	COUNT	BARS
Dance 1st half of Reverse Turn under Gentleman's raised right hand, finishing facing partner	1, 2, 3	1
		—
		8
Glide away from partner (L.F.), right hands joined		
Close R.F. to L.F. (weight on L.F.)	1, 2, 3	1
Step forward with R.F.		
Close L.F. to R.F. (weight on R.F.)	1, 2, 3	1

DORIS WALTZ

	COUNT	BARS
Step back with L.F.		
Close R.F. to L.F. (weight on L.F.)	1, 2, 3	1
Step forward with R.F.		
Close L.F. to R.F. (weight on R.F.)	1, 2, 3	1
		——
		12
Take Waltz Hold and Waltz (Natural Turn), opening-out at finish to original Starting Position ready to repeat the sequence *ad lib*.	1, 2, 3 four times	4
		——
		16

THE EVA THREE-STEP

THIS very attractive dance is usually omitted from books on Old Time dancing, possibly because it is extremely difficult to describe.

It was arranged by Sidney W. Painter, and it has remained steadily popular in the ballrooms, and has of late also been used with marked success in formation sequences.

The Eva Three-step introduces the Bower Position, a pleasing form of Allemande, and the dance is largely made up of Three-steps followed by a point. It is these Three-steps which are so difficult to describe, for the movements of the dancers' bodies and hands are important—not merely the foot-movements.

Below, I give a description which will enable those who have seen the Eva Three-step danced to recall the various figures and also to note the order in which they are danced.

It is not a difficult dance, but a fair amount of practice is usually necessary before the partners achieve the correct alignments during the first four bars, and maintain just the right distances from each other to ensure that the Three-steps are danced in the most effective manner.

Time: 4/4. *Tempo:* 32 bars per minute.

Starting position: Open.

GENTLEMAN

	COUNT	BARS
Three-step and Point—		
Step forward with L.F.	1	
Step forward with R.F.	2	

THE EVA THREE-STEP

	COUNT	BARS
Step forward with L.F.	3	
Turning slightly to R., point R.F. towards wall	4	1

Three-step Passing Partner—

Now facing wall,

Step diagonally forward with R.F., preparing to pass partner on her L. side, and taking her left hand in own left	1	
Step forward with L.F., passing partner	2	
Step forward with R.F., turning to L. Withdraw left hand and place it on hip	3	
Point L.F. forward. (Now facing diagonally to centre.)	4	1
		—
		2

Three-step Diagonally Forward—

With hand on hip (no hold throughout this bar):

Step diagonally forward with L.F.	1	
Step forward with R.F., and look towards partner	2	
Step forward with L.F., still looking towards partner, and turn slightly to R.	3	
Point R.F. forward (towards wall)	4	1
		—
		3

Three-Step Return to Place—

Turning slightly to L., so as to face L.O.D., Step back with R.F.	1	

	COUNT	BARS
Step back with L.F.	2	
Step back with R.F.	3	
Turning slightly to R.,		
Point L.F. towards wall, and take partner's left hand in own right	4	1 — 4

(Both partners should now be back, approximately, at the point from which they began the dance.)

Solo Waltz Outward—

Dance Solo Waltz, making one complete turn to L. Finish facing partner. Join both hands, raise arms shoulder high	1 and 2 3 and 4	1 — 5

The Swing Steps—

Step to L. side with L.F.	1	
Swing R.F. in front of L.F., and to L., foot raised from floor, toe pointed down	2	
Step to R. side with R.F.	3	
Swing L.F. in front of R.F. and to R., foot raised from floor and toe pointing down	4	1 — 6

THE EVA THREE-STEP

	COUNT	BARS
Waltz Finale—		
Taking Waltz Hold, dance two complete Waltz Natural Turns, opening-out at finish to original Starting Position ready to repeat the sequence *ad lib.*	1 and 2 3 and 4 twice	2
		8

LADY

	COUNT	BARS
Three-step and Point—		
Step forward with R.F.	1	
Step forward with L.F.	2	
Step forward with R.F.	3	
Turning slightly to L.,		
Point L.F. towards centre	4	1
Three-step Passing Partner—		
Now facing centre,		
Step diagonally forward with L.F.	1	
Step forward with R.F.	2	
Step forward with L.F., turning to L.	3	
Point R.F. forward	4	1
		2
Three-step Diagonally Back—		
Step diagonally back with R.F.	1	
Step back with L.F., and look towards partner	2	

	COUNT	BARS
Step back with R.F., still looking towards partner, and turn slightly to L.	3	
Point L.F. forward (towards centre)	4	1 / 3

Three-step Return to Place—

Turning slightly to R., so as to face L.O.D.,		
Step forward with L.F.	1	
Step forward with R.F.	2	
Step forward with L.F.	3	
Turning slightly to L.,		
Point R.F. towards centre and give left hand in partner's right	4	1 / 4

(Both partners should now be back, approximately, at the point from which they began the dance.)

Solo Waltz Outward—

Dance Solo Waltz, making one complete turn to R. Finish facing partner. Join both hands, raise arms shoulder high	1 and 2 3 and 4	1 / 5

The Swing Steps—

Step to R. side with R.F.	1
Swing L.F. in front of R.F., and to R., foot raised from floor, toe pointed down	2
Step to L. side with L.F.	3

	COUNT	BARS
Swing R.F. in front of L.F., and to L., foot raised from floor, toe pointed down	4	1
		—
		6

Waltz Finale—

Taking Waltz Hold, dance two complete Natural Turns, opening-out at finish to original Starting Position ready to repeat the sequence *ad lib.*	1 and 2 3 and 4 twice	2
		—
		8

THE BOWER POSITION

What is known as Bower Position occurs in Bar 2 when the partners pass each other. When the Gentleman gives his left hand to the Lady, as he steps forward with R.F. on the second beat, he turns his body towards her, and he still looks towards her as he steps forward with L.F. on the third beat. Provided that these movements are correctly made, it is natural and easy for the joined hands to be raised, thus producing the Bower Position, with the Lady passing under the Gentleman's left arm on the second step of Bar 2.

FLORENTINE WALTZ

THIS dance has been seen in our ballrooms for many years, but for some reason or other has never become generally popular. During the last year or two, however, there have been signs of a quickening of interest in it, and it has figured in the proceedings of some of the teachers' technical courses.

Nobody seems to know who arranged it. When, during 1950, it formed part of a refresher course given to teachers of the Victorian and Sequence Branch of the Imperial Society of Teachers of Dancing, the lecturer made no mention of the original arranger. I note, too, that although this dance is included in Mr. A. J. Latimer's *Bouquet of Old Time Dances*, he does not name the originator, as he does whenever the original arranger is known. Its source therefore remains a mystery.

The impression, widely held, that this is a somewhat difficult dance probably arises from the fact that it is often described in technical terms. If learned a figure at a time, as described below, it is easy to learn.

Time: 3/4. *Tempo:* 46 bars per minute.

Starting position: Waltz hold, in P.P.

GENTLEMAN

The Walk-Turn-Point Figure—	COUNT	BARS
Step forward with L.F. in P.P.	1, 2, 3	1
Step forward with R.F. in P.P.	1, 2, 3	1

FLORENTINE WALTZ

	COUNT	BARS
Step forward with L.F., turning to R. (Backing L.O.D.)	1, 2, 3	1
Point R.F. forward, toe to floor, heel slightly raised	1, 2, 3	1
		—
		4

Now in Contra P.P.,

Beginning with R.F. forward, dance the *Walk-Turn-Point* figure against L.O.D., finishing facing L.O.D., with L.F. pointed forward — 4

—
8

Solo Waltz Outward—

Dance one complete Waltz Turn, finishing facing partner, and joining hands — 1, 2, 3 twice — 2

—
10

The Swing Steps—

Step to L. side with L.F. (along L.O.D.)	1	
Swing R.F. over and across L.F., and to L.	2, 3	1
Step to R. side with R.F.	1	
Swing L.F. over and across R.F., and to R.	2, 3	1

—
12

Repeat Bars 8–12 — 4

—
16

	COUNT	BARS
The Change of Places—		
Taking partner's right hand in own right, Step forward with L.F., turning to R., right arm raised	1, 2, 3	1
Step forward with R.F., still turning	1, 2, 3	1
Step forward with L.F., still turning, slightly (now in partner's former position)	1, 2, 3	1
Close R.F. in front (3rd position) and bow slightly (Keep weight on R.F.)	1, 2, 3	1
		20
The Return to Place—		
Repeat the last 4 bars, stepping L.F., R.F., L.F., returning to original position, then closing R.F. to 3rd position in front, and bowing slightly. (Keep weight on L.F.)	1, 2, 3 four times	4
		24
Scissors Steps—		
Cross R.F. over L.F.	1, 2, 3	1
Cross L.F. over R.F.	1, 2, 3	1
Cross R.F. over L.F.	1, 2, 3	1
Point L.F. along L.O.D.	1, 2, 3	1
		28
Waltz Finale—		
Waltz (Natural Turn), opening-out at finish into original Starting Position ready to repeat the sequence *ad lib*.	1, 2, 3 four times	4
		32

FLORENTINE WALTZ

LADY

	COUNT	BARS
The Walk-Turn-Point Figure—		
Step forward with R.F. in P.P.	1, 2, 3	1
Step forward with L.F. in P.P.	1, 2, 3	1
Step forward with R.F., turning inward to back L.O.D.	1, 2, 3	1
Point L.F. forward, toe to floor, heel slightly raised	1, 2, 3	1
		4
Now in Contra P.P.,		
Beginning with L.F. forward (against L.O.D.) dance the Walk-Turn-Point Figure against L.O.D., finishing facing L.O.D., with R.F. pointed forward		4
		8
Solo Waltz Outward—		
Dance one complete Waltz Turn, finishing facing partner. Join hands	1, 2, 3 twice	2
		10
The Swing Steps—		
Step to R. side with R.F. (along L.O.D.)	1	
Swing L.F. over and across R.F. and to R.	2, 3	1
Step to L. side with L.F.	1	
Swing R.F. over and across L.F., and to L.	2, 3	1
		12

	COUNT	BARS
Repeat Bars 8–12		4
		—
		16

The Change of Places—

Give right hand in partner's right, and Step forward with R.F.	1, 2, 3	1
Step forward with L.F., turning to L.	1, 2, 3	1
Step to R. side with R.F., still turning (now in partner's former position)	1, 2, 3	1
Cross L.F. behind and to R. of R.F., and curtsey. Keep weight on L.F.	1, 2, 3	1
		—
		20

The Return to Place—

Repeat the last four bars, stepping R.F., L.F., R.F., returning to original position, then crossing L.F. behind R.F. as before, and curtsey. Keep weight on R.F.	1, 2, 3 four times	4
		—
		24

Scissors Steps—

Cross L.F. over R.F.	1, 2, 3	1
Cross R.F. over L.F.	1, 2, 3	1
Cross L.F. over R.F.	1, 2, 3	1
Point R.F. along L.O.D.	1, 2, 3	1
		—
		28

Waltz Finale— COUNT BARS

Waltz (Natural Turn), opening-out at finish into original Starting Position ready to repeat the sequence *ad lib.*   1, 2, 3 four times   4

$$\overline{32}$$

THE TANGO AS A SEQUENCE DANCE

THE Tango *as a sequence dance* finds no place in the Modern style, but in the Old Time ballroom various sequence dances are executed to Tango music—the Royal Empress Tango, Lola Tango, Square Tango, and also those which I describe later in this book. These sequence dances are generally based on the Tango as it was originally danced in Britain, but adapted in various ways so as to meet the requirements of the Old Time ballroom.

Those who have witnessed demonstrations of the Modern-style Tango, or who have learned the dance in that style, must remember that the *sequence* Tango is based on a totally different technique from that which underlies the Modern-style Tango. It is much easier to learn, and although it assumes various forms in the different Tango sequence dances, they are all based on the same fundamental principles, so that when you have learned one of them, you have learned much which will assist you when you attempt others.

THE TANGO HOLD is similar to that for the Waltz. The lady is held in front of the gentleman—not slightly to one side, on his right hip, as in the Modern-style Tango.

THE TANGO WALK is not the pronounced gliding movement of the Saunters; it is rather more like the ordinary everyday walk.

In this dance the feet are not turned out; they point directly ahead—*straight forward*. They remain parallel to each other all the time.

THE TANGO AS A SEQUENCE DANCE

THE WALK FORWARD is a natural-length step, taken from the hip, the leg swinging freely and the heel of the foot touching the floor first, then the whole of the foot touching the floor. When moving forward, the dancer should pass the moving foot very close to the other.

THE WALK BACKWARD is a natural-length step, taken from the hip, the leg swinging freely and the toe of the moving foot touching the floor first, then the whole of the foot touching the floor. When moving backward, the dancer should pass the moving foot very close to the other.

It is a good plan to practise the Walk to Tango music, swinging the legs well forward and backward. When you are able to Walk forward and backward, with a partner in front of you, and in time to the music, you can start to learn the steps of the different Tango sequence dances, but first make certain of your ability to Walk correctly.

Many dancers who are able to Walk forward easily and freely experience difficulty with the Walk backward. They tend to take a shorter step backward than forward. The reason for this is that they step first on to the ball of the foot instead of stretching well back on to the toes. This can make a considerable difference to the length of your stride —possibly as much as five inches.

BOTH PARTNERS should keep their weight forward. Thus, whenever your partner is in front of you, *your weight should be kept towards your partner*, whether you are moving forward or backward. Take care, however, not to lean forward. You should remain naturally erect.

When your partner is not in front of you—e.g. when in Promenade Position or Contra-Promenade Position, *your weight should still be kept forward*.

TANGO CLOSING STEPS—i.e. those in which one foot is placed close against the other, are made "broadside on," with the feet close together and parallel, toe-to-toe and heel-to-heel. In some of the earlier Tango sequence dances various somewhat eccentric ways of closing the feet together were tried, and occasionally attempts are made to revive these feeble imitations of the Modern style. Good dancers nowadays close the feet in the manner described above.

TIMING is as follows: A Slow step equals one beat of the music, and a Quick step equals half a beat of the music. It is easier to count in Slows and Quicks than in numbers of beats where the Tango is concerned, and in the following descriptions of Tango sequence dances I accordingly employ that method.

ELIZABETH TANGO

THIS is one of a number of successful dances arranged by Henry Clarke, and is unquestionably one of the easiest sequence dances of the Tango type.

Time: 2/4. *Tempo:* 32 bars per minute.

Starting position: Waltz hold. Gentleman facing L.O.D.

GENTLEMAN

Figure One—	COUNT	BARS
Step forward with L.F.	S.	
Step forward with R.F.	S.	
Short step forward with L.F.	Q.	
Short step to R. side, and slightly back, with R.F.	Q.	
Step forward with L.F.	S.	
Step forward with R.F.	S.	
Short step forward with L.F.	Q.	
Short step to R. side, and slightly back, with R.F.	Q.	
Step forward with L.F.	S.	
Step forward with R.F.	S.	4

SEQUENCE DANCING

	COUNT	BARS
Figure Two—		
Step diagonally forward with L.F. (short step), pivoting to L.	S.	
(Now with back to L.O.D.)		
Step diagonally back with R.F.	Q.	
Cross L.F. in front of R.F.	Q.	
(Now backing diagonally to centre.)		
Short step back with R.F.	S.	
Turning to L. (so as to back centre) step to L. side with L.F.	Q.	
Close R.F. to L.F.	Q.	2
Figure Three—		
Turning slightly to L., and opening-out into P.P.,		
Step forward with L.F. along L.O.D.	S.	
Step forward with R.F. in P.P.	S.	1
Figure Four—		
Turning slightly to R., now square with partner,		
Step to L. with L.F.	Q.	
Close R.F. to L.F.	Q.	
Step to L. side with L.F.	Q.	
Close R.F. to L.F.	Q.	1
Figure Five—		
Step forward with L.F. (towards wall)	S.	
Step to R. side with R.F.	Q.	
Close L.F. to R.F.	Q.	1

Figure Six—	COUNT	BARS
Step back with R.F. (towards centre)	S.	
Step to L. side with L.F.	Q.	
Close R.F. to L.F.	Q.	1

Figure Seven—

Short step forward with L.F., turning on it to face L.O.D.	S.	
Step to R. side with R.F.	Q.	
Close L.F. to R.F.	Q.	1

Figure Eight—

Short step back with R.F.	S.	
Step to L. side with L.F.	Q.	
Close R.F. to L.F.	Q.	1

Figure Nine—

Step forward with L.F.	S.	
Step forward with R.F.	S.	
Step forward with L.F., pivoting on it to R.	S.	
Step forward with R.F., pivoting on it to R., finishing facing L.O.D.	S.	2
		14

Figure Ten—

Short step forward with L.F.	Q.	
Short step forward with R.F.	Q.	
Short step forward with L.F.	Q.	
Close R.F. to L.F.	Q.	1

Figure Eleven—

	COUNT	BARS
Without moving L.F., place R. toe against L. heel, and turn body to L.	S.	
Close R.F. to L.F., and turn body to face L.O.D., now in original Starting Position ready to repeat the sequence *ad lib*.	S.	1
		16

LADY

Figure One—

	COUNT	BARS
Step back with R.F.	S.	
Step back with L.F.	S.	
Short step back with R.F.	Q.	
Short step to L. side and slightly forward with L.F.	Q.	
Step back with R.F.	S.	
Step back with L.F.	S.	
Short step back with R.F.	Q.	
Short step to L. side and slightly forward with L.F.	Q.	
Step back with R.F.	S.	
Step back with L.F.	S.	4

Figure Two—

	COUNT
Step diagonally back with R.F. (short step), pivoting to L. to face L.O.D.	S.
Step diagonally forward with L.F.	Q.
Cross R.F. behind L.F.	Q.

(Now facing diagonally to centre.)

	COUNT	BARS
Short step forward with L.F.	S.	
Turning to L. so as to face centre,		
Step to R. side with R.F.	Q.	
Close L.F. to R.F.	Q.	2

Figure Three—

Opening-out into P.P.,		
Step forward with R.F. along L.O.D.	S.	
Step forward with L.F. in P.P.	S.	1

Figure Four—

Turning slightly to L., now square with partner,		
Step to R. side with R.F.	Q.	
Close L.F. to R.F.	Q.	
Step to R. side with R.F.	Q.	
Close L.F. to R.F.	Q.	1

Figure Five—

Step back with R.F. (towards wall)	S.	
Step to L. side with L.F.	Q.	
Close R.F. to L.F.	Q.	1

Figure Six—

Step forward with L.F. (towards centre)	S.	
Step to R. side with R.F.	Q.	
Close L.F. to R.F.	Q.	1

	COUNT	BARS

Figure Seven—
Short step back with R.F., turning on it so as to back L.O.D. — S.
Step to L. side with L.F. — Q.
Close R.F. to L.F. — Q. — 1

Figure Eight—
Short step forward with L.F. (against L.O.D.) — S.
Step to R. side with R.F. — Q.
Close L.F. to R.F. — Q. — 1

Figure Nine—
Step back with R.F. — S.
Step back with L.F. — S.
Step back with R.F., pivoting on it to R. — S.
Step back with L.F., pivoting on it to R., finishing with back to L.O.D. — S. — 2

Figure Ten—
Short step back with R.F. — Q.
Short step back with L.F. — Q.
Short step back with R.F. — Q.
Close L.F. to R.F. — Q. — 1

Figure Eleven—
Without moving R.F., place L. toe against R. heel, and turn body to R. — S.
Close L.F. to R.F., and turn body (now backing L.O.D.) to original Starting Position, ready to repeat the sequence *ad lib.* — S. — 1

16

THE DONELLA TANGO

THIS Tango is a pleasant little dance, easily learned, but it has suffered (like many other dances) from attempts being made to incorporate in it part of the Modern-style technique, which is hopelessly unsuited to the Old Time ballroom.

Crude adaptations of the Modern-style Tango, especially when they assume the form of attempting to apply to an Old Time Tango one of the more difficult applications of the Modern-style technique, seem to me to deserve no encouragement. I therefore describe the dance below in its simple form, which is in harmony with the technique of the sequence dances based on the Tango as normally danced in the Old Time ballroom. This is the method invariably favoured by teachers today, and it is the one employed by good present-day dancers.

Many of our sequence dances have *evolved* to their present state. The cruder or less suitable movements have been modified or replaced as the result of experience. This is so in the case of the Donella Tango. Here, as in all the dances described in this book, I am not concerned with "original arrangements," but with the best present-day ballroom practice.

For that reason I ignore the freakish closing-steps which are sometimes taught for the Lady, and describe all closing steps for both partners in the generally-accepted Old Time Tango manner—the feet being closed broadside on, parallel, toe-to-toe and heel-to-heel.

Time: 2/4. *Tempo:* 32 bars per minute.

Starting position: Waltz hold. Gentleman facing L.O.D.

GENTLEMAN

The Walk and Close Steps—	COUNT	BARS
Step forward with L.F.	S.	
Close R.F. to L.F., keeping weight on L.F., feet together and parallel	S.	1
Step forward with R.F.	S.	
Close L.F. to R.F., keeping weight on R.F., feet together and parallel	S.	1
		—
		2
Repeat the above two bars		2
		—
		4

Outside Step (Right)—		
Step forward with L.F.	S.	
Pivoting slightly to L., step outside partner on her R. side with R.F.	S.	
Step back with L.F., pivoting on it to R. (Now square with partner.)	S.	
Step to R. side with R.F.	Q.	
Close L.F. to R.F., feet together and parallel	Q.	2
		—
		6

Outside Step (Left)—		
Step forward with R.F.	S.	
Pivoting slightly to R., step outside partner on her L. side with L.F.	S.	

THE DONELLA TANGO

	COUNT	BARS
Step back with R.F., pivoting on it to L. (Now square with partner.)	S.	
Step to L. side with L.F.	Q.	
Close R.F. to L.F., feet together and parallel	Q.	2
		—
		8

The Promenade—
Turning slightly to L., open-out into P.P.,
Step forward with L.F. in P.P.   S.
Step forward with R.F. in P.P.   S.   1
—
9

Backward and Forward Walk—
Turning to R., again square with partner.
Step back with L.F. (towards centre)   S.
Step back with R.F.   S.
Step forward with L.F. (towards wall)   S.
Step forward with R.F.   S.   2
—
11

The Pivot Turn—
Step forward with L.F., and swivel on it to R.   S.
Step forward with R.F., and swivel on it to R.
(Now facing L.O.D.)   S.   1
—
12

Forward Walk—
Step forward with L.F.   S.
Step forward with R.F.   S.

	COUNT	BARS
Step forward with L.F.	S.	
Step forward with R.F.	S.	2
		—
		14

Cross-over and Points—

	COUNT	BARS
Step over R.F. and to R. with L.F.	S.	
Point R.F. to R. side, and pivot slightly to L. on L.F.	S.	
Step over L.F. and to L. with R.F. (towards centre)	S.	
Point L.F. to L. side, and pivot slightly to R. on R.F., finishing facing L.O.D. in original Starting Position, ready to repeat the sequence *ad lib*.	S.	2
		—
		16

LADY

The Walk and Close Steps—

	COUNT	BARS
Step back with R.F.	S.	
Close L.F. to R.F., keeping weight on R.F., feet together and parallel	S.	1
Step back with L.F.	S.	
Close R.F. to L.F., keeping weight on L.F., feet together and parallel	S.	1
		—
		2
Repeat the above two bars		2
		—
		4

THE DONELLA TANGO

Outside Step (Right)—   COUNT   BARS

Step back with R.F.	S.	
Step back with L.F. (partner steps outside on your R. side)	S.	
Step forward with R.F. (partner now again in front)	S.	
Step to L. side with L.F.	Q.	
Close R.F. to L.F., feet together and parallel	Q.	2
		—
		6

Outside Step (Left)—

Step back with L.F.	S.	
Step back with R.F. (partner steps outside on your L. side)	S.	
Step forward with L.F. (partner now again in front)	S.	
Step to R. side with R.F.	Q.	
Close L.F. to R.F., feet together and parallel	Q.	2
		—
		8

The Promenade—

Turning slightly to R., open-out into P.P.		
Step forward with R.F. in P.P.	S.	
Step forward with L.F. in P.P.	S.	1
		—
		9

Forward and Backward Walk—

Turning to L. to face partner,		
Step forward with R.F. (towards centre)	S.	

	COUNT	BARS
Step forward with L.F.	S.	
Step back with R.F. (towards wall)	S.	
Step back with L.F.	S.	2
		——
		11

The Pivot Turn—

	COUNT	BARS
Step back with R.F. and swivel on it to R.	S.	
Step back with L.F. and swivel on it to R. (now with back to L.O.D.)	S.	1
		——
		12

Backward Walk—

	COUNT	BARS
Step back with R.F.	S.	
Step back with L.F.	S.	
Step back with R.F.	S.	
Step back with L.F.	S.	2
		——
		14

Cross-over and Points—

	COUNT	BARS
Step over L.F., and to L. with R.F.	S.	
Point L.F. to L. side and pivot slightly to R. on R.F.	S.	
Step over R.F. and to R. with L.F. (towards centre)	S.	
Point R.F. to R. side, and pivot slightly to L. on R.F., finishing with back to L.O.D., in original Starting Position ready to repeat the sequence *ad lib.*	S.	2
		——
		16

EUGENE TANGO

THIS is a sequence Tango which has attained considerable popularity in some parts of Britain. I am unable to state who arranged it, for its origin appears to be wrapped in mystery, but it is clear that it was inspired not only by the Tango as that dance originally appeared in Britain, but also by the Modern-style Quickstep. The Lock figure is, indeed, similar to the Lock Step Forward in the Quickstep.

The reader must not assume from this that the Eugene Tango is a Modern-style sequence dance. It is not. It is danced in accordance with the Old Time Tango technique, but is in some respects an unusual dance. For instance, whereas in the Old Time Tango sequence dances the Waltz Hold is generally used, here the Hold is similar to that of the Ladbroke, with both partners facing L.O.D.

The Lock Step, already mentioned, is another unusual feature. It is danced beginning with L.F. in Bar 5, and beginning with R.F. in Bar 6.

Time: 2/4. *Tempo:* 32 bars per minute.

Starting position: Partners stand almost side-by-side, the Gentleman's right shoulder being behind the Lady's left shoulder.

Gentleman holds his partner's raised right hand in his right hand, and her raised left hand in his left hand.

Both partners begin the dance with L.F., and the steps of both Lady and Gentleman are precisely similar throughout the dance.

STEPS FOR BOTH PARTNERS

The Square—   COUNT   BARS

	COUNT	BARS
Step to L. side with L.F.	Q.	
Close R.F. to L.F.	Q.	
Step back with L.F.	S.	
Step to R. side with R.F.	Q.	
Close L.F. to R.F.	Q.	
Step forward with R.F.	S.	2
Repeat Bars 1 and 2, i.e., dance the Square again		2
		—
		4

The Lock Step—

	COUNT	BARS
Step forward with L.F.	Q.	
Close R.F. loosely behind, and to the L. of L.F.	Q.	
Step forward with L.F.	S.	1
Repeat Bar 5, i.e., dance the Lock Step again, beginning with R.F.		1
		—
		6

The Aerial Turn—

	COUNT	BARS
Step forward with L.F.	S.	
Raise R.F. forward, off the floor, toe pointed down, and turn on L.F. to face opposite direction, keeping R.F. in front raised from floor	S.	1
Now with back to L.O.D., and starting with R.F.,		
Take 3 steps backward (along L.O.D.)	Q. Q. S.	1

EUGENE TANGO

	COUNT	BARS
Take 3 steps forward (against L.O.D.), turning to face L.O.D. on 3rd step	S. S. S.	
Close R.F. to L.F.	S.	2
		10

The Cross Steps—

Step over R.F. and across to R. with L.F.	S.	
Step with R.F. over L.F. and across to L.	S.	
Step with L.F. over R.F. and across to R.	S.	
Close R.F. to L.F.	S.	2
		12

The Double Twinkle—

Step forward with L.F.	S.	
Step forward with R.F., and raise L.F. in front, toe pointed down	S.	
Step back with L.F.	Q.	
Close R.F. to L.F.	Q.	
Step forward with L.F.	S.	2
Step forward with R.F.	S.	
Step forward with L.F., and raise R.F. in front, toe pointed down	S.	
Step back with R.F.	Q.	
Close L.F. to R.F.	Q.	
Step forward with R.F.	S.	2
		16

This sequence is repeated *ad lib.*

Notes on the Eugene Tango

The Square figure, danced twice at the beginning of this dance, owes its name to the fact that the partners both make the pattern of a square with their foot-movements during Bars 1 and 2, and again in Bars 3 and 4. Try to keep the correct alignment so that your foot-movements really do form a square.

As regards the Lock Step, both partners loosely close R.F. behind, and to left of L.F. on the 2nd step of Bar 5, like this—

Both partners loosely close L.F. behind, and to right of R.F. on the 2nd step of Bar 6, like this—

The Aerial Turn is often danced incorrectly, the dancer first turning *and then* raising the R.F. The R.F. must be raised *before* you swivel on L.F. to turn-about, and must be held in front of you, off the floor, throughout the turn.

Note, also, that the 3 steps backward which follow this turn are counted Quick, Quick, Slow, whereas the 3 steps forward (against L.O.D.) are all Slow. Correct timing is of the utmost importance if the Aerial Turn, and the Backward and Forward steps which follow, are to look well. The 3 Slow steps forward are normal walking steps; there is no dip in them.

THE MAZURKA AS A SEQUENCE DANCE

MAJOR CECIL H. TAYLOR, in his book, *Old Time and Novelty Dances*, describes the Mazurka as "a dance arranged in many figures for four or more couples." As such it finds no place in our present-day ballrooms. But the basic Mazurka Step is used in various sequence dances.

It is, for instance, the foundation step upon which the Varsoviana is built—a dance which was popular during the Victorian era, and which is often included in present-day programmes, besides being one of the dances included in the Amateur Tests (Gold Medal) of the Imperial Society of Teachers of Dancing, Victorian and Sequence Dance Branch. This dance is described in my book, *Old Time Dancing*.

The Mazurka Step is danced in 3/4 time, and is as follows—

	COUNT
Step forward with one foot . . .	1
Close other foot to 3rd position rear .	2
Hop lightly on foot last moved (i.e., the rear foot) and point the other foot forward, raised from floor and with toe pointed down, then bring it back sharply to the rear of the supporting leg, raised off floor, toe pointed down	3

The hop, made on the count of 3, is not a "moving" one—in other words, you do not make any progress along the ballroom when executing this hop-step, but bring the foot down on to precisely the same spot on the floor where it was when you started the hop.

In the sequence dances based on the Mazurka some slight variation of this basic figure often occurs. Thus while it is widely—and I believe generally—accepted that the forward foot should, on the count of 3, be brought sharply back to the rear of the supporting leg, in some sequence dances the forward foot is placed straight forward, just off the floor, and with toe pointed down. In others, (including the Oriental Mazurka and the Marie Mazurka) the forward foot is brought sharply back to a position *just above the instep* of the supporting foot.

In the two sequence Mazurkas described in the following pages the last-mentioned step—to just above instep of supporting foot—is employed. It is known as "a false finish" to the Mazurka Step—and so it is according to strict technique. But it is used in these sequence dances for two very good reasons. It suits their character. It does not hinder (as would the authentic finish), but promotes, the flow of the dance.

Other minor departures from the strictly authentic Mazurka Step occur when this figure is adapted for use in the sequence dances, and in the following descriptions I give the current ballroom practice.

THE SEQUENCE MAZURKAS ARE DANCES IN THE TRADITIONAL STYLE. The feet should be kept turned-out as in 1st Position throughout these dances.

ORIENTAL MAZURKA

THIS dance was arranged by Tom Almond, who introduced many sequence dances during the early years of the present century. Following inclusion in radio Old Time programmes it has experienced increased popularity in recent years, and a clear, helpful lesson on the dance, broadcast by Miss Cecil Ruault, in the course of a programme by Leonard Hayes and his Orchestra, revealed to thousands of listeners not only the charm of this dance, but the ease with which it can be learned. Thus powerfully aided by the radio, the Oriental Mazurka came very much to the fore during the 1949–50 dance season, much to the satisfaction of the keen minority of Old Time dancers who have long admired this engaging sequence.

Time: 3/4. *Tempo:* 46 bars per minute.

Starting position: Open. Partners half-facing each other, i.e., instead of facing directly along L.O.D., Gentleman turns very slightly to his right, Lady very slightly to her left.

GENTLEMAN

	COUNT	BARS
Pas de Valse—		
Step forward with L.F.	1	
Step forward with R.F., turning slightly to L.	2	
Close L.F. to R.F., 3rd position rear	3	1

SEQUENCE DANCING

	COUNT	BAR
Mazurka Step—		
Step forward with R.F.	1	
Move L.F. quickly but softly into position formerly occupied by R.F., and point R.F. forward, raised from floor, toe pointed down	2	
Hop on L.F. Simultaneously bring R.F. back (quickly) to position above left instep	3	1—2
Right Half Turn—		
Step forward with R.F., turning on it to the R.	1	
Step to L. side with L.F.	2	
Close R.F. to L.F. (Now facing partner.)	3	1—3
Take Lady's right hand in own left, and her left in own right.		
Pas Glissé—		
Glide L.F. to L. side (i.e., along L.O.D.)	1	
Close R.F. to L.F., keeping weight on L.F., raising left hand, inclining body to R., and swivelling slightly to R.	2, 3	1—4
(Now with back diagonally to centre.)		
Beginning with R.F., repeat Bars 1 to 4 in opposite direction—		
Pas de Valse (beginning with R.F.)		1

ORIENTAL MAZURKA

	COUNT	BARS
Mazurka Step (beginning with L.F.)		1
Left Half Turn (beginning with L.F.)		1
Pas Glissé (beginning with R.F.), finishing in original Starting Position, facing L.O.D.		1
		—
		8

Mazurka Step—

Taking Waltz Hold,

Step forward with L.F., inclining body forward and looking down at moving foot over left arm	1	
Move R.F. quickly but softly into position formerly occupied by L.F., and point L.F. forward, raised from floor, toe pointed down	2	
Hop on R.F. Simultaneously bring L.F. back (quickly) to position above right instep, and turning slightly to R., to face partner	3	1
		—
		9

Waltz (Natural Turn)—

Now facing wall,

Take Waltz Hold and dance one complete Natural Turn	1, 2, 3 twice	2
		—
		11

Glissade—

	COUNT	BARS
Still retaining Waltz Hold,		
Step to L. side with L.F. (along L.O.D.)	1	
Close R.F. to L.F., inclining body slightly to R., thus lowering arms towards the moving foot	2, 3	1
		—
		12

Waltz Finale—

	COUNT	BARS
Dance Waltz (Natural Turn), opening-out at finish into original Starting Position, ready to repeat the sequence *ad lib.*	1, 2, 3 four times	4
		—
		16

LADY

Pas de Valse—

	COUNT	BARS
Step forward with R.F.	1	
Step forward with L.F., turning slightly to R.	2	
Close R.F. to L.F., 3rd position rear	3	1

Mazurka Step—

	COUNT	BARS
Step forward with L.F.	1	
Move R.F. quickly but softly into position formerly occupied by L.F., and point L.F. forward, raised from floor, toe pointed down	2	

ORIENTAL MAZURKA

	COUNT	BARS
Hop on R.F. Simultaneously bring L.F. back (quickly) to position above right instep	3	1
		—
		2

Left Half Turn—

Step forward with L.F., turning on it to the L.	1	
Step to R. side with R.F.	2	
Close L.F. to R.F. (now facing partner)	3	1
		—
		3

Join right hand to partner's left, and left hand to his right.

Pas Glissé—

Glide R.F. to R. side (i.e., along L.O.D.)	1	
Close L.F. to R.F., keeping weight on R.F., raising right hand, inclining body to L. and swivelling slightly to L. (Now facing diagonally to centre.)	2, 3	1
		—
		4

Beginning with L.F., repeat Bars 1 to 4 in opposite direction—		
Pas de Valse (beginning with L.F.)		1
Mazurka Step (beginning with R.F.)		1
Right Half Turn (beginning with R.F.)		1
Pas Glissé (beginning with L.F.), finishing in original Starting Position, facing L.O.D.		1
		—
		8

	COUNT	BARS

Mazurka Step—

Release hold with left hand. (Partner takes Waltz Hold.)

Step forward with R.F., inclining body forward, and look down at moving foot over right arm	1	
Move L.F. quickly but softly into position formerly occupied by R.F., and point R.F. forward, raised from floor, toe pointed down	2	
Hop on L.F. Simultaneously bring R.F. back (quickly) to position above left instep, and turning slightly to L., to face partner	3	1
		—
		9

Waltz (Natural Turn)—

Now facing centre,

Take Waltz Hold and dance one complete Natural Turn	1, 2, 3 twice	2
		—
		11

Glissade—

Still retaining Waltz Hold,

Step to R. side with R.F. (along L.O.D.)	1	
Close L.F. to R.F., inclining body slightly to L., thus lowering arms towards the moving foot	2, 3	1
		—
		12

Waltz Finale—	COUNT	BARS
Dance Waltz (Natural Turn), opening-out at finish into original Starting Position, ready to repeat the sequence *ad lib.*	1, 2, 3 four times	4
		—
		16

How to Improve Your Dance

Most beginners impart a certain amount of violence into the Mazurka Step and similar figures involving the "cutting" of one foot from its position by the other foot, and hopping. Practice will, however, enable the dancer to achieve that free, light movement which is so admired in steps of this kind. Such steps look exceedingly easy and effortless when danced with perfect timing and a soft movement.

Take care to dance a correct *Pas Glissé* in bar 4; i.e. when closing one foot to the other, keep the weight on the foot first moved (Gentleman, L.F.; Lady, R.F.).

During Bar 12, the closing step completes a *Glissade*, and the weight should be transferred to the foot last moved—i.e. R.F. for Gentleman, L.F. for Lady.

The two figures mentioned provide a practical illustration of the difference between two gliding figures which occur frequently in sequence dancing, as follows—

Pas Glissé: A gliding step danced in any direction, the other foot then being closed to 3rd position, and *the weight kept on foot first moved.*

Glissade: A gliding step danced in any direction, the other foot then being closed to 3rd position, and *the weight taken on the foot last moved.*

MARIE MAZURKA

THIS dance was arranged by A. J. Latimer and Marie Latimer in 1906. The latter gave her name to this pleasant dance which, while numerous dances have come and gone, has maintained its place in the ballrooms, and in recent years has attained increased popularity.

The Marie Mazurka is built up on figures with which the reader is by now familiar, and it can therefore be learned from the following abbreviated description.

Time: 3/4. *Tempo:* 46 bars per minute.

Starting position: Open.

GENTLEMAN

	COUNT	BARS
Balancé Forward and Backward—		
Step forward with L.F.		
Close R.F. to rear of L.F., keeping weight on L.F.		
Step back with R.F.		
Close L.F. to R.F., in front, keeping weight on R.F.	1, 2, 3 twice	2
Mazurka Step (Twice)—		
Step forward with L.F.	1	
Move R.F. quickly but softly into position formerly occupied by L.F., and point L.F.		

	COUNT	BARS
forward, raised from floor, toe pointed down	2	
Hop on R.F. Simultaneously, bring L.F. back (quickly) to position above right instep	3	1
		3
Repeat Bar 3		1
		4

Now join both hands, and:

Pas de Valse Forward, then Backward — 2

— 6

Waltz (Natural Turn), opening out at finish to Open Position — 2

— 8

Balancé Forward and Backward, i.e., repeat Bars 1 and 2 — 2

— 10

Solo Waltz Outward — 2

— 12

Now take partner's right hand in own left, and

Glissade Forward (Twice)—
i.e., Forward L.F., Close R.F. to L.F., then repeat — 2

— 14

Waltz Finale—	COUNT	BARS
Take Waltz Hold, and Waltz (Natural Turn)		2
		16

The sequence is repeated *ad lib.*

LADY

Balancé Forward and Backward—	COUNT	BARS
Step forward with R.F.		
Close L.F. to rear of R.F., keeping weight on R.F.		
Step back with L.F.		
Close R.F. to L.F., in front, keeping weight on L.F.	1, 2, 3 twice	2
Mazurka Step (Twice)—		
Step forward with R.F.	1	
Move L.F. quickly but softly into position formerly occupied by R.F., and point R.F. forward, raised from floor, toe pointed down	2	
Hop on L.F. Simultaneously, bring R.F. back (quickly) to position above left instep	3	1
		3
Repeat Bar 3		1
		4

	COUNT	BARS
Now join both hands, and:		
Pas de Valse Forward, then Backward		2
		6
Waltz (Natural Turn), opening-out at finish to Open Position		2
		8
Balancé Forward and Backward, i.e., repeat Bars 1 and 2		2
		10
Solo Waltz Outward		2
		12
Give left hand to partner, and		
Glissade Forward (Twice)—		
i.e., Forward R.F., Close L.F. to R.F., then repeat		2
		14
Waltz Finale—		
Take Waltz Hold, and Waltz (Natural Turn)		2
		16

The sequence is repeated *ad lib*.

THE DUTCH FOURSOME

A Dance in Waltztime for Sets Composed of Two Couples

HERE is a dance which is totally different from all the others described in this book. Its inclusion in the dance programme helps to promote a pleasing variety. It is a progressive dance, the couples passing on to repeat the figures with other couples, and it therefore serves a useful social purpose. Moreover, this gay, colourful dance, which possesses an "atmosphere" which is all its own, is proving very useful for entertainment purposes, especially as an item in children's dancing displays. When used for this purpose it is generally danced by children in Dutch costume. The music is "Little Hollanders," by J. W. Tattersall, and was the prize-winning tune for the *Dance News* Trophy at the Congress of the International Sequence Dance Circle held at Blackpool in 1946.

The Dutch Foursome has been danced at many village open-air functions, including some to celebrate May Day, and the spectacle of large teams of well-trained child dancers executing this colourful dance on the village green has done much to increase interest in Old Time dancing in various localities.

The steps, arranged by F. J. Mainey, Founder and Director of the I.S.D.C., enable the dancers to weave pleasing patterns in the course of four sections which are repeated three times in all. Of course, where the dance is used for display purposes indoors or on the stage, it has to be adapted somewhat according to the amount of space

THE DUTCH FOURSOME

available. The description which follows is that of the Dutch Foursome as danced in the ballroom.

Not only is this lively dance popular within the I.S.D.C., where it originated; it has become generally popular, for all who see it danced invariably wish to learn it.

A detailed description of the dance would demand a great deal of space, but the following abbreviated description will enable those who have seen it danced to recall the various figures and to note the order in which they occur.

The novelty appeal of the Dutch Foursome is enhanced by the inclusion of the Dutch Kick Step. This occurs repeatedly throughout the dance, and gives it the characteristic Dutch atmosphere.

THE DUTCH KICK STEP takes two bars of the music. It may be begun with either foot. It consists of *stamp-swing, stamp-swing*, in Waltztime, the stamp taking up 1 beat, and the swing 2 beats.

Beginning with L.F., it is danced as follows—

	COUNT	BARS
Lift L.F. up slightly and bring it down fairly sharply, relaxing the knee	1	
Straightening left knee, swing R.F. across, in front of L.F. and to L. side, the foot just touching the floor as it moves to the L., and finishing with foot raised from floor, toe pointed down	2, 3	1
Bring R.F. down sharply to its original position, relaxing right knee	1	
Straightening right knee, swing L.F. across, in front of R.F., and to R. side, the foot just touching the floor as it moves to the R.,		

	COUNT	BARS
and finishing with foot raised from floor, toe pointed down	2, 3	1
		2

STEPS OF THE DUTCH FOURSOME

Time: 3/4. *Tempo:* 48 bars per minute.

Starting position: The dancers form sets of 4 around the room, each set consisting of 2 couples, the couples facing each other. One couple stand facing L.O.D., the opposite couple stand with backs to L.O.D.

Each Gentleman holds his partner's left hand in his own right hand, at shoulder height. His left hand is place on his left hip.

Each Lady holds her skirt with 1st finger and thumb of right hand, her left hand being joined to Gentleman's at shoulder height.

Four-bar Introduction—   BARS

The Gentlemen bow to their partners.
The Ladies curtsey to their partners.   4

Section One: The Dutch Glee Dance

All 4 begin the dance with—
Dutch Kick Step   2
Couples change places:
Gentlemen cross L.F., R.F., L.F.
Ladies cross R.F., L.F., R.F. (On Gentleman's R. side.)

THE DUTCH FOURSOME

	BARS
All face partners, point R.F. forward, and give right hand to partner	2
Balancé Forward (R.F.) and Rearward (L.F.)	2
Ladies dance Reverse Turn under partners' raised arms, each couple thus moving to occupy opposite couple's former place	2
	— 8
The Dutch Glee Dance is now repeated, i.e., all dance the above 8 bars, thus returning to the position from which they began	8
	— 16

SECTION TWO: THE WALTZ SQUARE

All face partners, and join both hands.

Dutch Kick Step—

The couple whose Starting Position was facing L.O.D., swing feet along L.O.D.

The couple whose Starting Position was backing L.O.D., swing feet against L.O.D. 2

—
18

Change places with Solo Waltz—

Gentlemen dance across outside Ladies;

Ladies dance across inside of Gentlemen;

Ladies join hands with opposite Gentlemen;

Gentlemen join hands with opposite Ladies. 2

—
20

	BARS
(All dancers are now standing sideways to L.O.D.)	
Dutch Kick Step	2
Solo Waltz across (thus rejoining own partner)	2
Dutch Kick Step	2
Solo Waltz across, then join hands with opposite partner	2
Dutch Kick Step	2
Solo Waltz across, to own partner and to position from which you began	2
	32

Section Three: The Dutch Mill

Join hands across.	
Ladies link right hands uppermost.	
Gentlemen link right hands undermost.	
Waltz Walk (1, 2, 3 each step) in a clockwise direction, beginning with outside foot	3
Turn inwards, releasing hands (Count 1); Clap hands (Count 2); Clap hands (Count 3)	1
Turn in opposite direction and join hands across.	
Ladies join left hands, again uppermost.	
Gentlemen join left hands, again undermost.	
Waltz Walk (1, 2, 3 each step) in anti-clockwise direction, beginning with inside foot	3
Turn inwards, releasing hands (Count 1); Clap hands (Count 2); Clap hands (Count 3)	1
	40

THE DUTCH FOURSOME

SECTION FOUR: FINAL PROGRESSION

	BARS
All join hands around, and Balancé Forward (R.F.) and Rearward (L.F.)	2
Turning to face partners, Gentlemen bow, Ladies curtsey	2
Taking Waltz Hold, Waltz with partner in direction faced at beginning of dance to meet next couple with whom the whole sequence is repeated from the beginning	4
	48

THE WESTERN SCHOTTISCHE

THIS is another dance which has enjoyed increased popularity following inclusion in various radio programmes. Although it is called the Western Schottische, actually the Gentleman does not dance any Schottische steps; only the Lady does so when, during the fourth and fifth bars, she moves some distance round her partner while he pivots.

This dance is easily learned, and most Old Time dancers who see it danced can learn the steps almost in a matter of minutes. Remember: *This is a dance in the traditional style, and the feet should be kept turned-out right through the dance.*

Time: 4/4. *Tempo:* 28 bars per minute.

Starting position: Waltz hold. Gentleman facing L.O.D.

GENTLEMAN

	COUNT	BARS
Step forward with L.F.	1	
Step forward with R.F.	2	
Turning slightly to R., step outside partner (on her L. side) with L.F.	3	
Without moving feet, relax left knee slightly	4	1
Balance back on to R.F.	1	
Step to L. side with L.F. (short step)	2	
Turning slightly to L., step outside partner (on her R. side) with R.F.	3	
Without moving feet, relax right knee slightly	4	1

THE WESTERN SCHOTTISCHE

	COUNT	BARS
Step back with L.F.	1	
Close R.F. back to L.F.	2	
Step forward with L.F.	3	
Close R.F. to L.F.	4	1
Swivel a quarter-turn to L., while partner dances to your L.		1
Swivel a quarter-turn to R., while partner dances to your R., and finish by taking Waltz Hold		1
Waltz (Natural Turn), ending facing L.O.D. in Original Starting Position, ready to repeat *ad lib*.		3
		8

LADY

	COUNT	BARS
Step back with R.F.	1	
Step back with L.F.	2	
Step back with R.F. (partner steps outside)	3	
Without moving feet, relax knees slightly	4	1
Balance forward on to L.F.	1	
Step to R. side with R.F. (short step)	2	
Step back with L.F. (partner steps outside)	3	
Without moving feet, relax knees slightly	4	1
Step forward with R.F.	1	
Close L.F. to R.F.	2	
Step back with R.F.	3	
Close L.F. to R.F.	4	1

	COUNT	BARS
Step to R. side with R.F.	1	
Close L.F. to R.F.	2	
Step to R. side with R.F.	3	
Place L.F. behind right heel, off the floor, toe pointed down, and hop on R.F.	4	1
Step to L. side with L.F.	1	
Close R.F. to L.F.	2	
Step to L. side with L.F.	3	
Place R.F. behind left heel, off the floor, toe pointed down, and hop on L.F.	4	1
Waltz (Natural Turn), ending facing L.O.D., in original Starting Position, ready to repeat the sequence *ad lib*.		3

$$\frac{}{8}$$

BLUE DANUBE WALTZ

THIS dance takes its name from the famous Waltz by J. Strauss to which it is danced.

The steps were arranged by F. J. Mainey, who has played so prominent a part in the revival of Old Time dancing, and this product of his inventive genius has received widespread recognition for not only is the Blue Danube Waltz popular at I.S.D.C. and other ballrooms in all parts of Britain, but it has found increasing favour in Old Time dance groups in the many countries which are now linked with the International Sequence Dance Circle.

As will be observed from the following description, this is an unusual Waltz-sequence dance. Throughout the greater part of the dance both partners execute similar steps, and I think it will prove an aid to simplicity if I describe the steps for both partners together, instead of separately.

Time: 3/4. *Tempo:* 46 bars per minute.

Starting position: Both partners face L.O.D., the Gentleman slightly behind the Lady.

The Gentleman's right shoulder is behind his partner's left shoulder.

The Gentleman holds his partner's right hand in his right hand, and her left hand in his left hand. The joined hands are held slightly above shoulder-level.

SEQUENCE DANCING

STEPS FOR BOTH PARTNERS

During the first 4 bars the Gentleman more or less remains still, simply swivelling slightly to his left, then to his right, with arms and hands moving as the Lady moves, and virtually guiding her in her movements.

During this opening phase the Lady's steps are as follows—

	COUNT	BARS
Step to L. side with L.F.	1	
Close R.F. to L.F.	2, 3	1
Step to L. side with L.F.	1	
Swing R.F. over and across, in front of L.F. and to L.	2, 3	1
Repeat to R. side, starting with R.F.		2
		—
		4
Both partners then repeat Bars 1-4, i.e., Glissade to L. and swing R.F., Glissade to R. and swing L.F.		4
		—
		8
The Lady (only) then dances the same steps (Bars 1-4), the Gentleman merely guiding her as before		4
		—
		12
Both partners—		
Step forward with L.F.	1, 2, 3	1
Step forward with R.F.	1, 2, 3	1
Point L.F. forward	1, 2, 3	1
Point L.F. back, toe to floor, with slight dip	1, 2, 3	1
		—
		16

BLUE DANUBE WALTZ

	COUNT	BARS
Both partners—		
Chassé diagonally forward:		
L.F. diagonally forward	1	
Close R.F. 3rd position rear	2, 3	1
L.F. diagonally forward	1, 2, 3	1
		—
		18
Lady turns to L., facing partner and with back to L.O.D.		
Gentleman dances Chassé rearward.		
Step back with R.F.	1	
Close L.F. to R.F.	2, 3	1
Step back with R.F.	1, 2, 3	1
Lady dances Chassé Forward (L.F., R.F., L.F.)		
		—
		20
Both partners—		
Chassé towards centre, i.e., Gentleman to his left, Lady to her right.		
Chassé towards wall, i.e., Gentleman to his right, Lady to her left		4
		—
		24
Both partners Waltz (Natural Turn), opening-out at finish to original Starting Position ready to repeat the sequence *ad lib*.	,	8
		—
		32

THE DREAM WALTZ

THIS dance was arranged by Major Cecil H. Taylor, who has been connected with the teaching of dancing for seventy years, thus carrying on the traditions of his ancestors who had taught dancing for two hundred years before he began!

He was for many years President of the world's largest society of dance teachers—the Imperial Society of Teachers of Dancing—and his enthusiasm for Old Time dancing in its correct figuration led him to found the Victorian Dancers' Society, which merged into the Imperial Society's Old Time Branch in 1950. After the second World War, when interest in the old dances was beginning to revive, he published a book, *Old Time and Novelty Dances*, which proved of great value to teachers.

The Dream Waltz is a simple combination of figures with which the reader is by now familiar, and it can therefore be easily learned from the following abbreviated description. The music is played slower than for most sequence Waltzes, the "dreamy" type of Waltz tune being ideal for this dance.

Time: 3/4. *Tempo:* 40 bars per minute.

Starting position: Open. Gentleman with L.F. 3rd position in front, Lady with R.F. 3rd position in front.

GENTLEMAN

	BARS
Pas de Valse (twice), starting with L.F.	2
Solo Waltz Outward	2

THE DREAM WALTZ

	BARS
Taking Waltz Hold, Waltz (Natural Turn), finishing by opening-out into P.P.	4
	— 8
Now facing L.O.D. in P.P.,	
Step forward with L.F. (Count 1)	
Step forward with R.F., foot raised from floor, toe pointed down. (Count 2, 3.)	1
Pas de Valse, starting with R.F.	1
Pas de Valse (twice), starting with L.F. (while partner Solo Waltzes)	2
Take Waltz Hold and Waltz (Natural Turn), opening-out at finish to original Starting Position, ready to repeat the sequence *ad lib.*	4
	— 16

LADY

	BARS
Pas de Valse (twice), starting with R.F.	2
Solo Waltz Outward	2
Taking Waltz Hold, Waltz (Natural Turn), finishing by opening-out into P.P.	4
	— 8
Now facing L.O.D. in P.P.,	
Step forward with R.F. (Count 1.)	
Step forward with L.F., foot raised from floor, toe pointed down. (Count 2, 3.)	1
Pas de Valse, starting with L.F.	1

	BARS
Solo Waltz (while partner dances Pas de Valse)	2
Take Waltz Hold and Waltz (Natural Turn), opening-out at finish into original Starting Position, ready to repeat the sequence *ad lib*.	4
	16

TANGO FASCINATION

HERE is a sequence Tango which richly merits the attention of all keen dancers who have learned the simple Tango sequence dances and wish to turn their attention to something rather more advanced.

Arranged by Fred Holmes, Tango Fascination has been acclaimed by experts as a notable contribution to the group of Tango sequence dances, and it has received much attention at teachers' technical courses.

Below, I describe this dance in considerable detail, and would mention that the description is necessarily somewhat lengthy in order to make the precise movements and alignments absolutely clear. Those who have learned the other Tango sequences described in this book should not fail to add this pleasing dance.

Time: 2/4. *Tempo:* 32 bars per minute.

Starting position: Waltz hold. Gentleman facing L.O.D.

GENTLEMAN

STEP	*The Lilt Chassé (Left)*—	COUNT	BARS
1	Step forward with L.F.	S.	
2	Step forward with R.F., turning to R. (facing diagonally to wall)	S.	1
3	Step to L. side with L.F.	Q.	
4	Close R.F. to L.F.	Q.	

STEP		COUNT	BARS
5	Step back with L.F. Raise R.F. slightly off floor	S.	1/2

The above figure, as its name suggests, is danced with a lilt. Steps 3, 4 should be danced on balls of feet, lowering on to flat foot on step 5.

The Lilt Chassé (Right)—

STEP			
1	Step on to R.F., diagonally to wall	S.	
2	Step forward with L.F.	S.	
3	Step to R. side with R.F.	Q.	
4	Close L.F. to R.F.	Q.	
5	Step to R. side with R.F., turning sharply to L., and opening-out into P.P. Raise L.F. slightly off floor	S.	2/4

(Now facing diagonally to centre, in P.P.)

The above figure, as its name suggests, is danced with a lilt. Steps 3, 4 should be danced on balls of feet, lowering on to flat foot on step 5.

Fallaway Diagonal Promenade—

STEP			
1	Step forward with L.F. in P.P. (diagonally to centre)	S.	
2	Step forward with R.F. in P.P., turning towards partner	S.	1

TANGO FASCINATION

STEP		COUNT	BARS
3	Step to L. side, and slightly back, with L.F., still turning	Q.	
4	Step back with R.F. (diagonally to centre). Place right hand on right hip	Q.	
5	Step back with L.F., turning slightly to R.	Q.	
6	Cross R.F. in front of L.F., keeping weight on L.F.	Q.	$\frac{1}{6}$

(Now facing diagonally to wall, against L.O.D. in Contra P.P.)

Fallaway Contra Promenade—

STEP			
1	Step forward with R.F., in Contra P.P.	S.	
2	Step forward with L.F. in Contra P.P., turning towards partner	S.	1
3	Step to R. side, and slightly back with R.F., (facing partner), still turning	Q.	
4	Step back with L.F., diagonally to wall, against L.O.D., and take Waltz Hold, in P.P. (Now facing diagonally to centre.)	Q.	
5	Step back with R.F., turning slightly to L.	Q.	
6	Cross L.F. in front of R.F., keeping weight on R.F.	Q.	$\frac{1}{8}$

(Now facing diagonally to centre in P.P.)

The Rondé Crossings—

STEP		COUNT	BARS
1	Loosening Hold slightly, Step forward with L.F. in P.P. (diagonally to centre)	S.	
2	Step over and across L.F. with R.F., turning to face partner	S.	1
3	With a circular movement, outward to L. and forward, cross L.F. well to the R. side of R.F.	S.	
4	Now facing partner, with a circular movement, outward to R. and forward, cross R.F. well to the L. side of L.F.	S.	1

10

The Sway Points—

STEP			
	Take Waltz Hold, facing diagonally to wall, and		
1	Step forward with L.F.	S.	
2	Point R.F. diagonally forward, toe to floor, heel slightly raised, raising left arm, and looking in the direction of the pointed foot and inclining body to the R.	S.	1
3	Step forward with R.F.	S.	
4	Point L.F. diagonally forward, toe to floor, heel slightly raised, raising right arm and looking in direction of the pointed foot, and inclining body to the L.	S.	1

12

For the above figure, the Hold must be compact, i.e., hold partner closely, but not tightly. On steps 2 and 4, do not look down at the pointed foot, but look at a point on the floor some yards away.

The Promenade Run and Allemande—

STEP		COUNT	BARS
	Facing diagonally to centre, in P.P.,		
1	Step forward with L.F. in P.P.	Q.	
2	Step forward with R.F. in P.P., turning to R. (Allemande)	Q.	
3	Step to L. side, and slightly back, with L.F., and place right hand on hip	S.	1

Contra Promenade Run and Allemande—

STEP			
	In Contra P.P.,		
1	Step forward with R.F. (diagonally to wall, against L.O.D.)	Q.	
2	Step forward with L.F., turning to L. (Now facing partner, who turns under your raised left hand.)	Q.	
3	Step to R. side, and slightly back, with R.F. Take Waltz Hold, in P.P.	S.	1
			—
			14

The Promenade Dip—

STEP			
	Facing diagonally to centre in P.P.,		
1	Step forward with L.F. in P.P.	S.	

STEP		COUNT	BARS
2	Step forward with R.F., with dip, and keeping knees relaxed	S.	1
3	Balance back on to L.F., straightening the knees	S.	
4	Place R.F. just behind L.F., with right instep a few inches from left heel. Raise L.F. just off the floor	S.	1
			16

The Gentleman steps forward, on to L.F., in the following bar, to repeat the whole sequence *ad lib.*

LADY

The Lilt Chassé (Right)—

STEP		COUNT	BARS
1	Step back with R.F.	S.	
2	Step back with L.F., turning slightly to R.	S.	1
3	Step to R. side with R.F.	Q.	
4	Close L.F. to R.F.	Q.	
5	Step forward with R.F. Raise L.F. slightly off floor	S.	1
			2

The above figure, as its name suggests, is danced with a lilt. Steps 3, 4 should be danced on balls of feet, lowering on to flat foot on step 5.

TANGO FASCINATION

The Lilt Chassé (Left)—

STEP		COUNT	BARS
1	Step back on to L.F. (now backing diagonally to wall)	S.	
2	Step back with R.F.	S.	
3	Step to L. side with L.F. (against L.O.D.)	Q.	
4	Close R.F. to L.F.	Q.	
5	Step to L. side with L.F., turning sharply to R., and opening-out into P.P. Raise R.F. slightly off floor	S.	2 / 4

(Now facing diagonally to centre in P.P.)

The above figure, as its name suggests, is danced with a lilt. Steps 3, 4 should be danced on balls of feet, lowering on to flat foot on step 5.

Fallaway Diagonal Promenade—

STEP			
1	Step forward with R.F. in P.P. (diagonally to centre)	S.	
2	Step forward with L.F. in P.P., turning towards partner	S.	1
3	Step to R. side and slightly back with R.F., still turning to R.	Q.	
4	Step forward with L.F. (diagonally to centre). Release partner's right hand	Q.	
5.	Step forward with R.F., turning slightly to R.	Q.	

STEP		COUNT	BARS
6	Cross L.F. in front of R.F., keeping weight on R.F.	Q.	$\dfrac{1}{6}$

(Now facing diagonally to wall in Contra P.P.)

Fallaway Contra Promenade—

STEP			
1	Step forward with L.F. in Contra P.P.	S.	
2	Step forward with R.F. in Contra P.P., turning towards partner	S.	1
3	Step to L. side, and slightly back with L.F. (facing partner), still turning	Q	
4	Step forward with R.F., and take Waltz Hold in P.P. (Now facing diagonally to centre.)	Q.	
5	Step back with L.F., turning slightly to L.	Q.	
6	Cross R.F. in front of L.F., keeping weight on L.F.	Q.	$\dfrac{1}{8}$

The Rondé Crossings—

(Now facing diagonally to centre, in P.P.)

1	Loosening Hold slightly, step forward with R.F. in P.P.	S.	
2	Step over and across R.F. with L.F., turning to face partner	S.	1
3	With a circular movement, outward to R. and forward, cross R.F. well to the L. side of L.F.	S.	

STEP		COUNT	BARS
4	Now facing partner, with a circular movement outward to L. and forward, cross L.F. well to the R. side of R.F.	S.	1
			—
			10

The Sway Points—

STEP

Take Waltz Hold, with back diagonally to wall, and
1. Step back with R.F. — S.
2. Point L.F. diagonally back, toe to floor, heel slightly raised, looking in the direction of the pointed foot, and inclining body to the L. — S. — 1
3. Step back with L.F. — S.
4. Point R.F. diagonally back, toe to floor, heel slightly raised, looking in the direction of the pointed foot, and inclining body to the R. — S. — 1

—
12

For the above figure, the Hold must be compact, i.e., Lady should be held closely but not tightly. On steps 2 and 4, do not look down at the pointed foot, but look at a point on the floor some yards away.

The Promenade Run and Allemande—

STEP

Facing diagonally to centre in P.P.,
1. Step forward with R.F. in P.P. — Q.

STEP		COUNT	BARS
2	Step forward with L.F. in P.P., turning to face partner under his raised arm	Q.	
3	Step to R. side, and slightly back, releasing Hold with left hand and taking dress therewith	S.	1
			——
			13

Contra Promenade Run and Allemande—

STEP			
	In Contra P.P.,		
1	Step forward with L.F., turning to L.	Q.	
	Now with back to partner,		
2	Step to R. side with R.F., and turn under his raised arm	Q.	
3	Step forward with L.F. in P.P.	S.	1
			——
			14

The Promenade Dip—

STEP			
	Facing diagonally to centre in P.P.,		
1	Step forward with R.F. in P.P.	S.	
2	Step forward with L.F. with dip, keeping knees relaxed	S.	1
3	Balance back on to R.F., straightening the knees and turning towards partner	S.	
	Now with back to L.O.D.,		
4	Place L.F. just in front of R.F., and raise R.F. just off the floor	S.	1
			——
			16
			==

THE FYLDE WALTZ

THIS dance has long been enjoyed by keen dancers who meet regularly in the Old Time clubs, but in recent years it has also become popular at the palais and other public dances, powerfully stimulated by inclusion in various radio programmes, and also by being given prominence at the teachers' conferences.

Arranged by the late Tom Almond, of Darwen, in 1902, it is built up entirely on figures with which the reader is now familiar, and can easily be learned from the following abbreviated description.

Time: 3/4. *Tempo:* 48 bars per minute.

Starting position: Open.

GENTLEMAN

	COUNT	BARS
Beginning with L.F.,		
Pas de Valse Forward	1, 2, 3	1
Balancé Forward on R.F., raising joined hands forward, and closing L.F. to 3rd position rear	1, 2, 3	1
Glissade Backward on L.F., lowering joined hands, and closing R.F. to 3rd position front	1, 2, 3	1

Waltz Inward—

Back L.F., turning to R.	1	
Place right toe behind left heel, still turning	2	

	COUNT	BARS
Pivot on balls of feet to R. Release partner's left hand. Take her right hand in own left	3	1
		—
		4
(Now with back to L.O.D., with R.F. in front, 5th position.)		
Beginning with R.F., dance Bars 1–4 against L.O.D., finishing facing L.O.D.		4
		—
		8
Releasing partner's hand,		
Waltz Outward, beginning with L.F. Finish almost back-to-back with partner, but facing diagonally to centre, against L.O.D. Take Lady's right hand in own left	1, 2, 3	1
		—
		9
Glissade Back on R.F., and close L.F. to 3rd position front	1, 2, 3	1
		—
		10
Beginning with R.F., *Waltz Inward*	1, 2, 3	1
		—
		11
Joining both hands, own left to partner's right, own right to her left,		
Step to L. side with L.F.		
Close R.F. to 3rd position front	1, 2, 3	1
		—
		12

	COUNT	BARS
Taking Waltz Hold,		
Waltz (*Natural Turn*), opening-out at finish to original Starting Position, ready to repeat the sequence *ad lib.*	1, 2, 3 four times	4
		—
		16

LADY

	COUNT	BARS
Beginning with R.F.,		
Pas de Valse Forward	1, 2, 3	1
Balancé Forward on L.F., raising joined hands forward, and closing R.F. to 3rd position rear	1, 2, 3	1
Glissade Backward on R.F., lowering joined hands and closing L.F. to 3rd position front	1, 2, 3	1
Waltz Inward—		
Back R.F., turning to L.	1	
Place left toe behind right heel, still turning	2	
Pivot on balls of feet to L. Withdraw left hand. Give own right hand in partner's left	3	1
		—
		4
(Now with back to L.O.D., with L.F. in front, 5th position.)		
Beginning with L.F., dance Bars 1–4 against L.O.D., finishing facing L.O.D.		4
		—
		8
Releasing partner's hand,		
Waltz Outward, beginning with R.F. Finish		

	COUNT	BARS
almost back-to-back with partner, and give right hand in his left	1, 2, 3	1
		—
		9
Glissade Back on L.F., and close R.F. to 3rd position in front	1, 2, 3	1
		—
		10
Beginning with L.F., Waltz Inward	1, 2, 3	1
		—
		11
Joining both hands, own right to partner's left, own left to his right, Step to R. side with R.F. Close L.F. to 3rd position in front	1, 2, 3	1
		—
		12
Taking Waltz Hold, *Waltz (Natural Turn)*, opening-out at finish to original Starting Position, ready to repeat the sequence *ad lib.*	1, 2, 3 four times	4
		—
		16

WALTZ SUPERBE

MANY dancers are under the impression that Waltz Superbe is a comparatively recent addition to the sequence dances, possibly owing to the fact that it has enjoyed a large-scale revival which has brought it to the notice of many for the first time.

It was introduced in 1909, when it won the first prize for its arranger, Charles W. Gardner, at the Annual Conference of the National Association of Teachers of Dancing.

On the whole, it follows familiar lines, except that Two Glissades are danced (during Bars 2 and 3) with the partners in a back-to-back position with both hands joined.

Time: 3/4.   *Tempo:* 46 bars per minute.

Starting Position: Open.

GENTLEMAN

	COUNT	BARS
Waltz Outward—		
(L.F., R.F., L.F., keeping hold of partner's left hand.)	1, 2, 3	1
Two Glissades—		
Now back-to-back to partner, take her right hand in own left, and—		
Step to R. side with R.F. (along L.O.D.)	1	
Close L.F. to R.F.	2, 3	1
Repeat the last bar, releasing partner's right hand at finish (still back-to-back)	1, 2, 3	1
		—
		3

	COUNT	BARS
Waltz Inward—		
Against L.O.D., keeping hold of partner's left hand. Finish facing partner	1, 2, 3	1
		—
		4
Two Glissades—		
Step to R. side with R.F. (against L.O.D.)	1	
Close L.F. to R.F.	2, 3	1
Repeat the last bar	1, 2, 3	1
		—
		6
Solo Waltz Outward—		
Along L.O.D., and at finish resume Open Position	1, 2, 3 twice	2
		—
		8
Pas de Valse along L.O.D.	1, 2, 3 twice	2
		—
		10
Pas Glissé (Twice)—		
Joining both hands,		
Pas Glissé along L.O.D., i.e.:		
Step to L. side with L.F.	1	
Close R.F. to L.F., keeping weight on L.F.	2, 3	1
Pas Glissé against L.O.D., i.e.:		
Step to R. side with R.F.	1	
Close L.F. to R.F., keeping weight on R.F.	2, 3	1
		—
		12

WALTZ SUPERBE

	COUNT	BARS
Waltz Finale—		
Taking Waltz Hold, Waltz (Natural Turn), opening-out at finish to original Starting Position, ready to repeat the sequence *ad lib.*	1, 2, 3 four times	4
		16

LADY

	COUNT	BARS
Waltz Outward—		
(R.F., L.F., R.F.) keeping hold of partner's right hand	1, 2, 3	1
Two Glissades—		
Now back-to-back to partner, give right hand in his left, and—		
Step to L. side with L.F.	1	
Close R.F. to L.F.	2, 3	1
Repeat the last bar, withdrawing left hand at finish (still back-to-back)	1, 2, 3	1
		3
Waltz Inward—		
Against L.O.D., keeping hold of partner's right hand. Finish facing partner	1, 2, 3	1
		4
Two Glissades—		
Step to L. side with L.F. (against L.O.D.)	1	
Close R.F. to L.F.	2, 3	1
Repeat the last bar	1, 2, 3	1
		6

	COUNT	BARS
Solo Waltz Outward—		
Along L.O.D., and at finish resume Open Position	1, 2, 3 twice	2
		—
		8
Pas de Valse along L.O.D.	1, 2, 3 twice	2
		—
		10
Pas Glissé (Twice)—		
Joining both hands,		
Step to R. side with R.F. (along L.O.D.)	1	
Close L.F. to R.F., keeping weight on R.F.	2, 3	1
Step to L. side with L.F. (against L.O.D.)	1	
Close R.F. to L.F., keeping weight on L.F.	2, 3	1
		—
		12
Waltz Finale—		
Taking Waltz Hold, Waltz (Natural Turn), opening-out at finish to original Starting Position, ready to repeat the sequence *ad lib.*	1, 2, 3 four times	4
		—
		16

OTHER SEQUENCE DANCES

THE reader who desires to learn additional sequence dances will find the following in my book, *Old Time Dancing*—

WALTZ SEQUENCE DANCES: Veleta, University Waltz, La Rinka, Rinking, Cuckoo Waltz, St. Bernard's Waltz, Pride of Erin, Wedding Waltz, Imperial Waltz, Destiny Waltz, Tango Waltz.

TANGO SEQUENCE DANCES: Square Tango, Royal Empress Tango, Lola Tango.

SAUNTERS AND FOXTROTS: The Saunter, Moonlight Saunter, On Leave Foxtrot.

ONE-STEPS AND MARCHES: Dinky One-step, Gay Gordons.

OTHER ROUND DANCES: Military Two-step, Barn Dance, Polka, Boston Two-step, La Mascotte, Maxina, Esperano Barn Dance, Schottische, Latchford Schottische, Varsoviana, Ladbrooke.

SQUARE DANCES, i.e. sequence dances executed by sets, usually of four couples: Lancers, Quadrille, Waltz Cotillon, Caledonians, The Alberts, Carnival.

CIRCLE DANCES: Grand March, Circassian Circle, Progressive Barn Dance, Dashing White Sergeant.

Lightning Source UK Ltd.
Milton Keynes UK
UKOW04f1805151214

243186UK00001B/38/P

9 781445 511665